AF335215

The Cornucopian Mind
and the Baroque Unity
of the Arts

The Cornucopian Mind and the Baroque Unity of the Arts

Giancarlo Maiorino

The Pennsylvania State University Press
University Park and London

Library of Congress Cataloging-in-Publication Data

Maiorino, Giancarlo, 1943–
The cornucopian mind and the baroque unity of the arts
Giancarlo Maiorino.

p.   cm.
Bibliography: p.
Includes index.
ISBN 0-271-00679-X
1. Arts, Baroque.   2. Ut pictura poesis (Aesthetics)
3. Humanism in art.   I. Title.
NX451.5.B3M35 1989
700′.1—dc20   89–3894
CIP

Copyright © 1990 The Pennsylvania State University
All rights reserved
Printed in the United States of America

For my parents
Anna and Ciro (1908–1986) Maiorino;
from Nocera Inferiore,
where Spanish roots and Neapolitan soil have nourished
our baroque souls

Because this study has led me to the core of
the Counter-Reformation Baroque, I have
found that its artforms echo a cultural way of
life ingrained in the food, faith, and wisdom
of my family. From Nocera Inferiore and
Salerno to Ravello, Rome, and Caracas, the
Maiorinos (in presence and memory) have
been a cornucopian source for this project,
which has matured my own sense of identity.

Contents

PART III:
Conclusion: The Progress of Perfectibility

List of Illustrations

Acknowledgments

For their help and encouragement, I am grateful to Luis Beltran, Eugene Eoyang, Frank Warnke, Ulrich Weisstein, and the students of my seminar on the Baroque (1985): Peggy Bola, John Berks, and Thomas Mussio.

For plates and permissions, I would like to thank the following: Archivi Alinari, Art Resource, The Louvre, National Gallery (London), Museo del Prado, The Metropolitan Museum of Art, Mauritshuis (The Hague), National Galleries of Scotland, Victoria and Albert Museum, Alte Pinakothek (Munich), and Staatliche Kunstsammlungen Gemäldegalerie (Dresden).

Introduction

If academic tradition and routine did not pre-
vent us from seeing things as they are, and did
not insist in classifying the types of mind ac-
cording to their means of expression instead
of grouping them according to what they
have to express, a single history of the mind
would replace the various histories of art, of
literature.

—Paul Valéry

I

To date, the Baroque still remains one of the least tamable beasts in the wilderness of criticism. By and large, the synchronic approach has been predominant, and a number of thematic studies have dealt with the beast at the peak of adulthood.[1] By contrast, I have centered my diachronic approach on developments from infancy toward maturity.[2] This study offers neither a synopsis nor a history of the age; instead, its aim is to interpret the period through the paramount concept of form as "process."

In such a dynamic perspective, I have set matters of origin and originality against the poetics of Humanism, whose rediscovery of antiquity fostered models of self-fulfilled maturity. From Petrarch and Leon Battista Alberti to Raphael and Castiglione, analogical models in history, the system of linear perspective, and a host of treatises molded reality into forms of theoretical certainty.

Although a source of much inspiration, the *aemulatio* of antiquity played itself out once artists and theorists set up canons of presumed, if not achieved, perfection. At its best, art shaped intellectual forms of trans-historical plenitude.

Throughout the *Cinquecento,* Humanism inspired filial needs of obedience and rebellion. Slowly, however, the Copernican revolution brushed aside the Ptolemaic faith in a man-centered universe, and Pascal took a new measure of anthropomorphic constructs:

> Let us take our compass; we are something, and we are not everything. The nature of our existence hides from us the knowledge of first beginnings which are born of Nothing; and the littleness of our being conceals from us the sight of the Infinite. . . . This is our true state; this is what makes us incapable of certain knowledge and of absolute ignorance. . . . Let us therefore not look for certainty and stability. Our reason is always deceived by fickle shadows; nothing can fix the finite between two infinites, which both enclose and fly from it. (*Pensées,* 72)

Fifteenth-century orations on human dignity were muted in a limitless cosmos where a systematic multipolarity spanned the horizons of art, truth, and knowledge.[3] As a mode of human experience, infinity broke open the finiteness of classical and humanist worldviews.

To orient readers toward the shift from Humanism to the Baroque, Werner Weisbach's distinction is still helpful: "The classical ideal of even balance, harmonious proportions and unobtrusive decoration has given way to something *mouvementé,* dynamic, exuberantly ornamental—a contrast which has been expressed in German by describing the first as *ein Stil des Seins* (literally, "a style of being"), and the second as *ein Stil des Werdens* ("a style of becoming")."[4] The intellectual measurability of the humanist cosmos could not keep pace with the progress of science.

Once it was set against the measureless, certainty made

room for search, and the clarity of the known for speculations about the unknown. By the turn of the *Seicento,* art had to probe into the shapelessness of the ever-unfolding matter of life amidst an open universe without ends in sight. The very concepts of unity and wholeness had to accommodate styles of becoming, since infinity could admit of no fixed frames of order. Creation came to depend more on commitment than celebration, and on attempts rather than results.

From a baroque standpoint, the Copernican "breaking of the circle" fostered exploration instead of nostalgia. Regrets about the "Old Philosophie" aside, infinity set up the challenge of endlessness as a mental attitude striving to feel at home in a universe where discovery itself became a form of epistemological certainty.

Growth overwhelmed measurement. As never before, the future stood midway between golden ages and utopian fictions, much as models of *imitatio* and *aemulatio* had to be bathed in the contradictory brew of the human condition. The future held promises; often, process itself turned into an operative structure of hope. The capacity-to-be made possibility more attractive than achievement.

II

This study does not challenge the validity of the Baroque as a period-concept that extended from the last quarter of the sixteenth to the end of the seventeenth century. And it need only be mentioned that most histories of art and literature take the term for granted. In spite of its rampant eclecticism, the Baroque stemmed from a unitary and unitive view of art and knowledge that set royalty next to poverty and folklore not too far from classicism. However heated, debates on the subject have sharpened its legitimacy.

Since skepticism on matters as complex as those concerning the Baroque has produced more confusion than viable alternatives, I have set out to interpret some of its cohesive aspects. Throughout, my approach shall favor relevance over range.

Instead of narrowing the age to significant traits such as magic (Hocke), alienation (Hauser), images-themes (Rousset), "isms" (d'Ors), or a-temporal (Focillon) and stylistic categories of Wölfflinian extraction (Buffum), I have linked thematic choices to the poetics of artists who built the historical framework of the period. My inductive method has focused on the emergent concept of form as "process," which touched on concerns with the boundless furtherance of life (Part One), the formative unity of the arts (Part Two), and the evolution of human perfectibility (Conclusion) as they came to the fore through a cluster of founding fathers—Michelangelo, Giordano Bruno, and, beyond the Alps, Montaigne and Cervantes—during the second half of the *Cinquecento*.[5]

III

At the earliest stage, Michelangelo brought the restlessness of his probing Neoplatonism to the baroque cradle (chapter 1). His *non-finito* opened up form, much as the inner vitality of his sculptural "process" inspired artists who were to test external boundaries of all kinds. The sheer longevity of the sculptor's creative activity linked Humanism and what art historians call the High Renaissance to Mannerism and, I submit, to the Baroque.

It is in the context of "open" forms within an "open" universe that the first part of this study moves from Michelangelo to Giordano Bruno, who in fact adapted humanist notions of art and philosophy to the culture of the "New Science."

After the Michelangeloesque prelude, Neoplatonism also inspired Bruno's poetics of immeasurable abundance, which set "process" at the heart of the baroque worldview (chapter 2). As the "ideological link" running through the whole study, his *Italian Dialogues (Dialoghi italiani)* touched on poetry, criticism, and the arts in 1584–85, before Marino, Caravaggio, and Bernini made their impact felt.

The Nolan's (Bruno's literary *persona*) prominence has been ascertained in science, philosophy, and the history of ideas.[6] His rightful place on the baroque map of art criticism, however, has not brushed aside outdated prejudices (stemming from Benedetto Croce's reference to the Baroque as a form of artistic ugliness) that have confined him to the literary *pre-barocco* and *anti-barocco*. By contrast, his affiliation with the Baroque is central to this study.[7]

Although familiar with the waning tradition of Humanism, Bruno was among the first to celebrate Copernicus's *De revolutionibus orbium caelestium* (written in 1530 and published in 1543). Amidst many who doubted any form of progress, the Nolan's optimism gave direction to a culture set to maintain science at pace with art and faith. In his case, form as process was but a vehicle for the ever-unfolding progress of humankind at the edge of infinity.

Even though it may appear to be "monographic," my analysis of Bruno's works is comprehensive but not exhaustive. His "recurrent" presence in most chapters is but a measure of his contribution to the wider context of the Baroque.

Since I believe that Bruno and Michelangelo spearheaded the cornucopian growth of baroque culture, their works have been set at the axial core of this study. Bruno's texts, in fact, paved the way for choices that would be developed under the mounting leadership of Montaigne and Cervantes before the end of the sixteenth century.

Part Two extends the range of form as process to shared concerns that affected the baroque landscape of the arts.

Chapter 3 links faith in an ever-expanding concept of knowledge to the chronotype of formation, whose ground-breaking vitality enacted the very growth of form.

Once artists set out to portray chronotopic changes, denial and renovation verged on the threshold between shape and shapelessness. At the edge, artists tested their own authority to the point where the creative act could enhance fiction just as easily as it could hinder it. Often, life let its own forms make artistic claims by shifting in and out of aesthetic boundaries. Whether it be in picaresque Spain or middle-class Holland, styles of becoming emerged amid the operative forms of social intercourse. With ease, artists stood inside and outside fictional frames in which creation and criticism took each other up (chapter 4).

In the Conclusion, Rembrandt's *Aristotle Contemplating the Bust of Homer* (chapter 5) brings to the fore an indelible image of process as a conciliatory form of human communication. Within the unitive nomenclature of this study, the Dutch canvas could stand as a symbol for an age whose legacy of humanist learning gave way to dialogues that valued human understanding on islands and continents alike.

At the end, chapter 6 takes up the growth of human perfectibility through the impact that the temporal (process) and spatial (infinity) coordinates of a progressive culture has had on mythic and myth-making concepts of perfection. In an earlier study, the notion of "new born and perfect" has foregrounded my own critical overview of a central aspect of Humanism. And I do think that these two endeavors ought to be viewed in a kind of diachronic relationship.[8]

IV

As to geographical boundaries, my focus falls along Mediterranean shores, where matters of influence drew strength from both Humanism and the Counter-Reformation. It suffices to mention that Montaigne was steeped in humanist culture, and Guicciardini was one of his favorite historians. Cervantes and Velázquez were familiar with Italian approaches to chivalric literature (Ariosto) and "realistic" painting (the Caravaggesque tradition) long before they went to Italy, where Ribera (known as *lo Spagnoletto*) found that Spanish rulers had created a congenial environment in Naples. I need only mention that Spanish theologians dominated at the Council of Trent, while Italian influences on Spanish spirituality could be traced back to Savonarola.[9]

Like Humanism, the Baroque stemmed from the mainstream of the Italian tradition, which led Michelangelo and Bruno to set up the artistic cornerstones of an epoch that was to peak outside Italy. From a diachronic standpoint, epistles and commentaries nurtured French *essais,* while *novelle* (Boccaccio) and *poemi cavallereschi* (Ariosto) stood in the background of picaresque and Cervantine literature in Spain. On the artistic front, Ribera, Poussin, and Rubens led the way for artists who exported the Italian lesson across the Alps, where they were joined, among others, by Giambattista Marino, Gianlorenzo Bernini, and Titian.

It is probably less than accidental that novelty found it easier to plow its way in cultures more remote from, and independent of, the classical-humanist stronghold. For that very reason, Italian theorists ruled on dramatic unities, but the theater flourished elsewhere.

Only on thematic grounds have references been made to the Reformation culture of northern Europe.

V

Because of "underlying shared spiritual preoccupations," dissonant voices produced a baroque harmony that drew literature and the visual arts together. The literary critic therefore would agree with the art historian that, "if unity is to be discovered within this diversity . . . what we must look for is not any well-defined uniformity of style, but the embodiment of certain widely held ideas, attitudes and assumptions."[10] From *studioli* and workshops to building sites, the arts responded to clashes of common energy.

It is less than an overstatement to claim that period concepts ought to be drawn from the totality of culture rather than parts thereof, and scholarship has urged us to focus on interdisciplinary points of connection.[11] Instead of setting up a theoretical overview, my treatment of the sister arts draws from their "integrated" coexistence. In terms of interdisciplinary terminology, I would find confirmation to my approach, and guidance to this field of studies, in what Murray Roston calls a "process of inferential contextualization." Unequivocally, he rejects any "broad premiss defining the spirit of the age" in the attempt to demonstrate how works of art conform to it. Instead, research ought to begin "from a literary text and, even more specifically, often from a particular problem related to it."[12] Hoping to be inclusive without edging on superficiality, my cultural perspective favors historical fluency over systematic juxtapositions.

I do expect readers of this manuscript to be somehow familiar with the "challenge" of the Baroque. In a baroque spirit, I call on them to set up provocative exchanges with this text, whose goal is to initiate further explorations into one's special field of interest.

This is the point at which I have to comment on methodology, which stems from my experience as a literary and interdisciplinary comparatist. I believe that my approach ought to be a synthetic one; for me, comparison is an act of synthesis, not of analysis. For me, "how," "what," and "where" are instrumental; "why" is teleological. Because I expect comparatists to evaluate "as many modes of human understanding as possible in a single act of the mind," I agree with R. P. Blackmur that comparatists, master-laymen, and their ideological cohorts cannot train "in caution, reserve, and the sin of over-scrupulosity in every matter not directly warranted by fact. It is mere facts that make mere scholarship; it is the mere facts about the work that fail to tell us what the work is about."[13]

Perhaps edging on the higher grounds of aesthetics and the history of ideas, I center on leading trends and major developments; particular issues are acknowledged but could not be treated as thoroughly as the specialist would. The risk lurking over my shoulder is always that of getting trapped into problems of specialized competence, which tend to cut into my speculative discourse. The kind of *inter*-disciplinary research I am engaged in must weigh quite heavily on the interpretative potential that the *inter*-connectedness of artistic forms has to offer. Therefore, it is for the specialist to develop more thorough treatments of specific problems. My comparative "mode" must channel into a comprehensive overview the scholarship available in the individual disciplines (from literature and art history to philosophy and the history of science). At best, I hope to offer leads, instead of chasing them. Because of the depth and range that interdisciplinarity usually entails, my expository strategy tends to be concise by choice as well as by need. It is shaped, or at least I would like it to be shaped, into a rhetoric whose main thrust lets insight and suggestions branch out in a plurality of directions.

I do understand that there are times when specialists would like to see more space given to issues raised on their own turf, but it is for them to explore those issues further. My task is to lead them to take the initiative. To go beyond, I would court incompetence and presumption. If at all successful, my aim is to offer an interpretative overview. That way, specialists and comparatists can better define their respective fields of competence. As a result, a more cooperative distribution of labor could be undertaken. At best, we would enhance our credibility vis-à-vis an interdisciplinary map whose territory would otherwise be too vast for anyone to explore with any expertise.

VI

For Jean-Paul Sartre, "there must be always a difference of position" between the pastness of artworks and the presentness of a viewer's criticism of them. The artist knows "what he wanted to do and we don't; but we know what he has done and he doesn't."[14] The hindsight of our privileged stand ought to further critical discovery. If it is true that the present of creation cannot be severed from the present of culture in the historical study of literary systems,[15] it is likewise plausible—and necessary—that interpretation should not relent in upgrading our experience of art.

After much "breaking" and "untuning," it is still useful to be reminded that doubt, denial, and paradox are not unique to modern consciousness. As moderns, we have much to learn from Michelangeloesque unrest and Cervantine parody. In dealing with a past pregnant with the possible,[16] interpretation ought to remain tentative.

Domestication of elusive beasts through the numbing captivity of either indifference or intransigence is not the aim of this study.[17] To avoid that, Jean Rousset has recommended that "the idea of the Baroque should remain a working hypothesis."[18]

While making dialogue possible, the *différence* between past and present should discourage single-minded stands that often have created unwarranted tensions between originality and understanding.

Four authors are quoted throughout. References to Montaigne and Cervantes, with page numbers indicated in the texts, are to *The Complete Essays of Montaigne* (Stanford, 1965; trans. Donald Frame) and *The Adventures of Don Quixote* (New York, 1980; trans. J. M. Cohen). Among Donne's works, the following recur in several chapters: *Devotions* (Ann Arbor, 1959), with page numbers indicated in the text, and *The Sermons of John Donne,* ed. George R. Potter and Evelyn M. Simpson (Berkeley, 1953), with shortened titles (*Devotions, Sermons*), volume, and page numbers indicated in the text. In Bruno's case, the following texts have been used: *The Heroic Frenzies,* trans. Paul Memmo (Chapel Hill, 1964), *The Expulsion of the Triumphant Beast,* trans. Arthur Imerti (New Brunswick, 1964), *Cause, Principle, and Unity,* trans. J. Lindsay (Westport, 1976), *On the Infinite Universe and Worlds,* trans. D. W. Singher in her volume *Giordano Bruno: His Life and Thought* (New York, 1950), *The Ash Wednesday Supper,* trans. S. L. Jaki (The Hague, 1975). References are to these editions, with shortened titles (*Frenzies, Expulsion, Cause, Infinite, Ash*) and page numbers indicated in the text. For other Italian and Latin works, references are to *Dialoghi italiani,* ed. Giovanni Aquilecchia (Florence, 1972), and *Opere latine,* ed. Carlo Monti (Turin, 1980), with shortened titles (*Dialoghi, Opere*) and page numbers indicated in the text. Translations are by author. Other texts are referred to in the Notes. Throughout, I have made an effort to use translations that are reliable as well as easily accessible. In a few instances, I have given passages without translations, which would have blatantly tampered with the character and texture of the text. Yet, I have been careful not the let those "bonuses" interfere with the contextual flow of the argument.

PART I

Life's Boundless Furtherance

Neoplatonism at the Crossroads: Michelangelo's Power of Expression and the *Non-Finito*

> *The cast only reproduces the exterior; I repro-*
> *duce, besides that, the spirit which is certainly*
> *a part of nature. I see all the truth, and not*
> *only that of the outside.*
> —Auguste Rodin

I

Under the aegis of Florentine Neoplatonism, interactions between art and philosophy affected much of sixteenth-century culture. In Rome, sculpture "redeemed" the wounds of life through the transcendental forms of Michelangelo's first *Pietà* (1498–99). While sharing the brightest stillness of youth, mother and son have muted emotions into an image of aloof spirituality. "Among all his contemporaries," Erwin Panofsky insists, Michelangelo "was the only one who adopted Neoplatonism not in certain aspects but in its entirety, and not as a convincing philosophical system, let alone as the fashion of the day, but as a metaphysical justification of his own self."[1]

At the turn of the *Cinquecento,* however, the Florentine leadership in the cultural landscape of the peninsula declined. Raphael and Michelangelo settled down in papal Rome, where the sculptor slowly matured into the unfinished style of *St. Matthew* (after 1506), *Captives* (1513–27/28?), and *Florence* and *Rondanini Pietàs* (before 1555, 1563–64). What emerged was an approach to art more typical of the latter part of the sixteenth century, when Neoplatonism evolved from Ficino's commentaries on Plato to the *Italian Dialogues* of Giordano Bruno. In the 1530s, therefore, Michelangelo was as retrospectively distant from the philosophy of the Florentine Academy as his *non-finito* foreshadowed things to come.

Keeping the Humanism-Baroque trajectory in mind, I think that Neoplatonism could serve as a signpost for testing sculptural *non-finito* against the future instead of the past.

With an eye to distant things to come, Henry Moore's remarks on the *Rondanini Pietà* (Fig. 1) updated the relevance of the unfinished as a mode of creation:

> Also, there is a fact, for me a strange fact, about the really great artists of the past: in some way their late works become simplified and fragmentary, become imperfect and unfinished. The artists stop caring about beauty and such abstract ideas, and yet their works get greater. . . . Beauty in the later Greek or Renaissance sense, is not the aim of my sculpture. Between beauty of expression and power of expression there is a difference of function. The first aims at pleasing the senses, the second has a spiritual vitality which for me is more moving and goes deeper than the sense.[2]

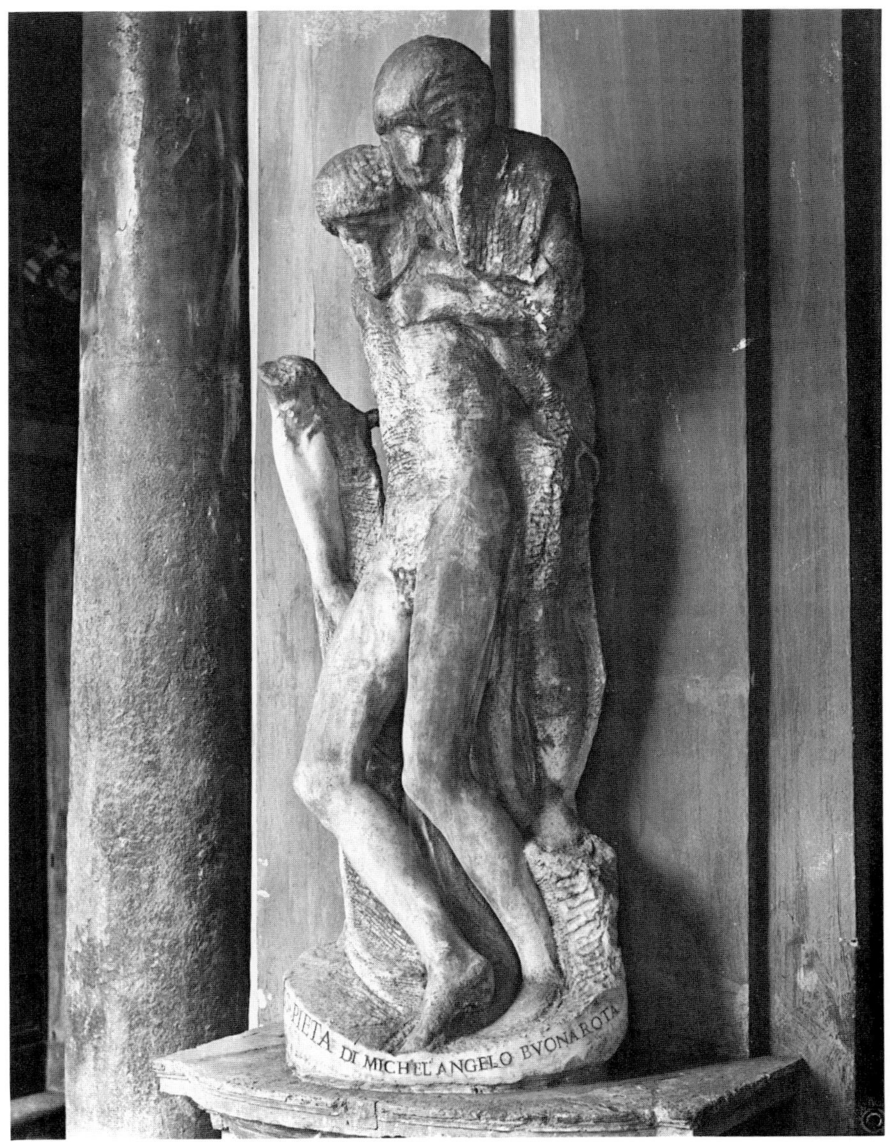

Fig. 1. Michelangelo, *Rondanini Pietà*, 1563–64. Castello Sforzesco, Milan

II

After such aloof works as the *Saint Peter's Pietà* and the *David* (1501–4), power of expression (in Henry Moore's sense) became predominant in Michelangelo's art, which grew away from the static ideals of proportion typical of fifteenth-century sculpture. By contrast, the Florence *Captives* body forth clashes between "power" and "beauty." At the same time, inner energy struggles out of the adamantine block through unmolded shapes that resist completion.[3]

Neoplatonists had claimed that "we, undisciplined in discernment of the inward, knowing nothing of it, run after the outer, never understanding that it is the inner which stirs us" (Plotinus, *Enneads,* V,8,2). Centuries later, it was stated that "form is an act, since it is the principle of acting. Again, form bursts forth into action and motion, and never stops operating." Wherever "the inexhaustible act reigns, there reigns infinity and the entire light of the intellect."[4] Equally convinced that "form manifests itself in the Act" (*Opere,* 326), Bruno equated creation with *potenza,* in which "act and power are the same thing. . . . Every potency and act, then, which in the principle are as enfolded, united, and one, are unfolded, dispersed, and multiplied in other things" (*Cause,* 111–12).

Michelangelo translated power and act into *terribilità,* which blended fear and sublimity into a unique style. By popular acclaim, his awesome talent overshadowed that of ancient sculptors.[5] Actually, the modern artist dared to replace the ideal of beauty with that of vitality.[6] At the threshold of representation, sculpture thrived on tensions between external appearance and internal energy. At all times, form brought to the fore power of expression without vilifying its undefinable interiority.

Although critical of artists who would "leave the rough and scarcely begun work to take up new things," the humanists maintained that "it is best to avoid the vitiating effect of those who wish to eliminate every weakness and make everything too polished."[7] To that concern, they found classical precedents: "It often happens that our writings are ruined by excessive care, and the file does not refine, but damages them. This is what the great Apelles intended to say when he claimed to surpass

Protogenes in one thing, namely in knowing when to turn his hand away from the painting."[8]

At times, the *finito* could be troublesome. Alberti's concept of architecture was focused on design, and execution amounted to no more than a menial task. Widening the gap between mental construct and artistic form, the execution of Michelangelo's plan for the tomb of Julius II would have required more than a lifetime. From plan to practice, his early *Madonna della scala* (1489–92) already bore signs of a reluctance to complete the two figures in the background.[9]

Once volumetric masses began to overshadow anatomical details in the Florentine *Captives*, the *non-finito* brought to the fore power of expression. Whereas concerns with anatomy exhausted creation into finished shapes, formlessness left inner vitality untamed. Sculpture thus unveiled living forms.

The time was ripe for looking at the human body as an organism rather than a construct. And Bruno was among the first to outline two modes of creation: "Art begets form out of matter by subtraction, as when it makes a statue out of stone, or by apposition, as when by joining stone to stone, earth, and wood, it constructs a house; but nature makes everything out of its matter by means of separation, birth, effluxion—*di separazione, di parto, di efflussione.*" Such terms do not refer to interchangeable modes, since "art cannot operate except on the surface of things formed by nature, such as wood, iron, stone, wool, or the like. But nature works, so to speak, from the centre of its subject or matter, which is throughout formless" (*Cause*, 131, 102). Effluxion thus points to emanation (or flowing out), a metaphor familiar to the Neoplatonists ("fountain-of-forms" or "formal principle which becomes and informs everything"; Bruno, *Cause*, 106).

In the language of sculpture, subtraction and apposition are techniques whereby an external design gives form to unartistic stone or clay. Birth and effluxion, instead, respond to internal laws of growth that are analogous to nature's way of producing forms out of its own matter. In terms of artistic parallels, marble is matter, and it is form. Once they became predominant in the *Captives*, rough textures brought to the surface the inner core of sculpture.[10] Michelangelo, in fact, never dealt with form and antiform.

Since an excellent artist "knows better how to do what he has not done than the others know what they do,"[11] Michelangelo's *non-finito* heightened the potential for form. In Bruno's words, "only outer forms change and are even destroyed . . . they are not substances, but accidents and circumstances of substances" (*Cause,* 89). Form longs for "matter in order to perpetuate itself. For, separated from matter, form loses its being, and not matter, which has all it had before the form was found, and still can have other forms" (*Cause,* 134). By analogy, sculptural matter imposes its own structure upon form.[12]

To make itself perceptible, however, matter must submit to the "evil" of mimesis; an evil Michelangelo became immediately aware of. At the earliest stage, the *rilievo schiacciato* of the *Madonna della scala* kept the figures within the flat planes of the imaginary cube.[13] Accurate renditions of external details were sacrificed to the geometric oneness of the archetypal block. Commenting on Vasari's reaction to the *Captives* (models "lying in a tub of water"), Erwin Panofsky writes that they "are not conceived in relation to an anatomical axis but in relation to the surfaces of a rectangular block."[14] Stylistic fluidity thus affected the unity of block, mass, and shapes.

Beauty could not be severed from figuration in Neoplatonic poetics, since nothing "grows old more slowly than shape and more quickly than beauty. From this it is clearly established that beauty and shape are not the same."[15] Shape consists of "unfabricated" mass, whereas arrangement, proportion, and adornment refer to external criteria of beauty whose futility Michelangelo pinned to empty skulls, fleshless skins (*Last Judgment*), and poetic lines:

> Once on a time our eyes were whole,
> > Every socket had its light.
> > Now they are empty, black and frightful,
> > This it is that time has brought.[16]
>
> (Già fur gli occhi nostri interi
> > con la luce in ogni speco;
> > or son voti, orrendi e neri,
> > e ciò porta il tempo seco.)

Inevitably, the process of time eats away at beauty.

III

The Neoplatonists insisted that form, upon entering matter, "loses its simplicity and becomes divisible, and, therefore, impure; it changes from active to passive, just as its readiness for action is followed by incapacity of movement."[17] In the language of sculpture, the indulgent lifelessness of Michelangelo's *Dying Slave* (Fig. 2) betrays the agony of energy (internal) drained by beauty (external), a tendency that led to the stylized *maniera* of the *Apollo-David* (1523–32) and the *Victory* (1527–28).

Asked why he liked the unfinished *Captives*, Henry Moore answered: "I prefer them because they have more power in them, to me, much more power than the finished ones. The one in the Louvre is much too weary and sleepy and lackadaisical."[18] Such a weariness calls to mind the *Night* (*La notte*) in the Medici Chapel (church of San Lorenzo, Florence). As part of a symbolic whole, the reclining figure has consumed the bulging and knotted restlessness of the *Day*, which came to light as a sad and fettered (across her chest) *Dawn*. Inevitably, the experience of time rushed in a state of captivity.

For Charles de Tolnay, the band of cloth across the *Dying Slave*'s breast "seems to be a materialization of the weight oppressing his soul . . . there is no apparent logic in the placing of these different bands. . . . It is already the soul which is here prisoner of the body."[19] From the *Dawn* to the Paris *Slave*, cloth bands seem to suggest that form has been incarnated into existence. The soul's prison is not the brutish matter of the block but the human body itself.

At this point, we ought to keep in mind that the Florence *Captives* were to be shown as if bound to pilasters on the lower level of the tomb for Julius II. Iconography therefore placed them at a physical threshold where they would be symbolic of humanity's effort to raise itself toward heaven. At that boundary, the *Atlas Captive* resists gravitational pulls away from and back into the block.

At the very edge of human form, the *Crossed-Leg Captive* (Fig. 3) strives to break free of his own physical being. Early in his career, Michelangelo had tested humanist canons of stability when he sculpted the drunken *Bacchus* (1496–97). Without

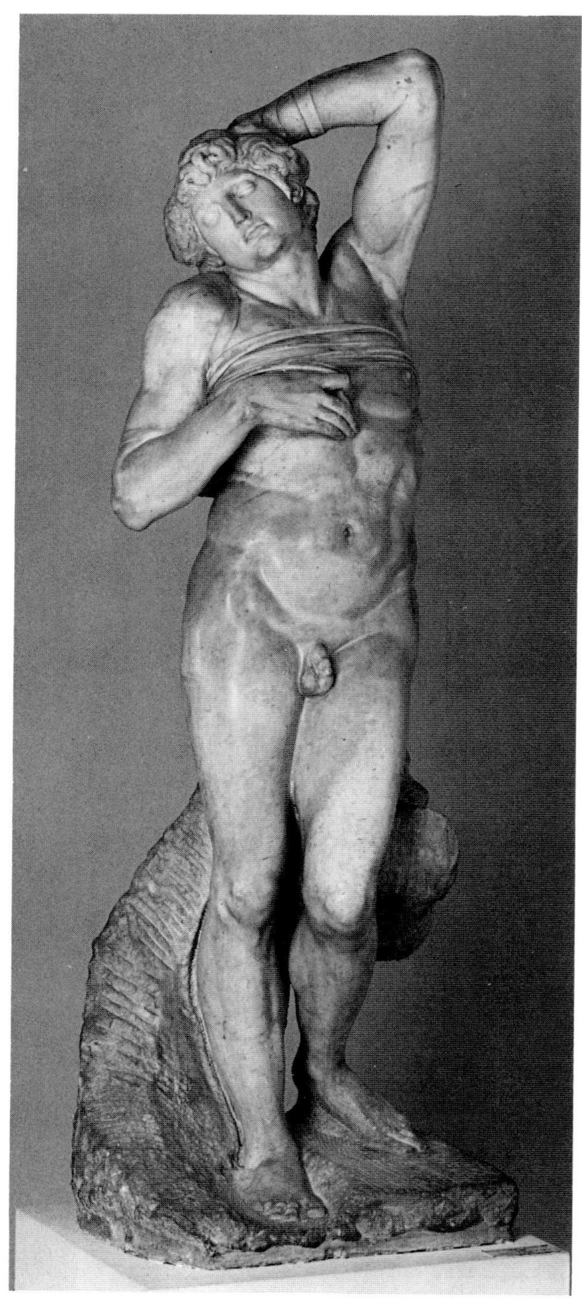

Fig. 2. Michelangelo, *Dying Slave*, before 1513.
Louvre, Paris

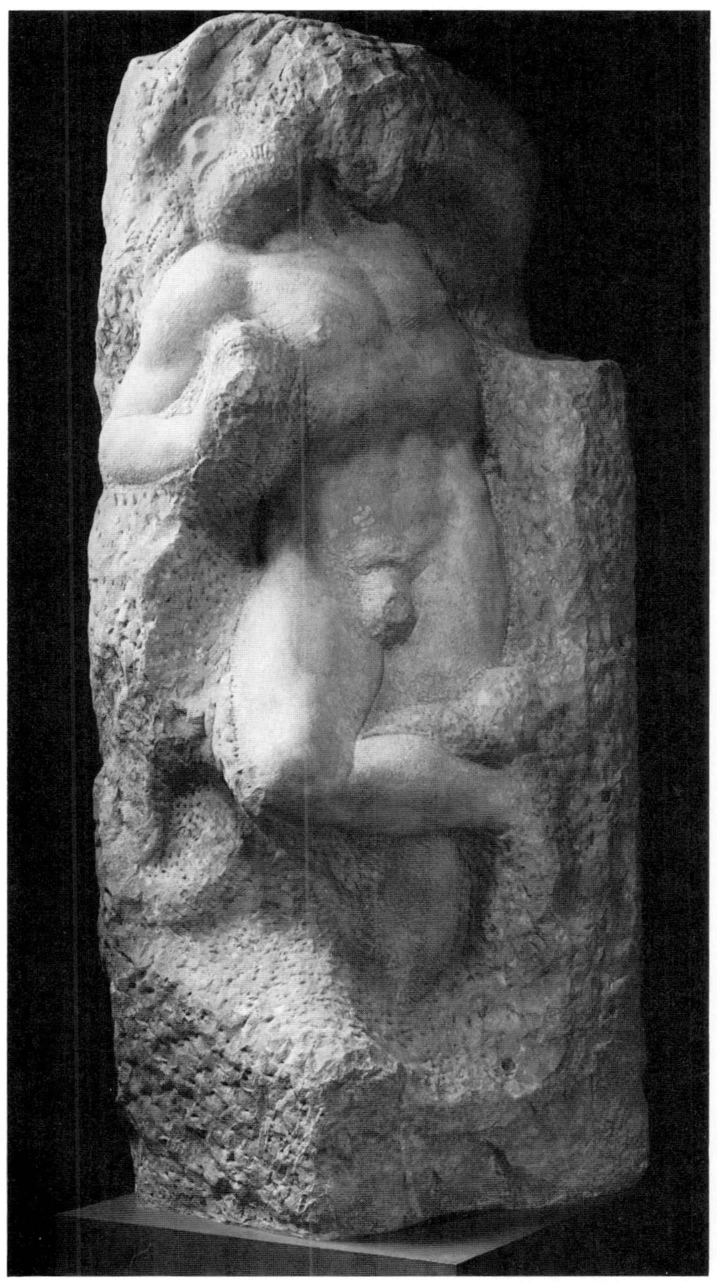

Fig. 3. Michelangelo, *Crossed-Leg Captive*, 1527–28. Accademia, Florence

thematic references, however, the Florentine *Captive* floats in a state of weightlessness bound to marble itself. Sculpture thus enacted the Platonic struggle of creation; from unity to diversity and back toward unity again.

What, then, are the *Captives* chained to? If captivity implies constriction, why would they be trying to rid themselves of formless matter, which is whole and perfect? I would like to suggest that captivity stirs their souls to overcome the flesh without rejecting human power.

As a supernal unity, essence calls for representation. Devoid of unity, existence in turn reaches out toward transcendence. At the same time, the *Captives* long for, and are afraid of, completion. Relevant are Bruno's words: "When the intellect wants to grasp the essence of a thing, it proceeds by simplifying as much as possible. I meant that it moves away from composition and multiplicity, rejecting corruptible accidents, dimensions, figures, and turning to what lies under these figures . . . when we aspire and strive to the principle and substance of things, we make progress toward indivisibility—*quando aspiriamo e ne sforziamo al principio de le cose, facciamo progresso verso la indivisibilità*—" (*Cause*, 143–44). Art brought out a conflict at the heart of human nature.

While remaining in progress, the *non-finito* of the *Captives* adds the power of a slow uncoiling to the ideal oneness of the block. Tensions between rough mass and anatomical forms bulging in space foreground the Platonic dilemma of figures forever on the edge of loss and recovery. Since they still partake of the primeval stuff,[20] the *Captives* have entered the world of matter without exhausting their strength into the inanity of a hopeless thinker (*Last Judgment*).

At that stage in his artistic growth, Michelangelo tormented the shell of form, for he wanted it to unveil layers of rough and smooth degrees of finish. The ideal transparency of the *Saint Peter's Pietà* yielded to deeper contrasts of light and shadows in the *Madonna Pitti*. The artist brought out the very technique of the life of forms, the biological process of sculptural growth.[21] And once the *non-finito* began to shape forms as tentative and problematic as the very depths of human nature, Michelangeloesque art paved the way for the Baroque.

IV

Poetry and sculpture alike took on sacrificial overtones when Michelangelo put the technique of representation on trial:

> Just as we put, O Lady, by subtraction,
>> Into the rough, hard stone
>> A living figure, grown
>> Largest wherever rock has grown
>> Most small.

> (Sì come per levar, donna, si pone
>> in pietra alpestra e dura
>> una viva figura
>> che la più cresce u più la pietra scema).

However unconsciously, compensation between growth (living figure) and loss (rock-block) frustrated Platonic artists averse to carving away from the universal form. They had been warned that beauty "does not come over integrally into the work; that original beauty is not transferred; what comes is a derivative and a minor; and even that shows itself upon the statue not integrally and with entire realization of intention, but only in so far as it has subdued the resistance of the material" (Plotinus, *Enneads*, V,8,1).

Reticence to waste sculptural matter also affected Michelangelo's treatment of the base, which imitated naturalistic details in the *David* and *Bacchus*. Later, however, the block absorbed base and body within the cubic geometry of the Florentine *Captives*. Technical and conceptual problems thus began to converge; art gave absolute form and absolute idea a guise more akin to sculptural "making."

Because they are roughly carved, the *Captives* enhance the conceptual aspect of the block, which takes on a poetic voice in a sonnet fragment:

> Down from a great cliff, from the highest mountain,
>> where I was cloaked and hidden by great rock,
>> I came to be exposed in this low spot,

> In such a tiny stone, and still unwilling,
> Born with the sun, and, as decreed by Heaven . . .
>
> (Dagli alti monti e d'una gran ruina,
>   ascoso e circunscritto d'un gran sasso,
>   idiscesi a discoprirmi in questo basso,
>   contr'a mie voglia, in tal lapedicina.
>   Quand'el sol nacqui, a da chi il ciel destina.)

The speaking "I" could be the *blocco,* which shared in the un-flawed wholeness of its natural environment as long as it was kept hidden by a great rock on top of a mountain. Unfortunately, that primeval oneness broke down. Unwillingness either to sculpt the whole statue or to write the entire sonnet made of the unfinished a matter of spiritual integrity.

At this point, we ought to turn to a poem that Bernini wrote from the marble's point of view. The subject is a block meant to become a companion piece to *Truth Unveiled by Time:*

> From my ancient rock,
>   To give me life and voice,
>   And not only voice and life but also motion, flight,
>   An artist, unique in this world,
>   One day drew me forth; his hand once wished
>   With its busy chisel
>   And its careful hammer
>   To strike upon me blows of life
>   And thus to make of Time a thing stupendous.

Although form belongs to the representational, the life-giving power of time is immediately undermined:

> But when content and satisfied
>   To hold the concept in his mind,
>   He turned aside and said thus to himself:
>   Will then your hands trained to immortalize
>   Heroes only be able
>   To reveal here among us

> Glories made ready for a cruel tyrant
> Who, in destroying, brings about
> So many injuries to art and Nature?
>
> .   .   .   .
>
> With him my hope took flight
> Of having life, alas, then I lament
> That I forever must remain a stone.

The finished is ephemeral, time destroys what it gives, and execution breaks down the unity of the "concept." For once doubtful, the sculptor left the stone untouched. Clearly, the Michelangeloesque lesson was beyond Bernini's range.

As a practical test, Auguste Rodin wrote that "the art of Michel Angelo created statues all of a size, in a block. He said himself that only those statues were good which could be rolled from the top of a mountain without breaking; and in his opinion all that was broken off in such a fall was superfluous. His figures surely seemed carved to meet this test; but it is certain that not a single antique could have stood it; the greatest works of Pheidias, or Praxiteles, or Polycletus, or Scopas and of Lysippus would have reached the foot of the hill in pieces."[22] One might guess that such a fall would have done no harm to the body-block compactness of the *Captives* (and of Rodin's own armless and headless figures).

For certain, the *Captives* do not enact a story (the humanist *istoria*), but utter a sculptural language at the very edge of expression. If at all possible, the work of art is to body forth the humanization of matter still as matter. Even though captivity could not be conquered, each figure embodies an act of tormented freedom. Narration thus yielded to the presence of figures consumed by a search dubious in outcome and yet irrepressible. Martin Heidegger would suggest that Michelangelo's *non-finito* enacts the classical process of *aletheia,* as truth "emerging into the unconcealedness" of a reality in which the technical "shaping" of the creative act brings knowledge "out of concealedness."[23] Hence, the *non-finito* brought out concerns with the hidden un-hiddenness of divinity.

Once the world of the spirit made more forceful demands, Michelangelo came to accept the idea that vitality could grow only at the expense of beauty. As never before, human forms were pushed back into the block that bore them to life.

Conflicts between representation and expression surfaced in poetry as well:

> If my rough hammer in hard stone can form
>> A human semblance, one and then another,
>> Set moving by the agent who is holder,
>> Watcher and guide, its course is not its own.

> (Se'l mie rozzo martello i duri sassi
>> forma d'uman aspetto or questo or quello
>> dal ministro che 'l guida, iscorge e tiello,
>> prendendo il moto, va con gli altrui passi.)

Dissatisfaction with the "making" of human semblances also shed doubts on the validity of the sculptural act. Since excellence rested with the *concetto,* mental acts could be more essential to creation than physical efforts. A split thus occurred between craft and thought.

> In the multitude of lower things,
>> . . . a blow will have the greatest force
>> As at the forge it's lifted up the highest,
>> This above mine to Heaven has run and flown.

> (E perchè 'l colpo è di valor più pieno
>> quant'alza più se stesso alla fucina,
>> sopra 'l mie questo al ciel n'è gito a volo.)

Emotional intensity raised the agent toward a spiritual realm at odds with the practice of art. While the hammer's blow struck incorporeal sparkles, poetry thrived on the ineffability of thought.[24]

Somehow, hammer and chisel were expected to carve human and spiritual semblances alike. But how? How could ever-deepening emotions be forced into finished shapes? Poetry voiced a dilemma Michelangelo could only hope to solve:

> Wherefore with me, unfinished, all is lost.
> Unless the divine workshop will assist
> In making it; on earth it was alone.

> (Onde a me non finito verrà meno,
> s'or non gli dà la fabbrica divina
> aiuto a farlo, c'al mondo era solo.)

Although he was yet to discover that all was not lost, the artist could not let go of a creative act which he forever held in his hands. He did not cut the umbilical cord between the block and the finished figures. While separation was avoided, effluxion produced statues in which act and form would conquer and defeat each other endlessly.

In the case of Donatello's *David* (marble and bronze), the block delimited a space independent of medieval walls and portals. Nevertheless, relief sculpture on churches and baptistries continued to prosper throughout the fifteenth century.

Michelangelo transferred such a contextual dependence to a background of Platonic ideas. As an early form of that symbolism, the shining transparency of the *Saint Peter's Pietà*—what has been called *troppo finito*—seems to have dissolved the body into the pure light of transcendence; suffering attained sublimity. The sculptor therefore brought a rather medieval spirituality to the humanist block of space. For Paul Klee, in fact, Michelangelo was a transformer of styles who should have "baroquized" the Gothic.[25]

It is a fact that affinities between Gothic and baroque art stemmed from stylistic continuity in northern Europe, where the waning of the Middle Ages lingered on until it reached baroque crossroads.

While providing a more spiritual alternative to Renaissance classicism, chivalric and religious literature (romance, *autos sacramentales*, mystic poetry) in medieval Spain directly linked up with the Counter-Reformation, what Menéndez Pidal has called its *fruto tardío*. On artistic grounds, Gothic styles (*flamboyant* in France and *florido* in Spain) were quite akin to baroque taste north of the Alps. For Michelangelo, however, such contacts turned into lifelong endeavors to grow out of the intellectual isolation of David and Adam. With a view to the Baroque, he stood midway between Savonarola and the *Controriforma*.[26]

V

Inevitably, the openness of Michelangelo's *non-finito* modified the concept of organic unity insofar as it set completion against process. Of Platonic origin, the axiom that parts contribute to the superior unity of the artistic whole was central to the humanist treatises on the arts. For later Neoplatonists, however, the artist himself goes back to the wisdom of nature, which does not consist of "manifold detail coordinated into a unity but rather a unity working out into detail" (Plotinus, *Enneads,* V,8,5). Furthermore, the idea, "as it communicates itself to the corporeal . . . has more of non-being than of being" (Bruno, *Frenzies,* 222). Effluxion and execution cause loss. In the vocabulary of sculpture, the unfinished brings out the resistance that the oneness of matter upholds against fragmentation into details.

Humanist postulates aside, Ficino set the unity of the artwork in the creative act, to which nothing has to be added "to make it better. . . . Unity consists in act."[27] Without necessarily aiming at mimesis, the organic whole obeys laws of its own making. In a figurative sense, completion of the human body became troublesome in the *Florence Pietà* (Fig. 4). After his irate attack, Michelangelo instructed Calcagni not to restore the damaged leg, for he realized that expression could take exceptions with anatomy. Often, tensions between conventional and artistic wholes could enhance each other. Much as the mutilated leg does not hinder the stylistic and psychological unity of the Florentine sculpture, the unfinished state of the body's left side in the drawing *Male Figure Seen from the Back* (1496–1500, Fig. 5) heightens the arching outline from arm to foot on the other side. Points of reference had changed; inner vitality tampered with external appearance. Equally compelling is *Studies for the Crucified Haman* (1511), in which the two arms projected in opposite directions do not interfere with the powerful twist of

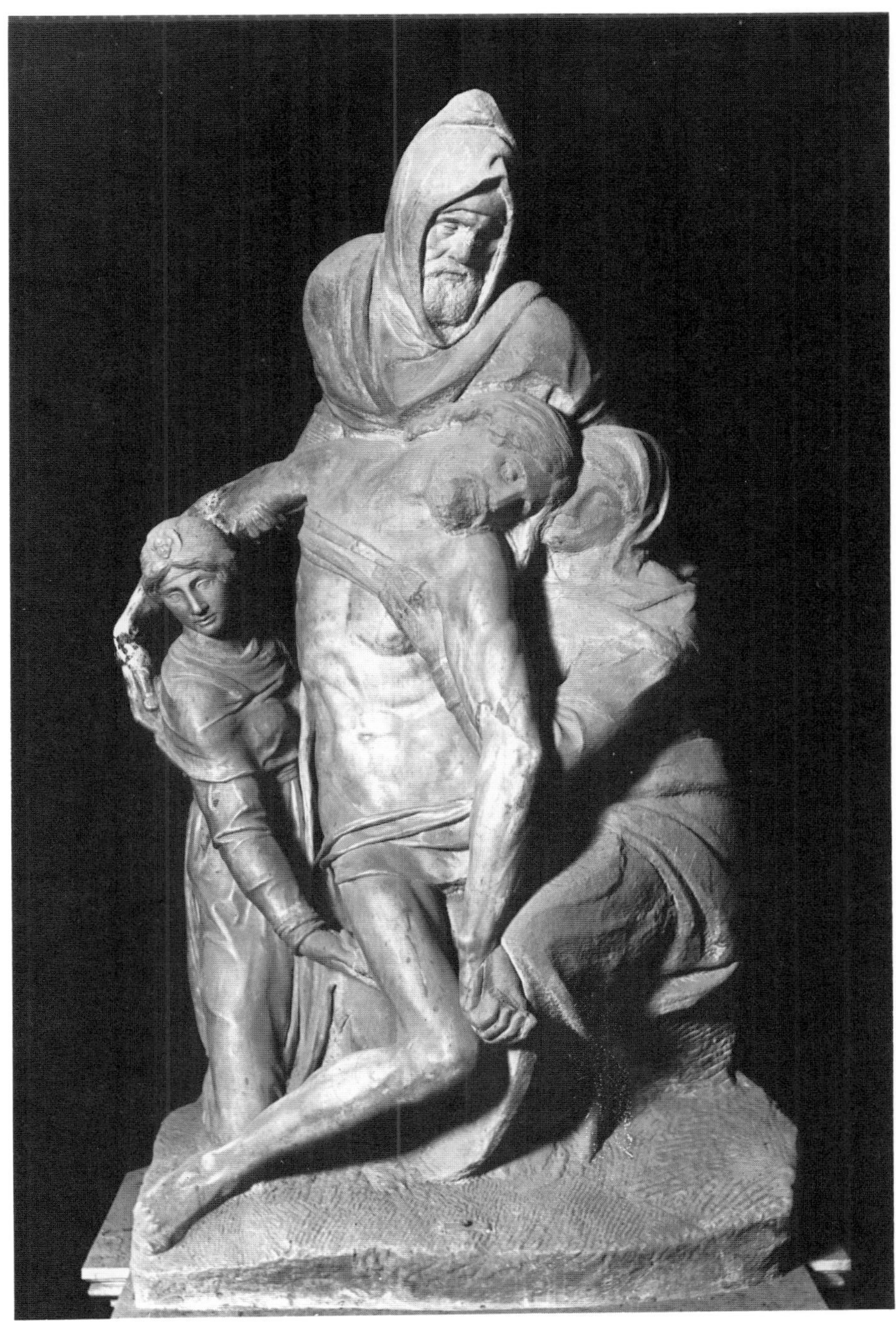

Fig. 4. Michelangelo, *Florence Pietà*, before 1555. Duomo, Florence

the head. Facial tensions would have been covered by the hand, but Michelangelo did not draw it. He did not claim priority for anatomical accuracy. When the drawing became part of the fresco of one of the four spandrels on the Sistine ceiling (Fig. 6), the hand was restored in a position that covered most of the face. Anatomy hindered expression.

The critical notion that nothing can be added or taken away from the artistic whole without destroying it should not be taken as an absolute, since form is adaptable to less than ideal conditions. And the *Torso Belvedere* had taught Michelangelo that the whole could survive damage and afterthoughts. Later, the ravages of external circumstances did not weaken Winckelmann's comments on such a version of Hercules, which he restored to its symbolic integrity: "Abused and mutilated to the utmost, and without head, arms, or legs, as this statue is, it shows itself even now to those who have the power to look deeply into the secrets of art with all the splendor of its former beauty." Beyond mutilation, we can see Hercules surrounded by all his labors; he is again the hero and the god. It suffices to add here that the truncated parts of the *Florence* and *Rondanini Pietàs* spearheaded an artistic approach which Rodin updated in *Torse d'Homme, The Walking Man,* and *Le Serf.* In the name of what has been called the fragmentary aesthetic, such sculptures have told us that an artistic whole need not necessarily coincide with the complete thing. And Marguerite Yourcenar has reminded us that a statue's life begins the day after it is completed. Through erosion, accidents, and abuse, time—*ce grand sculpteur*—keeps the process of artistic creation alive.[28]

VI

Since antiquity, Kenneth Clark writes, ideal beauty and high finish have hindered aesthetic vitality. Whether it be action or the rhythmic sweeping of clothes, classical sculptors enhanced energy through movement; and so did their fifteenth-century heirs.

For a sculptor who, after the *Saint Peter's Pietà,* made of

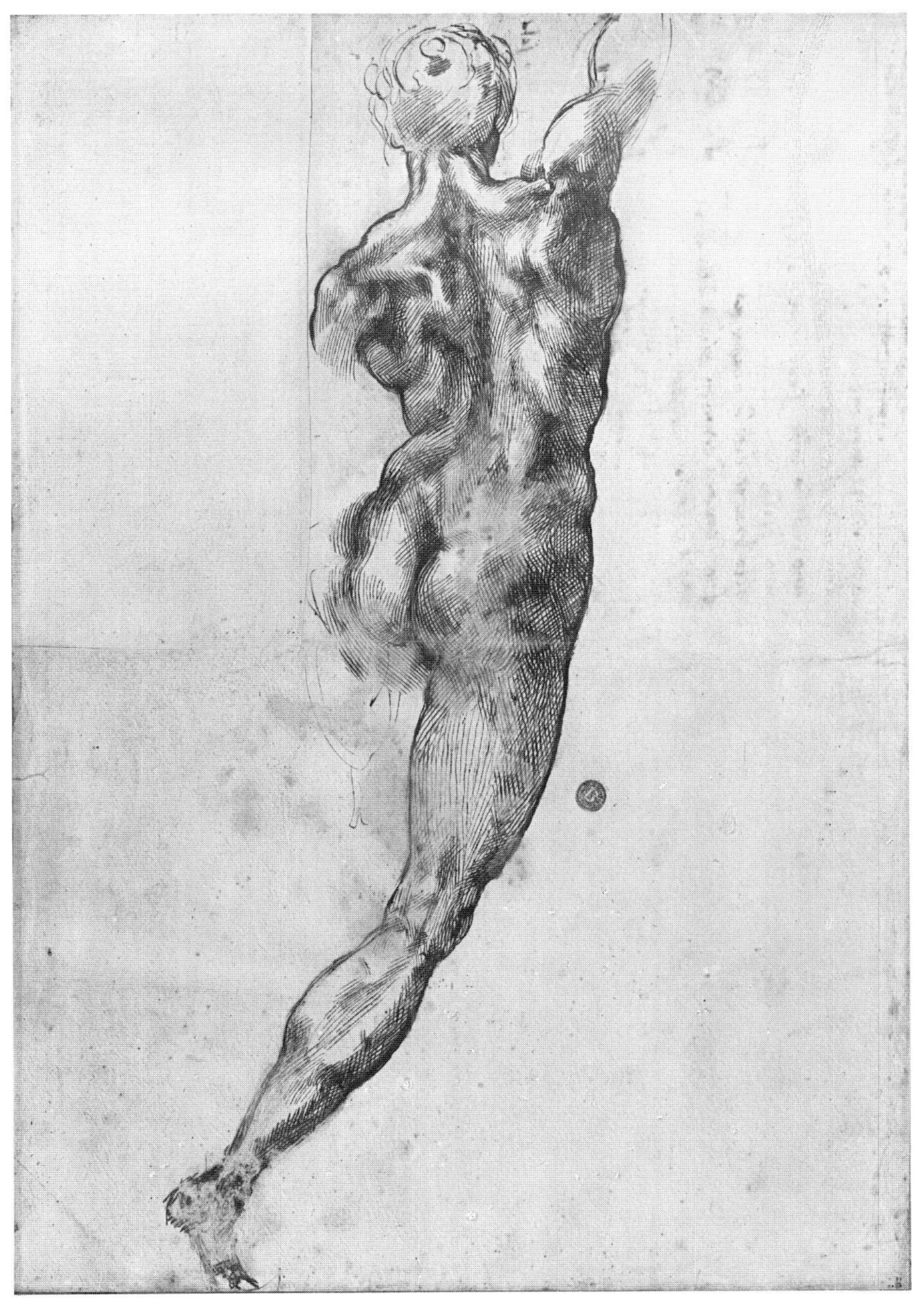

Fig. 5. Michelangelo, *Male Figure Seen from the Back*, 1496–1500. Casa Buonarroti, Florence

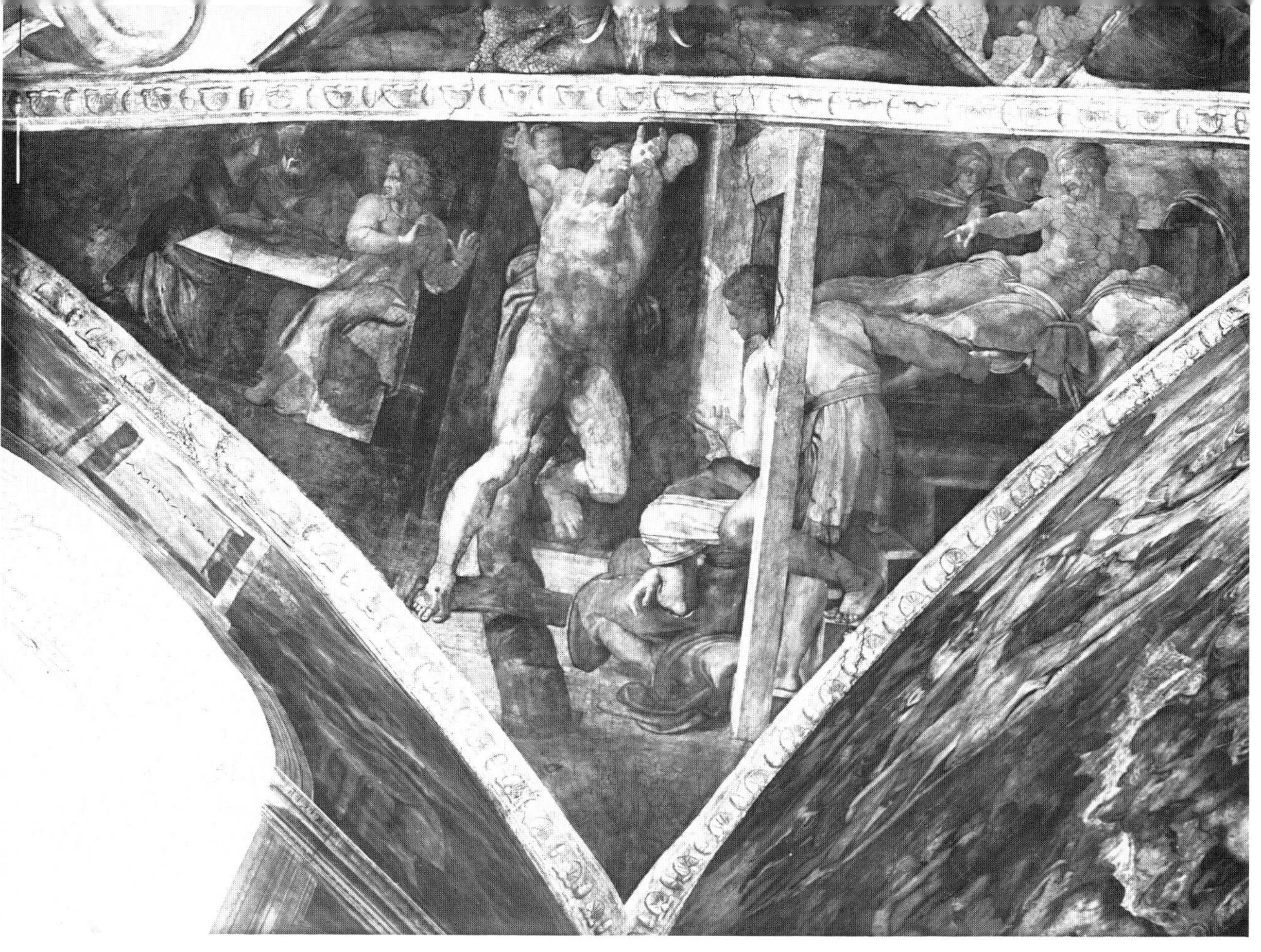

Fig. 6. Michelangelo, *The Crucifixion of Haman*, 1511. Sistine Chapel, Rome

the nude the only carrier of inner strength, ancient and modern statues were both inspirational and challenging. Muscular tensions and twisting bodies uncoil energy in the drawings of the bathing nudes for the fresco of the *Battle of Cascina* (which was never executed). On the Sistine ceiling, the nudes-athletes also struggle toward some bodiless future. Because they "exist as vehicles of expression,"[29] those figures are so distorted that in real life they would appear disproportionate.

There is, Kenneth Clark adds, also a nude "that expresses defeat. The beautiful body, which seemed secure and serene, is defeated by pain. . . . This nude embodiment, which I have called pathos, is always the expression of the same idea, that man in his pride has suffered the wrath of the gods."[30] Michelangelo had to transcend beauty and pathos. Either through agony or sleep, that was the dilemma he wrestled with at the time of the *Dying Slave,* whose slumping body edged on exhaustion.

For a sculptor who elected to keep human forms within the ideal boundaries of the block, an altogether new approach was needed. Contortions, action, and power of expression could not be unleashed through figures interacting with space (as Giambologna and Bernini would do). In Michelangelo's case, solutions of that kind had produced a drunken *Bacchus,* agonizing *Slaves,* and a stylized *Victory.* A new correlation between energy and pathos emerged the moment the block itself was identified with the contextual and ideal matter of art; one grew in direct proportion as the other dwindled. Changes in that relationship affected the vitality of the human spirit.

VII

For Bruno, the renewal of forms stood as a criterion of excellence. More than a decade before his Italian dialogues were written, Michelangelo sculpted his last unfinished piece, the *Rondanini Pietà.* The empty space hovering over Christ's broken arm is saturated with intimations of fall and violence. Before Giacometti, Michelangelo equated existence with perceptual space, which became a cancer out to destroy the essence of being. For them, to sculpt was to trim the fat from space.[31]

   In the world of real life, that cancer consumed the body:
      Time passes on, distributing each hour,
      A very harmful poison in our Life; . . .

   (Muovesi 'l tempo, e compartisce l'ore
      al viver nostr'un pessimo veneno; . . .)

Always living in a state of "great physical anxiety and of the greatest physical fatigue," Michelangelo wore himself "to the bone with every kind of labour." Yet, he would not have wanted it any other way: "I have no friends of any sort and want none. I haven't time enough to eat as I should." Day by day, the loss of his father taught him "to die, not with regret, but with a desire for death." And "the greater part" of his own humanity went with him. When his faithful servant Urbino passed away, the artist wrote: "Of this God has given me a sign in the happy death he died; for he was far less grieved at dying than at leaving me here in this treacherous world with so many burdens; though the greater part of me has gone with him, and nothing but unending wretchedness remains to me."[32] Once alone, the master became servant. As an old sculptor, however, he caught enough of the body to make the moment comprehensible. He was answering Paul's question: "Who will deliver me from this body of death?" (Romans 7.24). At last, physical decay was about to let the soul show forth.

   Michelangelo's attacks on the leg (*Florence Pietà*) and arms (*Rondaninin Pietà*) of Christ scarred art with the wounds that time had inflicted on his own body:

   I am broken up, ruptured and cracked and split
      From my labors so far; death is the inn
      Where I by paying rent can live and eat.

   My honored art, wherein I was for a time
      In such esteem, has brought me down to this:
      Poor and old, under another's thumb,

I am undone if I do not die fast.

(Dilombato, crepato, infranto e rotto
    Son già per le fatiche, e l'osteria
    è morte, dov'io viv' e mangio e scotto.

L'arte pregiata, ov'alcun tempo fui
    di tan'opinion, mi rec'a questo,
    povero, vecchio, e servo in forz'altrui,
    ch'i' son disfatto, s'i' non muoio presto.)

Near the final hour of his last sculpture, the crushing pressure of space devoured the bodily frame; sculptor, sculpture, and sculpting were being undone in art and life alike.

What endured was a process similar to what Manuel García Morente has phrased as *"vivir desviviéndose:"*

> . . . vivir la vida como si no fuera vida temporal, sino eternidad. Santificarse es . . . despojarse, desnudarse, reducirse a lo más hondo y escueto del yo . . . por eso decíamos antes que el hombre hispánico no vive viviendo, no se vive, sino que se desvive; o, dicho de otro modo, que vive muriendo . . . desnudar de materialidad y de vida temporal la persona humana . . . la salvación eterna no es para él solamente un objeto de contemplación; ni tampoco solamente una norma de conducta, sino que es, ante todo y sobre todo, lo que da sentido y finalidad concreta a cada uno de los actos en que se descompose la vida terrestre.[33]

Vivir desviviéndose was echoed in Michelangelo's poetic *discresce,* that is to say, the unraveling of growth itself:

What kind of biting file
    Makes your tired carcass shrivel and decrease,
    Sick soul, forever? When will time release
    You from it, back to where you were in Heaven.

(Per qual mordace lima
    discresce a mance ognor tuo stanca spoglia,
    anima inferma? or quando fie ti scioglia
    da quella il tempo, e torni ov'eri, in cielo.)

The human form could survive the process of age only by sacri-
ficing all but its skeletal core. In Donne's words, he still had
enough body to destroy his soul. The final challenge was at
hand: "I must have this body with me to heaven, or else salvation itself is not perfect; And yet . . . I have too much body for
my soul." Before the writer, the sculptor set out to "attenuate"
his body "by mortification" (*Sermons* II, 63). The chisel thus
made its way through the skin, to the flesh, the bones, and down
to the naked soul of the artwork. Time let go of all its claims,
and the soul foreshadowed forms of divinity.

To unravel growth itself became as compelling an impera-
tive for Michelangelo as it had been for John the Baptist, whose
words seem to have paved the way for *discresce:* "He must
increase, but I must decrease" (Saint John 2.3). In a biblical
spirit, John had to "decrease" his prophetic influence not to lead
followers to believe so much in him as to slight the coming
Christ. His prophetic reflection is confessional; pride must not
come in the way of both Christian destiny and personal salvation. The text presents a moment of crisis, when the epiphany of
self-illumination steers the Baptist toward a transcendental kinship with the ever-fulfilling coming of the Lord.

That moment of crisis was Michelangelo's own. He had
to "decrease" his youthful pride, which had led him to sign his
name of *artifex* on the Virgin's robe (*Michael Angelus Bona-
rotus Florent Faciebat*) alongside the dead Christ. Later, identification with Nicodemus in the *Florence Pietà* enacted the artist's
own redemptive growth. Still in Saint John (2.3), the old man
asks: "How can a man be born when he is old? Can he enter the
second time into his mother's womb, and be born?" Birth thus
opened up to a quest for a new beginning in the realm of the
spirit. At the time of the Florence group, Michelangelo asked the
question, but the gravitational pull of the dead body could only
weigh on the deposition of hope. He could identify with Nicodemus, but was yet to find a way of "increasing" into a resurrec-

tion he could share with Christ himself. Art had reached a point where its mode and tone anticipated forms of the secretive spirituality of later decades.

In the mystic experience of Saint John of the Cross, the ultimate paradox was at hand. Between construction and destruction (sculpture), affirmation and denial (poetry), art could utter a suspended state of eternity:

> God, hear me, what I say is true:
>> I do not want this life of mine,
>> and die because I do not die.
>>> (Trans. Willis Barnstone)

> (Oye, mi Dios, lo que digo,
>> que esta vida no la quiero;
>> que muero porque no muero.)

After the turn of the seventeenth century, even baroque prose echoed the poetic forms of the sculptor's spiritual ordeal:

> I feele that originall canker corrode and devoure me,
> and therefore *Defenda me Dios de me,* Lord deliver
> me from my self.
>> (Thomas Browne, *Religio Medici,* II, 10)

VIII

In one of his sonnets (1509–12) on the Sistine ceiling, Michelangelo wrote:

> In front of me my skin is being stretched
>> While it folds up behind and forms a knot,
>> And I am bending like a Syrian bow.

> (Dinanzi mi s'allunga la corteccia,
>> e per piegarsi adietro si ragroppa,
>> e tendomi com'arco soriano.)

Even at that early stage, art tested human commitment. Effort and pain dug into the physical self, until no more skin was left by the time the torso of the last *Pietà* was sculpted.

What remained was human matter somehow "redeemed" of its own corporeality, which became so unsubstantial that the bent knees uplift the weightless Christ. As a fetal image of transcendence, anatomy seems to verge on the a-gravitational threshold before birth and after death. Christ's hollowed torso therefore stood as a shadow of eternity bending (see the arched and tensive side view of the sculpture) toward its supernal womb.

> A prayer voiced hopes of resurrection:
> Lord, in the final hour,
> Stretch out thy pitying arms to me, take me
> Out of me, make me one that pleases Thee.

> (Signor, nell'ore streme,
> Stendi ver' me le tuo pietose braccia,
> Tomm'a me stesso a famm'un che ti piaccia.)

At once sacrificial and redemptive, Michelangelo's surrender to the Lord gave art a total image of life and death.

Expansion to the limits of matter also marked stages in the life of the Brunonian spirit, which, "once time has run its course and the stem of life has been cut, recoils on its center and again projets itself toward the infinite space. That event is usually identified with death; since we move toward an unknown light, few people can in fact realize the extent to which our life really means death, whereas death really means a new life" (*Opere*, 100).

In light of its death-resurrection symbolism, the *Rondanini Pietà* first responds to gravity and then defies it. Set against empty space, the broken arm is all the more impressive when one understands that it draws on the disintegration of the upper torso of an earlier design of the Christ figure. Although truncated, that robust limb was a last tribute to a proud *artifex* who once had believed that physical beauty (*Saint Peter's Pietà*) could edge on immortality.

The theme of creative power was played against destruction in an unfinished sestina written between 1525 and 1529:

Even if, besides my own, all other arms
    Seem to defend all my most precious things

    .   .   .   .

    Love, I feel myself now being turned to nothing

.   .   .   .

    While my soul from my body is not yet taken,
    Lord, who can turn the universe to nothing,
    Maker and governor, King of all things,
    It's little to you in me to take a place,
    As . . . these are mortal arms
    That . . . and always be your shield.

    .   .   .   .

    For every virile man the genuine arms,
    Not having which all men turn into nothing.

(Sie pur, fuor di mie propie, c'ogni altr'arme
    difender par ogni mie cara cosa;

    .   .   .   .

    Amore, i' sento già di me far nulla;

    .   .   .   .

    Mentre c'al corpo l'alma non è tolta,
    Signor, che l'universo può far nulla,
    fattor, governator, re d'ogni cosa,
    poco ti fie aver dentr'a me loco;

    .   .   .   .

    che d'ogn' uomo veril son le vere arme,
    senza le quali ogn' uom diventa nulla.)

The breaking down of the body follows that of language. Discourse falters, while unspoken fragments of hope emerge. For the *homo artifex,* the hand was a creative analogue through which God gave power to Adam and strength to David. As he was about to rid scuplture of the cancer of physicality, Michelangelo made of the broken arm his farewell to David, Adam, and his youthful forms of human dignity.

In the *Rondanini Pietà,* the arm's fleshy presence vis-à-vis the emaciated torso suggests a process of reduction, a hopeful disvestiture of the physical self echoed in a poetic fragment (1552):

> The soul gains more the more it's lost the world,
>   And death and art do not go well together.
>   What should I of myself then hope for still?
>
> (Più l'alma acquista ove più 'l mondo perde;
>   l'arte e la morte non va bene insieme:
>   che convien più che di me dunche speri?)

If at all possible, the highest beauty could be conquered only through the sacrifice of art to death, since Michelangelo no longer needed to sculpt what he himself was becoming.

As a form of that longing, the shrinkage of the torso in the last *Pietà* brought up the very likeness of the sculptor's own corpse.[34] That image best illustrates Leonardo da Vinci's vision of a body reduced to *"ispogliate, spolpate, e ignude ossa."* In fact, Leonardo insisted that anatomy should "represent all the stages of the limbs from man's creation to his death, and then till the death of the bone; and which part of him is first decayed and which is preserved the longest."[35] For Michelangelo, growth and decay set forth a spiritual process at the end of which a transcendental pull lifted him toward heights where Neoplatonic souls found "light in darkness, life in death, eternity in time, the infinite among finite things."[36]

The old sculptor ended his earthbound journey in the metaphysical drama of his last *Pietà,* which presented mother and son as figures of growth, death, and renewal. At the earliest stage, the Child had struggled to move away from her mother in the *Bruges Madonna,* as if urged on by destiny. But in the higher realm of Platonic ideas, birth itself carried fetters. In Donne's words, captivity started there: "Wee are all conceived in close Prison; in our Mothers wombes, we are close prisoners all" (*Sermons* II, 197). Only poetry could give a better sense of Christ's nativity:

> *Immensitie cloystered in thy deare wombe,*
>   Now leaves his welbelov'd imprisonment,
>   There he hath made himselfe to his intent
>   weake enough, now into our world to come
>   (*Holy Sonnets*, I)

We grow prisoners "within larger walls," until we get to "the place of Execution, to death," which seized Christ in the *Florence Pietà*. Slowly, Michelangelo understood that, "if we be dead with him, we shall be raised with him." Since life's journey is "from the womb to the grave" (*Sermons* II, 196–97), it was in the womb that the flesh of separation was born. And only a return to the womb could foster a unity that would not die. At the beginning, the Virgin was

>   Thy Makers maker.
>   (*Holy Sonnets*, I)

At the end, they sustained each other, while "glottonous death" would "instantly unjoynt" their bodies (*Holy Sonnets*, VI). Yet, death could not conquer their unfettered power within; theirs was the bond that could not be captive, the knot that would not be untied. In that last sculpture, the Christian drama would not become a tragedy. The earth claimed the earthborn, but art gave birth to a dawn that would last forever. Beyond the last fragments of sculptural solidity, only the poet's words could spell the triumph of faith:

>   we wake eternally,
>   And death shall be no more; death, thou shall die.
>   (*Holy Sonnets*, X)

Within the boundaries of the intrinsic time of forms evoked, retained, and overcome,[37] it is fit to remember that Michelangelo worked on the *Rondanini Pietà* down to the last days of his life. At that point, "sculpting" traced the story of man as memory and hope, loss and search. Nicodemus's question came back: "How can a man be born when he is old? Can he enter the second time into his mother's womb, and be born?"

Christ had died, and his resurrection had showered new light; death escaped the grip of age. The sculptural unity of the Christ-Virgin in the ascending trunk of the last *Pietà* gave presence to the face and word of Christ's answer to the old man: "Ye must be born again." In the blindness of his last days on earth, when memories and hopes were disintegrating the remnants of existence, the artist bodied forth a prophetic image of his own rebirth in eternity's womb.

At last, the truncated limb of youth yielded to the "piteous" and "trusty" support enfolding mother and son in the Milan sculpture. An old prayer was answered:

> Like an old serpent through a narrow place
> > So may I pass, discarding my old arms,
> > My soul's behavior be renewed, and taken
> > During my lifetime from all human things.

> (Quel vecchio serpe per istretto loco
> > passar poss'io, lasciando le vecchie arme,
> > e dal costume rinnovata e tolta
> > sie l'alma in vita e d'ogni umana cosa.)

At the time he wrote those verses, Michelangelo had the words and the *concetto,* but the sculptural form was missing.

At least in poetry, the soul could seek renewal where the hand no longer was of any use:

> The causes yield and bow to the results;
> > Hence it is art that overpowers nature.
> > I know, I've tested it in beautiful sculpture,
> > Time and death to the work will not keep trust.
> > . . . .
> > By either means, with carving or with paint,
> > Portraying both the faces of us two.

> (La causa a l'effetto inclina e cede,
> > onde dall'arte è vinta la natura.
> > I' 'l so, che 'l pruovo in la bella scultura,
> > c'all'opra il tempo e morte non tien fede.
> > . . . .

> in qual sie modo, o di colore o sasso,
> di noi sembrando l'uno e l'altro volto . . .)

Art had overpowered nature at the time of Adam and David. Later, age and faith led from effects to the cause:

> Searching through many tests and through much time,
>> The wise man will attain the true idea,
>> Only when death is near,

> (Negli anni molti e nelle molte pruove,
>> cercando, il saggio al buon concetto arriva
>> d'un'immagine viva, vicino a morte.)

The true idea ("*buon concetto*") conquered false beliefs ("*falsi concetti*"), but only near death could eternity filter through time:

> There's no painting or sculpture now that quiets
>> The soul that's pointed toward that holy Love
>> That on the cross opened Its arms to take us.

> (Né pinger né scolpir fie più che quieti
>> l'anima, volta a quell'amor divino
>> c'aperse, a prender noi, 'n croce le braccia.)

As a sublime paradox, the last unfinished *Pietà* was Michelangelo's most complete sculpture, for it encompassed—to use a Brunonian phrase—"man's attempt to capture human totality" (*Opere*, 420).

At that final stage, the sculptor could lean on both sides of death. Anticipating a baroque choice, Michelangelo brought to light restless forms that were to inspire the poetics of formation.[38] If art is a means for a better understanding of the endless challenge of life, then one can agree with Jean Rousset that "the Baroque carries within itself an innate hostility toward the completed work; because it antagonizes any stable form, its own demons drive it beyond form the moment it has been produced, so as to move toward another form."[39]

IX

Having conquered his own captivity, Michelangelo died in the spirit and image of Christ. He set himself free of earthbound fetters, and fulfilled a quest undertaken as early as 1520:

> I see myself as yours, from far invoke
>> My own approach to Heaven, my derivation,
>> And reach the bait, you, through the imitation.

> (Di te me veggo e di lontan mi chiamo
>> per appressarm'al ciel dond'io derivo,
>> e per le spezie all'esca a te arrivo.)

At the outer limits of the human spirit, art would help him to cross the line between resemblance and identity.

Keeping classical fatalism aside, Michelangelo turned to the un-Greek patterns of the Christian ascent from doom to grace:

> And single phoenix cannot live again
>> Unless it first burns. So, if I die burnt,
>> Brighter I hope among those to come back
>> Whom death enhances, time does not demean.

> (ne l'unica fenice se riprende
>> se non prim'arsa; ond'io, s'ardendo moro,
>> spero più chiar resurger tra coloro
>> che morte accresce e 'l tempo non offende.)

Life must be described in terms of death, and death must be phrased in terms of rebirth. In losing his life, the Christian hero finds it. One must die to be born again.[40]

Beyond the reach of broken arms, beyond Adam and David, the hollowed Christ-Michelangelo arched between time and eternity. The sculptor thus overcame the realm of tragedy, which had weighed down the slumping body of Christ at the time of the *Florence Pietà:*

I live, dying for me, for sin alive,
　　My life's indeed not of me, but of sin;

　　·　·　·　·　·　·　·　·　·　·　·　·　·

　　My mortal part of a good, freedom a slave
　　For me is made; O terrible condition!

(Vivo al peccato, a me morendo vivo;
　　vita già mia non son, ma del peccato:

　　·　·　·　·　·　·　·　·　·　·　·　·

　　Serva mie libertà, mortal mie divo
　　a me s'è fatto. O infelice stato!)

Michelangelo's earlier identification with Nicodemus had finally turned toward the Savior, whose Passion and Resurrection were reenacted:

For he who lives on death will never die.

(che chi vive di morte mai non muore).

A line that paved the way for the mystic verses of Saint John of the Cross:

I live yet do not live in me,
　　am waiting as my life goes by,
　　and die because I do not die.

(Vivo sin vivir en mí,
　　y de tal manera espero,
　　que muero porque no muero)

While retaining figurative vestiges, the *Rondanini Pietà* raised power of expression toward spiritual heights. Since, according to Michelangelo,

No one has mastery
　　Before he is at the end
　　Of his art and his life, . . .

> (non ha l'abito intero
> prima alcun, c'a l'estremo
> dell'arte e della vita . . .)

It was at the end of his own life that he mastered *finito* and *non-finito*. Beauty was undone to the point that power of expression bathed in sublimity the truest form of spiritual plenitude. Whether it be wood or the block of marble, the unconquerable form of matter, Bruno wrote, truly "is all that it can be; and so it has all measure, has all species of figures and dimensions" (*Cause*, 126) in the artistic realm of the unfinished.

In the aphoristic style of a modern Platonist, the *Ronda-nini Pietà* gave presence to that stage of human experience where duration edges on the metaphysical form of process. For Nicolas Berdyaev, Michelangelo succeeded better than most in sculpting the renewal of spiritual becoming, which is "eternal newness, eternal creative ecstasy, the dissolving of being, in divine freedom."[41]

The Breaking of the Circle: Giordano Bruno and the Poetics of Immeasurable Abundance

A Dominican monk, a gypsy professor, a commentator of old philosophies and a deviser of new ones, a playwright, a polemist, a counsel for his own defense, and, finally, a martyr burned at the stake in the Campo dei Fiori—Bruno, through all these modes and accidents (as he would have called them) of being, remains a consistent spiritual unity.

—James Joyce

I

After its publication, Torquato Tasso put his *Jerusalem Delivered* (*Gerusalemme liberata* 1575) to the test of critical standards, and he complied with them.

Such a precedent, however, did not stop Bruno from writing a few years later (1584–85):

> Poetry is not born of rules, except by the merest chance,
> but that the rules derive from the poetry. For that reason
> there are as many genres and species of true rules as
> there are of true poets. (*Frenzies*, 83)

Against the grain of humanist ideology, form and content coexisted within acts of creation that tested norms of style, genre, and language. The Brunonian seed soon yielded a baroque harvest that was to nurture later commitments not to oppose genius to rules (Coleridge), for the meaning of the work is to be found within the work itself (Croce).[1]

Whereas the humanists (Alberti, Bruni) quickly set up models that stifled their *aemulatio* of antiquity, Bruno never tired of giving precedence to originality over conformity. In fact, "Homer was not a poet who depended upon the rules, but he is the cause of the rules." In turn, Aristotelian precepts were "drawn up by an author who was not a poet of any sort but who knew how to assemble rules of that particular kind (that is, rules of Homeric poetry) for the benefit of one who would wish to be not another poet with a muse of his own, but an imitator of Homer and the ape of Homer's muse." Actually, rules are useful to "those who cannot, as Homer, Hesiod, Orpheus and others could, be a poet without the aid of Aristotle" (*Frenzies*, 82–83). The scoundrels were the Aristotelians, that is to say, the imitators and traditionalists of all ages. In an equally polemical vein, Montaigne claimed that "the honor of invention is greatly and incomparably preferable to the honor of quotation" (809).

Critical as he was of models of any kind, Bruno "could not find a part similar to another part nor atoms like other atoms" (*Opere*, 148). Just as "the irregularity of a stone does not fit, coincide, and join with the irregularity of any other stone (but only where the reliefs and the hollows best correspond), in the same way any appearance will not strike just any mind."[2] At all levels, emphasis was placed on the individual.

Antinormative at heart, Bruno found unconventional forms attractive: "Whether it consists in some kind of proportion or in something incorporeal which shines through physical nature, beauty is manifold and works on countless levels."[3] In fact, the beautiful in nature is "far better presented in innumerable individuals than in those which are numbered and finite" (*Infinite*, 257). As Yeats later put it, "two and two must make four, though no two things are alike." In spite of mathematical symmetry and beyond humanist proportion, nature proves that "everything is unique and nothing unique is measurable."[4]

Variety also attracted Montaigne in those final decades of the sixteenth century: "Both the Greeks and the Latins, as we ourselves, use eggs for the most express example of similarity. However, there have been men, and notably one at Delphi, who recognized marks of difference between eggs, so that he never took one for another; and although there were many hens, he could tell which one the egg came from" (815).

In the realm of visual forms, Bernini said that in making a portrait from life it was necessary to be able to recognize "the unique qualities of individuality that nature gives to each person rather than the generality common to all."[5] Classical and humanist conformity to models of "sameness" gave way to the baroque preference for diversity, what Arthur Lovejoy would have called an abundance of differentness.[6]

On baroque grounds, differentness is central to the semantic meaning of that much debated "cultural" word: *barocco*. It suffices to mention here an etymology falling within the province of syllogism (from medieval logic) and deceit (*baroco*, with regard to shady commercial practices). More important is the Spanish *barrueco-berrueco*, namely, a node or pearl of irregular shape. Whereas the adjective *barrueco* underlines a physical-psychological-stylistic reality, the Italian substantive *barocco* indicates a metaphysical-intellectual-polemical reality vis-à-vis tradition. From atoms and stones to eggs and pearls, irregularity undermined uniformity. The ugly stood next to the beautiful, and mixture legitimized a world of bizarre forms.[7]

At a time when progress was being measured "by disagreement more than by agreement, by difference more than by similarity" (Montaigne, 703), art conceded that the true "rule consists in knowing how to break rules according to contemporary taste—*la vera regola è saper rompere le regole a tempo e luogo*."[8] In his life of the artist, Baldinucci tells us that even Bernini liked to say that going beyond the rules is sometimes necessary.

Misplaced in a center-less universe, and challenged by a

world of appearances, certainty gave way to "relativism in relations."[9] Since it could not be based on reason, value was founded on consensus. Each individual could define beauty and become its critic. However anti-Michelangeloesque, "realistic" paintings gained popular approval in Rome and elsewhere (Caravaggio and the Caravaggeschi). Seeking acceptance, artists often surrendered to opinionated audiences (Bacon's *sons of science*), the effluvia of mobs (Gracian), and the acclaim of crowds (Lope de Vega). Playwrights transferred successful sketches from one comedy to another (Bernini), while prologues and epilogues courted readers on and off stage (Cervantes's "idling reader," Ben Jonson's "reader extraordinary").[10]

II

Having set the old apart from the new, Bruno also drew a wedge between professional imitators and true poets. In the latter's camp, love poets (myrtle) were set apart from those of the laurel, "who instruct heroic souls through speculative philosophy." Stating a preference for the latter, *The Heroic Frenzies* (81–82) pivot around a group of poems followed by critical and philosophical commentaries. Analysis and invention met in the same text. At last, the Nolan became "Guide, Law, Seer, Father, and Author" (*Opere*, 418).

    Such an assertive spirit guided Bruno's approach to myth as well. Humanist transcendence set the Icarus legend on a mountaintop where a wise man was about to leap "through the superior world."[11] Bruno later compared that Neoplatonic symbol to a frenzied ascent (*Frenzies* 1, dialogue 3):

> Since I have spread my wings toward sweet
>   delight, the more do I feel the air beneath my
>   feet, the more I spread proud pinions to the wind,
>   and contemn the world, and further my way toward
>   heaven.
>   Nor does the cruel fate of Daedalus's son
>   burden me, on the contrary I follow his way the
>   more: that I shall fall dead upon the earth I am

well aware; but what life compares with this
death?

I hear the voice of my heart upon the wind:
where do you take me, adventurous one? Resign
yourself, for too much temerity is rarely without
danger.

I reply: fear not noble destruction, burst
boldly through the clouds, and die content, if
heaven destines us to so illustrious a death.

(Poi che spiegat'ho l'ali al bel desio,
    Quanto più sott'il piè l'aria mi scorgo,
    Più le veloci penne al vento porgo,
    E spreggio il mondo, e vers' il ciel m'invio.
      Nè del figliuol di Dedalo il fin rio
    Fa che giù pieghi, anzi via più risorgo.
    Ch'i' cadrò morto a terra, ben m'accorgo;
    Ma qual vita pareggia al morir mio?
      La voce del mio cor per l'aria sento:
    —Ove mi porti, temerario? China,
    Che raro e senza duol tropp'ardimento.—
      Non temer, respond'io, l'alta ruina.
    Fendi sicur le nubi, e muor contento,
    S'il ciel si illustre morte ne destina).

Actually, Bruno phrased his endless pursuit of knowledge
through a love sonnet which Luigi Tansillo had written for Maria d'Aragona. While the latter joined the life-cycle of the poet-
as-poet in a text where he is both creator ("guest"—author) and
creation (interlocutor), the former availed himself of a power
absent in the parent poem proper.[12]

At first, Benedetto Croce detected two different poems in
the same set of words. Later (1944), he read the sonnet as a
single poem expressing a state of mind that could be either
emotional (Tansillo) or intellectual (Bruno). Since "words are
inasmuch as they signify something, whoever reads different
meanings in them is confronted with different words."[13] Often
parodic, individual readings (or adaptations thereof) could multiply meaning at will.

At the heart of the humanist frame of mind was a sustained dialogue with the past, and Petrarch set up a mode of learning when he wrote to Boccaccio (1359):

> I have read Virgil, Horace, Livy, Cicero, not once but a thousand times, not hastily but in repose, and I have pondered them with all the powers of my mind. I ate in the morning what I would digest in the evening; I swallowed as a boy what I would ruminate upon as a man. These writings I have so thoroughly absorbed and fixed, not only in my memory but in my very marrow.[14]

Bearing on *aemulatio,* mistranslations of older texts produced nodes of diachronic interactions between individuals and cultures.

Because of a lapse of time, lexical indeterminacy allowed Bruno to rewrite Tansillo's poem with a different meaning. Literature, more than writers, was the essential thing, and textual interactions of that sort became a baroque cornerstone. For Bruno, the old world of words uttered modern prophecies:

> There will come an age
>   In the far-off years, when the Ocean
>   Shall unloose the bonds of things
> (*Ash*, 59)

> (Venient annis
> Saecula seris, quibus Oceanus
> Vincula rerum laxent)
> (Seneca, *Medea,* 378–80)

The poetry of the Argonauts "foretold long ago" Columbus's journey. Instead of causing anxiety, influence kept the formal process of creation open. From Bruno to Montaigne, glosses, quotes, and commentaries made of language an epistemological activity always prone to test its semantic range.[15]

In the Brunonian cosmology, literature itself could undergo rebirth; it called for misreadings. Because of a common "Fate of Mutation," poetry would "incur many other worse and better species of life and fortune" (*Expulsion,* 78). Aiming at an epiphanic convergence of tradition and individual talent, Bruno drew from Plato, Tansillo, and Copernicus. Even myth enhanced the legitimacy of a new worldview wherein Icarus's initial ascent toward "sweet delight" (*The Heroic Frenzies*) finally turned to boundlessness:

And while I rise from my own globe to others
    And penetrate ever further through an eternal field,
    That which others saw from afar, I leave far behind me.
                                    (*Infinite*, 249)

(E mentre dal mio globo a gli altri sorgo,
    E per l'eterio campo oltre penetro:
    Quel ch'altri lungi vede, lascio al tergo.)

The poet's death could not mute his poetry. And when the heart failed writing, the power of creation was passed on to the mourning tongues of admirers who scattered his ashes into the soul of futurity. As W. H. Auden wrote,

      The words of a dead man
        Are modified in the guts of the living.
             (*In Memory of W. B. Yeats*)

In the more competitive jargon of literary indebtedness, such a transformation of the precursor's lines validates Harold Bloom's claim: "When you read, you confront either yourself, or another, and in either confrontation you seek power."[16]

From precursors back to archetypes, Bruno's treatment of Icarus, Actaeon, and the phoenix pointed toward a distinction between poetry and history: "It is certainly an appropriate way, when someone intends to present history and give laws, to speak according to the general understanding." While ideas fall back on mythic images, the details of life belong to verbal discourse. Accordingly, Jove warns not to "expect an ornate contexture of words . . . and, according to the institute of orators, conceits sooner placed three times to the file than once on the tongue." As a matter of fact, "Giordano speaks in a vulgar manner. . . . He calls bread, bread; wine, wine . . . and all other parts by their own names" (*Expulsion*, 104–5, 71). Since he believed in the growth of language, the Nolan mixed Latin and vernacular, literal and figurative levels of expression.[17]

While calling himself *Academico di nulla Academia* in *The Candle Bearer* (*Il candelaio*, 1582), Bruno would not "undermine the edifice of good discipline to establish the frame of perversity" (*Infinite*, 230). Opposition was stated against sixteenth-century critics who did not—or chose not to—understand that Aristotle's comments "are there only to show us the kind of epic poet Homer was, and not to serve as modes of instruction to other poets who could in other veins, skills, and frenzies be in their several kinds equal, similar or even greater than Homer" (*Frenzies*, 82).

At the beginning of the *Cinquecento*, Aretino had set scholars of art (imitators) against disciples of nature (true artists), and a line was drawn between true poets and those who practice the art of writing verses (Fracastoro's *Il Navagero*). At the height of the baroque season, it was generally acknowledged that Aristotle "taught oratory, but never exercised it . . . taught poetics, but never wrote a poem . . . taught conceits, but never composed one."[18] The result was the downfall of man's faith in the postulates of humanistic poetics.

Without rejecting genre altogether, Bruno wrote dialogues containing internal monologues, comedic altercations, and even narrative passages. Coleridge found Theophil's journey through London in *The Ash Wednesday Supper* "curious for its lively accounts of the rude state" of the city, "both as to the streets and the manners of the citizens."[19] In the spirit of *imitazione rappresentativa mista*, the Nolan mixed narrative, argumentative, critical, and satirical modes in his dialogues, which misinterpreted Plato, Lucian, and Erasmus. Consistent with contemporary statements on the dialogue form (Tasso's *Discorso dell'arte del dialogo*, 1585), Bruno approached the genre by standing midway between poets and dialecticians. His sonnets in fact shed light on the exemplary status that lyric poetry had achieved (side by side with epic and drama) late in the sixteenth century.

Discussion in humanist dialogues could not fail to reach clarity. On balance, the interlocutor-protagonist of Alberti's treatise *On the Family* (*Della famiglia*) asserts, does not suggest, and the interlocutor-listener accepts, does not share. Disagreements sharpen authorial stands, while inconsequential objections do not distract a receptive (if not already convinced) audience.

In the Socratic sense, the dialogic means of seeking truth is counterposed to "official monologism, which pretends to possess a ready-made truth." Because of its leveling authority, monologic space recognizes another person as an object of consciousness, but not as another consciousness. The Albertian truth was ready-made. By contrast, dialogic truth is born between people committed to mutual interactions.[20]

For Bruno, the expression of thought was one with its tentative making. His "are dialogues, wherein are interlocutors, who make their own speeches, and by whom are reported the discourses of many, many others, who equally abound in their own meanings, reasoning with that fervor and zeal which, especially, can be and are appropriate to them" (*Expulsion*, 73). Knowledge is memorized, interpreted, and transferred from one interlocutor to the next.

Bruno entrusted readers with gathering from the genre what they could "according to the capacity of their bowls." Even Copernicanism unveiled "contradictions and oppositions . . . he who doesn't like one thing may take another" (*Cause*, 60). While no text was sacred, every reader had to upgrade his understanding of it. Actually, "there is nothing so wicked that it may not be converted to the profit and usefulness of good people; and there is nothing so good and worthy that it cannot be the cause and material of scandal." The dialogue therefore tends to convert one extreme into its opposite, "that which satisfies" into "that which wearies" (*Expulsion*, 74, 90). As such, the dialogic mode has been typical of writers particularly aware of human fellowship.[21]

III

In the Platonic tradition, poetry is inspired by the Muses. Although the poet "is a light and winged and holy thing," there "is no invention in him until he has been inspired and is out of his sense, and the mind is no longer in him" (*Ion, 534*). Furthermore, "he who, having no touch of the Muses' madness in his soul, comes to the door and thinks that he will get into the temple by that help of art—he, I say, and his poetry are not admitted" (*Phaedrus, 250*). Since they "are simply inspired to utter that to which the Muse impels them, and that only" (*Ion, 534*), poets become divine mouthpieces. Emphasis is placed on communicative—rather than creative—powers. In a Neoplatonic key, the "poetic frenzy springs from the Muses; but he (Plato) considers both the man and his poetry worthless who approaches the doors of poetry without the call of the Muses, in the hope that he will become a good poet by technique."[22]

Passivity, however, was only one aspect of the Platonic heritage. Since antiquity, creation out of nothing has been a divine prerogative. Mortals, on the other hand, could make something out of something else (Philo, Augustine, Athanasius), namely, mimesis and the materials of the craft. The concept of art as imitation (Plotinus, Philostratus, and Longinus) gave way to that of art as expression. Steadily, recognition of the mind's autonomy made of the artist an analogue to God.

Inspired as they were by Cicero's *Pro Archia*, the humanists (Petrarch's *Invectiva contra medicum*, Boccaccio's *De genealogia deorum*, Coluccio Salutati's *De fato et fortuna*) made poetry depend on an inborn faculty:[23]

> And the Greeks say "poet" from the verb "poiein," which is half-way between "creating," which is peculiar to God when out of nothing he brings forth anything into being, and "making," which applies to men when they compose with matter and form in any art. It is for this reason that, although the feigning of the poet is not entirely out of nothing, it nevertheless departs from making and comes very near to creating. And God is the supreme poet, and the world is His poem.[24]

Philosophy, art, and language stood at a turning point, where the Platonic-classical *making* (out of already existing materials) met with the Hebraic-Christian *creating;* the artist became a semi-Creator.

Although in the epistolary form, Ficino treated the simile with panegyrical enthusiasm:

> The philosophic spirit imitates, and expresses exactly, the secret works of the Almighty God, making them manifest in thought, words and letters, through different instruments and materials. But I think one thing, especially, should be appreciated; not everyone can understand the principle or method by which the marvellously fashioned work of the all-skilled creator has been constructed, but only he who has the same genius for the art . . . who can deny that his mind is virtually one with the author of the heavens himself? And that in a sense he would be able to create the heavens and what is in them himself, if he could obtain the tools and the heavenly material. For he does now create them, albeit of another material, nevertheless on the same design.[26]

By humanist standards, that was creation in an analogical mode blessed with, rather than diminished by, God's presence.

A century later, Bruno praised individual geniuses:

> Tansillo—because of a custom or habit of contemplation, and because they are naturally endowed with a lucid and intellectual spirit, when under the impact of an internal stimulus and spontaneous fervor spurred on by the love of divinity, justice, truth and glory, by the fire of desire and inspired purpose, they make keen their senses and in the sulphurous cognitive faculty enkindle a rational flame which raises their vision beyond the ordinary. And these do not go about speaking and acting as mere receptacles and instruments, but as chief inventors and authors. (*Frenzies*, 107–8)

In his own case, the Nolan added: "I won't speak like a holy prophet, an abstracted diviner, an apocalyptic visionary, or the angelic she-ass of Balaam. I shall not discourse as if inspired by Bacchus, nor as if swoln-up with wind through the prostituted

Muses of Parnassus. . . . I'll speak, I say, like a man who has no other brain than his own" (*Cause,* 59).

As such, frenzies and ecstasies involve a movement from one time frame (*stasis*) to another (*ekstasis*). For Bruno, "he who is moved is always another, and he who is another always bears himself and behaves otherwise than he did before" (*Frenzies,* 255). The result is a displacement (in Greek *ekstasis* means "to stand elsewhere") whereby one moves into the wonder of otherness, into the ecstatic.[27] Since heroic frenzies "do not arise from forgetfulness, but from remembrance" (*Frenzies,* 115), the human will "govern the affections of the inferior potencies against the surge of their natural violence." If "it is unjust that the sense outrage the law of reason, it is equally blamable that the reason tyrannize the law of the senses." The rational faculty reconciles the "one with the many, the same with the diverse, motion with position, the inferior with the superior" (*Frenzies,* 87, 135, 121). Beyond clashes between sense and mind, the frenzy unraveled a heroic activity at the threshold of intuitive knowledge.

From a literary standpoint, Bruno's leanings toward the Platonic world of ideas (*Phaedrus*) stood against the ever-growing influence of Aristotle's *Rhetoric.* At the height of the baroque season, Tesauro tried to reconcile the two in *Il cannocchiale aristotelico,* in which *ingegno* and *furore* made poetic conceits out of hidden relationships. Actually, madness was an apt condition of art insofar as it led to taking one thing for another; insanity was metaphorical.[28]

Ultimately, art and mind came together in the Brunonian experience of spiritual heights:

> This phoenix which kindles itself in the
>> golden sun and bit by bit is consumed, while it
>> is surrounded by splendor, returns a contrary
>> tribute to its star;
>>   because that which ascends from it to the
>> sky, becomes tepid smoke and purple fog, which
>> cause the sun's rays to remain hidden from our
>> eyes, and obscure that by which it glows and
>> shines.

Thus my spirit (which the divine splendor
inflames and illumines), while it goes about
explaining that which flows so brightly in its
thoughts.
   sends forth verses from its high conceit,
only to obscure the shining sun, while I am
completely consumed and dissolved by the effort.
   Ah me! This purple and black cloud of
smoke darkens by its style what it would exalt,
and renders it humble.

(Questa fenice ch'al bel sol s'accende,
   E a dramma a dramma consumando vassi,
   Mentre di splendor cint'ardendo stassi,
   Contrario fio al suo pianeta rende;
      Perchè quel che da lei al ciel ascende,
   Tepido fumo ed atra nebbia fassi,
   Ond'i raggi a' nostri occhi occolti lassi
   E quello avvele, per cui arde e splende.
      Tal il mio spirto (ch'il divin splendore
   Accende e illustra), mantre va spiegando
   Quel che tanto riluce nel pensiero,
      Manda da l'alto suo concetto fore
   Rima, ch'il vago sol vad'oscurando,
   Mentre mi struggo e liquefaccio intiero.
      Oimè! questo adro e nero
   Nuvol di foco infosca col suo stile
   Quel ch'aggrendir vorrebbe, e 'l rend'umile.)

Since poetic similes reveal by hiding, truth is simultaneously
apparent and obscure.
   For Bruno and the Spanish mystics, art was to express
transcendental intuitions through images meant to defy imagery
itself. Saint John of the Cross anguished over the inadequacy of
language:

   y todos más me llagan,
      y déjame muriendo
      un no se qué que quedan balbuciendo

(yet each word is a blow,
and they keep babbling bits
of mystery—leaving me near death)

The three *ques* convey the stammering efforts of those who try
to say what cannot be said.[29] The numinous exceeded words,
and memory alone could awaken it from within.[30]

While Michelangelo portrayed the divine as a human
analogue (*Creation of Adam,* Sistine Chapel), Bruno wrote that
"divinity can be the object in similitude, and not a similitude."
Because of a "lack of proportion" between object and means,
the inherent plenitude of analogical constructs gave way to indeterminacy: "One must believe that the highest and most pro-
found knowledge of divine things is negative and not affirmative" (*Frenzies,* 115, 253). Emphasis shifted from likeness to
reduction and transference, which also drew strength from the
hermetic and kabbalistic tendency to be different, to be elsewhere. At the brink of what discursive forms could offer, art
was consumed in the workings of its own best effects.[31]

Because of their metaphysical thrust, heroic frenzies grew
to a point where the image of light became light itself. Once
infinite potency and infinite act coincided, the mind could "lose
love and affection for every other sensible as well as intelligible
object, for joined to that light it becomes that light, and conse-
quently becomes a god." In the process, man would hold "his
tongue from speaking to whom he most longs to speak, for fear
that some defect of his glance or of his word might debase him,
or in some way cause him disgrace. And this is what happens
when the excellence of the object is so far superior to the power
of apprehension" (*Frenzies,* 115, 257). Against the negative way
(*via negativa*) of apprehending God by means of either silence or
paradox, there stood a *via eminentiae* that set up a typology of
"images," "shadows," archetypal figures, and scriptural allego-
ries symbolic of God's presence in the world.

Such a code of signs gave evidence to God's verbal and
historical action. In fact, they were actual (not literary) events
foreshadowing numinous encounters at the boundary between
human invention and divine revelation.[32] The baroque mind
was therefore struggling between Cicero and Plato, the elo-

quence of words (*verba*) and the greater truth of realities (*res*) that had clashed in Augustine's *De doctrina christiana* and *De vera religione.*

IV

Beyond language and earthbound concepts of knowledge, Bruno made of the infinite a spiritual landscape. Long after Leonardo da Vinci had raised a provocative question on the subject ("What is that thing which does not give itself, and which if it were to give itself would not exist? It is the infinite, which if it could give itself would be bounded and finite"),[33] the Nolan insisted that "it is neither fitting nor natural that the infinite be understood, or that it present itself as finite, for then it would cease to be infinite" (*Frenzies,* 129). Understanding of the "sublime order" exceeds myth and history, for the realm of infinity thrives on the "imaginative daring" of minds capable of "investigation and research that will not be exhausted through the attainment of limited truths and finite goods. It is innate to man to long for the totality" (*Opere,* 420), namely, the synthesis, the whole. Unity itself is "in infinite number, and the infinite number is unity; that besides, unity is an implicit infinite, and that the infinite is explicit unity" (*Expulsion,* 135).

Much against humanist abstractions, Bruno favored "mathesis," a kind of magic-symbolic knowledge (or religious philosophy) replete with metaphorical ambiguity. He did not treat the idea of infinity as a philosopher afraid of ornament, but as one to whom metaphor was natural. Because he was critical of Copernicus's trust in "mathematics more than nature" (*Ash,* 28), the Nolan drew a line between mathematical and scientific-philosophical views of the infinite.[34]

The new science delivered man to a realm as heroic as the mind's ability to confront it. Superior minds (Donne, Pascal) wondered, and the Church feared. Where others faced chaos, Bruno found that the mind could keep at pace with nature and religion. Infinity was the only measure for the eternal metempsychoses of the spirit: "We shall advance to the discovery of the infinite *effect* of the infinite cause, the true and living evidence of the infinite vigor" (*Ash,* 62). A vigor that spearheaded Christian perfectibility, that is to say, perfection as process.

V

It was inevitable that mutability and growth would affect Bruno's concept of love, which Neoplatonism had traditionally linked to the beautiful. In Bembo's *Asolani* (1505), "beauty is a kind of grace which is born of proportion and the harmony of things; the more nearly perfect it is in its embodiments, the more lovely it renders them to us; and in human beings it is an attribute of the mind no less than of the body." Arguments in favor and against love (first two books) are followed by attempts at reconciliation (third book). Accordingly, "natural desires, such as love of life, of understanding, of self-perpetuation, of children, and of useful things, are those which nature gives without intermediary, which suffer no abatement, and which are the same in all of us." Before Bruno, Bembo praised natural love: "If virtuous love is the desire of beauty and we are led to beauty only by our eyes and ears and thoughts, all that lovers seek with their other senses, unless they seek it in order to nourish life, is evil and not virtuous love."[35] Like other Venetian artists who stood at bay of Florentine intellectualism, Bembo was aware that his ideal would not quite square with life as he knew it. In the hedonistic culture of Venice, sensuous Venuses (Giorgione, Titian) overshadowed warring Davids (Donatello, Michelangelo).

For Bruno, spiritual love is due to God, and its human counterpart to man. The Petrarchists, instead, intellectualized one and debased the other:

> What a tragicomedy! What act, I say, more worthy of pity and laughter can be presented to us upon this world's stage, in this scene of our counsciousness, than of this host of individuals who became melancholy, meditative, unflinching, firm, faithful, lovers, devotees, admirers and slaves of a thing without trust-worthiness. (*Frenzies,* 59–60)

Love bears out the effects of hearts caught in intricate webs of fidelity and rejection.

Conversely, sexual love could be holy for Bruno, who did not want "to be second to any one who worthily breaks bread in the service of nature and the blessed God" (*Frenzies*, 61). Because it turns mind and body away from the flux of life, virginity "is neither a virtue nor a vice, and does not contain goodness, dignity or merit; and when she does not serve governing Nature, she becomes crime, expressed impotence, madness and foolishness" (*Expulsion*, 231).

In a playful key, Donne echoed similar concerns: "I call that *Virginity a vertue* which is willing and desirous to yeeld its self upon honest and lawful terms, when just reason requireth; and untill then, is kept with a modest chastity of Body and Mind." Unquestionably, Bruno would have shared his conclusion: "The name of *Virgin* shal be exchanged for a farre more honorable name, *A Wife*."[36]

VI

Committed as he was to variety rather than uniformity, Bruno found that mutability is necessary to man and nature alike. Even "God createth harmony out of sublime contraries," and the universe owes its "existence to the strife of the concordant and the love of the opposed" (*Infinite*, 324). During those decades, Montaigne wrote that "there were never in the world two opinions alike, any more than two hairs or two grains. Their most universal quality is diversity. . . . Whoever should remove the seeds of these qualities from man would destroy the fundamental conditions of our life" (600). Attraction of contraries stood as a principle of human and universal relationships whereby justice and knowledge—and by extension art and beauty—depend on the experience of their opposites.

Although it could secure "an even conservation of things," concord inevitably would lead to exhaustion. For Donne, discord is "never so barren that it affords no fruit, for the fall of one State is at worst the increase of another; because it is as impossible to find a discommodity without any advantage as corruption without generation."[37] Such a diversitarian assumption aimed at fullness and variety without end.[38]

Much like an energetic sparkle at the core of universal relationships, the Brunonian *potenza* thrived on the attraction of contraries:

> Potency is commonly divided into active potency, by means of which the subject is able to operate, and passive potency, by means of which it is able to exist or to receive or to possess or to be the subject of the efficient cause in any way. . . . Therefore, there is nothing which can be said to exist, if it cannot also be said to own capacity of existing. And this aspect corresponds so precisely with active potency that passive and active cannot exist in any way without one another. (*Cause,* 111)

Keeping formal concerns in mind, emphasis shifts from external appearance to inner function: "The soul is an internal force that shapes itself from the inside like a snail; because of its own impulses it can stretch or retract into a compact mass; it can offer no image of itself, but it then can let little horns emerge from its forehead, and it can elongate its body again as it unfolds from its center." As an organism, the snail's form is a "living art" (*Opere,* 805) shaping itself from within.

In the tradition of organic analogues, Coleridge later compared Shakespearean plays to a serpent, "which makes a fulcrum of its own body, and seems forever twisting its own strength."[39] Literary texts recommended to observe *"sveltezza nel serpeggiare*—quickness in a snake-like or curvilinear execution of forms,"[40] insisted on the verb *riserpendo* ("twisting back like a serpent"; Bruno, *Dialoghi,* 1173); associated "that serpentine and crooked line" with "Meanders," "Labyrinths," and those difficult paths on which Fortune has set the "obscure method of his providence" (Thomas Browne, *Religio Medici,* I, 17); and illustrated the Machiavellian conflict between what men ought to do and what they actually do in terms of "serpentine wisdom" and "columbine innocence" (Francis Bacon, *The Advancement of Learning* II, xxi, 9). *Serpentina* forms also were typical of seventeenth-century sculpture (Bernini's *Pluto and Persephone* 1621–22) and architecture (Borromini's *lanterna* on Sant'Ivo alla Sapienza, Rome; Fig. 7).[41]

Actually, it was a twisted and bent cone, the *cornucopia,* that embodied the baroque line of beauty.[42] Its spiral thrust was repeated by Angelo Vannelli and Bernini in the *Lumaca* fountain, at one time in Piazza Navona and now in Villa Pamphili (Rome, Fig. 8).

Dissatisfaction with the planimetric and enclosed form of the circle led Bruno to focus on the spiral, which, being "visible on the surface and in depth," uncoils in space. In fact, the whole cosmic motion "pushes all things in an eternal trajectory that is spiral and that could not be explained through a geometric rule" (*Opere,* 538–51). Giving visual form to a progressive (rather than repetitive) measure of time, the spiral became symbolic of an expanding spirit that the Nolan handed down to Vico.

VII

Emphasis on inner growth plunged art within the self. For Bruno, the poet is neither a liar nor an idle "priest of the muses," but the very creator of a new Parnassus:

My heart is in the place and form of Parnassus, which
    I must ascend for my safety; my muses are the thoughts
    which at every hour reveal to me their glorious tale;

My heart, my thoughts and my tears themselves cause the
    laurel to bear leaves for my adornment.

(In luogo e forma di Parnaso ho 'l core,
    Dove per scampo mio convien ch'io monte,
    Son mie muse i pensier ch'a tutte l'ore
    Mi fan presenti le bellezze conte;

Ma di lauro m'infronde
    Mio cor, gli miei pensieri e le mie onde.)

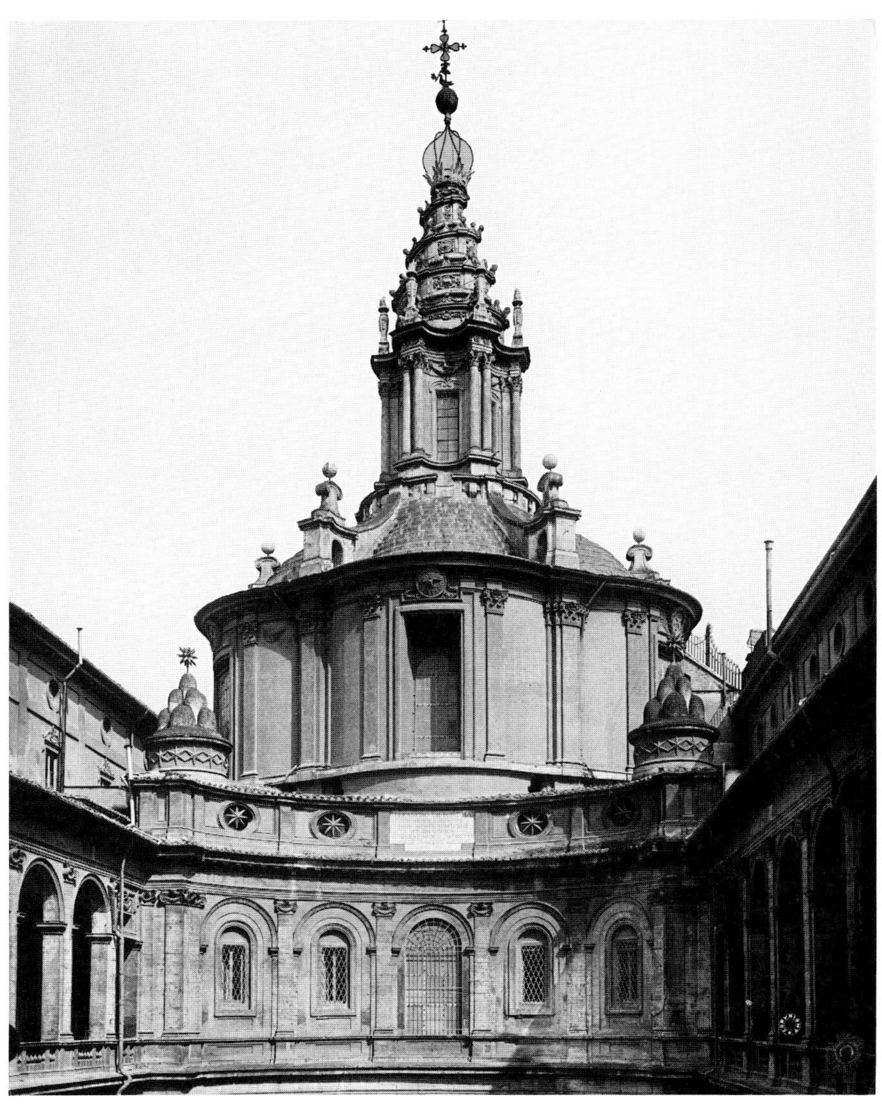

Fig. 7. G. Della Porta and Borromini, *Saint Ivo alla Sapienza*, 1642–50. Rome

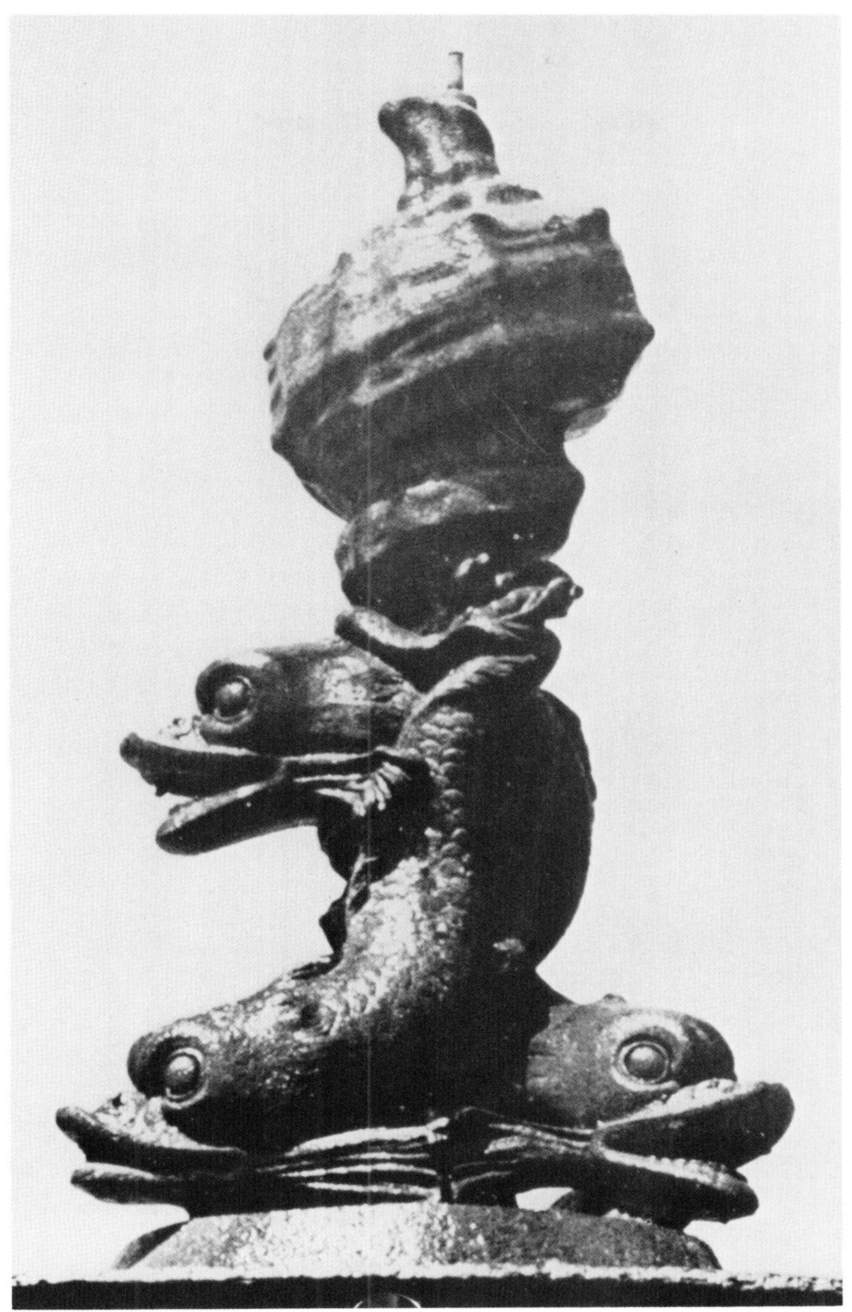

Fig. 8. Angelo Vannelli and Gianlorenzo Bernini (bozzetto), The *Lumaca Fountain*, 1652(?). Villa Pamphili, Rome

The prose commentary adds that "in this way he deems himself no less able to be crowned illustriously through his own heart, thoughts and tears, than others who are crowned by the hands of kings, emperors and popes" (*Frenzies*, 81, 85). The descent from heaven was under way. As the *Seicento* approached, revolt brewed on Parnassus; the Muses became forms of the poet's self.

Even Bruno's treatment of mythology echoed a subjective posture. Having caught sight of the nude Diana, Actaeon is converted from hunter into prey: "Therefore, Actaeon, who with these thoughts, his dogs, searched for goodness, wisdom, beauty and the wild beast outside himself, attained them in this way. Once he was in their presence, ravished outside of himself by so much beauty, he became the prey of his thoughts and saw himself converted into the thing he was pursuing." Of his dogs, the mastiffs stand for the will, and the greyhounds for the intellect; human love "spurs the intellect to go before it (the will), like a lantern." Through achievement and renovation, the mind becomes its own limitless object. The essence of genius feeds on the inexhaustible interplay between intellect and will, which bestows power "to itself, when it reflects upon itself and increases itself" (*Frenzies*, 124–25, 68).[43] Nature is absorbed by the mind, which can generate life.

Instead of a *via resolutionis*, myth became a *via explicationis*. To that extent, Actaeon and the phoenix bore promises of renewal, and Bruno's comments on such myths of transformation changed the narrating consciousness. Poetry gave a new flavor to the ancient fable. In turn, prose measured the modernity of the mind's growth in a dialogic form that linked past to present along the path of progress.

Myth reflected personal achievements as well. Bruno wrote in a Latin ode late in his life:

For we have known the Gift of Genius.
. . . .
We do not care at what low price fools rate us
Nor mind how mad we look in the eyes of the world.
We soar on stronger wings: we penetrate
Beyond the cloudy pathways of the winds
By power of vision—that is enough for us.[44]

To "achieve a goal at ease with, and inspired by, a sublime order," the heroic mind "has dispersed the clouds and destroyed Olympus, which brings others to a common prison." It was indeed possible "to reach out with the wings of the mind there where one cannot go on foot" (*Opere,* 417–18, 453). The artist was about to shape a poetics no longer measurable by finite standards.

In the larger framework of baroque culture, Bruno's contribution to the poetics of the infinite ought to be related to Henry More's *Psychathanasia* and *Democritus Platonissans; or, An Essay upon the Infinity of Worlds out of Platonick Principles* (1646). Throughout Marjorie Nicolson's fundamental essay on the "New Philosophy," quotes and comments remind us of Bruno. A few samples will suffice. In his *Divine Dialogues,* More allowed full play to his natural enthusiasm, his love of variety, diversity, and irregularity as principles of Nature. More felt the Copernican psychology of infinity, responding with joy to man's pursuit of what he can never reach. The combination of awe and delight that Christians had long felt when they worshiped God, More felt as he worshiped infinity.[45] Matters of direct influences aside, analogues of that sort can only strengthen the unity of baroque culture.

The "mountain glory" which so fascinated English writers in the seventeeth and eighteenth centuries (Traherne, Burnet, Dennis, Shaftesbury, Addison) eventually shifted the concept of infinity from God through vast Nature to the soul of man, and vice versa. That process became typical of "The Aesthetics of the Infinite,"[46] which Bruno anticipated to a significant extent: "In eternity, the infinite provides new nourishment for the finite, and strengthens the rigor of this body according to its need, since a body takes on more power in relation to the tenacity of an innate potency" (*Opere,* 485).

Since he could not develop a vocabulary suited for the measureless, the Nolan fell back on abstract language ("infinite cause"), rhetorical questions, geometric concept-images ("center is everywhere and circumference nowhere"), and myth. His sublime was discursive.

Yet, traditional discourse defied its own limits when Donne projected man's unity with God in the heavens "for ever, and ever, and ever, and infinite, and super-infinite evers" (*Sermons* VIII, 92). Less than tautological, the repetition of ever and evers unleashed a temporal coil of energy toward infinity, where the linguistic crescendo was just about to break free of the man-bound world of words. The geocentric pull of discourse caved in, while literary acceleration kept at pace with the Brunonian ascent toward a heroic stratosphere. The singular grew into a plural expansion that muted language toward the outer distances of ineffability.

Since he was equally aware of the boundless forms of reality, Bruno saw in Mount Vesuvius a symbolic analogue to his own eruptive energy. Believing as he did that "the object of the mind is infinite," pursuits of such an object were conceived in the spirit "of a positive affirmation of an end, infinite and without limit" (*Frenzies*, 236–37). Elsewhere, it was added that human understanding "cannot stop or rest, and still presses onward. Therefore it is that we cannot conceive of any end or limit to the world, but always as of necessity it occurs to us that there is something beyond" (Bacon, *Novum Organum*, 1, 48).

In a memorable comment, Marjorie Nicolson wrote that the more minds like Bruno "discovered about the new world and the universe, the more insatiably they labored to tear down the rotten buildings and replace them with a grander structure. The more imagination strove to grasp the astounding new universe, the more truly man realized his own potentialities, and the vaster his soul grew with that too much that was not enough. Poets, scientists, philosophers, of a newer 'new philosophy'—these were the first Romanticists."[47] Bruno's heroic flight blew up the Ptolemaic universe, but the Church did not foresee that Christianity would survive the explosion.

VIII

It is indeed indicative that Bruno set his concept of art against the limitless landscape of *De immenso:*

As an operative form of expression, art conceives and realizes itself discursively—Nature operates intensively, not discursively. Art manipulates extraneous matter, but nature its own; art is applied to matter whereas nature is intimately united to matter; indeed, it is matter itself.

Art is inferior to nature: "We cannot imagine that the state of nature is so poor that it could be surpassed by art." At first, this statement seems to deny Bruno's inclusive spirit. Yet, poet and philosopher are one and the same, even though their means of expression have been traditionally different. In nature, fire shapes and burns itself from within; as a "living art," the soul also consists of a "shaping power that forms its matter from within itself" (*Opere*, 805–6). The parallel between nature and mind makes creation individual, autonomous, and purposive.

The very growth of knowledge unlocks spiritual realms where discourse fails to unlock the mind's inner vitality. Although he rejected "Platonic techniques and archetypes" (*Opere*, 805) as rhetorically static, Bruno fell back on philosophical myths and metaphorical language. Actually, he wrote on philosophy and metaphysics in intensely allusive poetry, for he believed that only silence and a suggestive vocabulary could foreshadow the highest truths. Cognition itself "can never be perfect to the extent that it shall be able to understand the highest object; but only to the extent that our intellect has the power to understand this object" (*Frenzies*, 117). Instead of producing rest and completeness, poetry shares in a reality where the very growth of the mind sheds light on the unforeseeable. The meaning of poetic language rests with the depth of individual readings.

Conversely, the rhetorical explicitness of discursive art is so mechanical that it hinders the vitality of nature and thought alike. At the edge of mimesis, heroic frenzies did not fall prey to language. Because he was willing to conquer the idea that "in us alone doth nature live," the Nolan turned to spaces farther than Xanadu and higher than Mount Abora, taking on the immensity of planetary systems.

The process of internalization soared toward unknown heights when Bruno returned for the last time to the Icarus myth in his Latin ode:

> Let others lust to bind to naked shoulders
>   Daedalus' wings, to fly with the clouds' strength
>   And seek the buffeting impulse of the winds—
>   Hunger to be hurled, like Pegasus, beyond
>   The hollow confines of the flaming world.
>   .   .   .   .
>   We soar on stronger wings: we penetrate
>   Beyond the cloudy pathways of the winds
>   By power of vision—that is enough for us.

A daring act has yielded to an uplifting state of spiritual power. Language and images exude energy:

> Following us the multitude will rise,
>   Climbing the path that leads from each man's heart.
>   No auguries by fire or bird or cloud,
>   No necromancers' forecasts show the way,
>   But Genius bestowed out of the treasure of God.

A revelation follows in the last quatrain:

> Wings are not for mortals. Let the sun
>   Go naked, unadorned by any cloud.
>   Vision of truth! quested, found, revealed,
>   Take me—though none may follow where I go.
>   If I am wise with Nature by God's bounty
>   That is enough indeed, more than enough.

By God's grace, the absolute beauty of the naked sun makes it possible for the poet to withstand "the hollow confines of the flaming world." The closing line seems to betray a sense of expectation, a final human test about to seal the poet's own sacrificial quest.

Surely, Bruno foresaw the necessity of keeping the Genius' godlike potential in check:

> Not the bright quality of polished wit,
>   Nor vivid mind nor reason, can betray us;
>   But only the shifty trickster's arrogance,

> A blind, unbalanced, groundless confidence
> In self-created seeds of miracles.

Lines of that sort introduced symptoms of a "lofty *daemonic* freedom" at the heart of souls out to "experience . . . the sight of unlimited distances, and heights lost to view."[48]

Confidence in self-created seeds of miracles pointed to times when more Faustian minds would not resist arrogance. And it was in Bruno's days that Icarus's ill-fated challenge lured Christopher Marlowe:

> His waxen wings did mount above his reach
> And melting, heavens conspired his overthrow.
> (*Doctor Faustus*, I, i, 20–21)

Groundless confidence plunged the infinite within the self, which could consume, and even damn itself. For the Nolan, instead, subjectivity still partook of a universe in which "every contrary is reduced to friendship . . . every discord to concord, every diversity to unity" (*Frenzies*, 67). The artist's beauty-making power included all; it was poetry, nature, and metaphysics.

IX

Certain as he was that the "death of one century brings life to all the others" (*Frenzies*, 85), and confident that "we are all subject to a perfect Power" (*Infinite*, 244), Bruno believed that "the great age" had not passed, but was about to come. For the Christian mind, no philosophical consciousness of history is possible without consciousness of the future.[49] The Nolan left it for later writers to envision man rolling on an inclined plane (Nietzsche); nor could he accept the idea that the center no longer would hold (Yeats). And John Donne was just as confident that geographic discoveries did not break up man's faith in the unity of creation. Ulyssean challenges could test boundaries without breaking down the "Compass" of life. At the surface, human destiny was chartered out through a cartographic metaphor: "Take a flat Map, a Globe *in plano,* and here is East, and there is West, as far asunder as two points can be put: but reduce this flat Map to Roundnesse, which is the true form, and East and West touch one another, and are all one: So consider mans life aright, to be a Circle." In spite of doubts of all sorts, microcosm and macrocosm could still be rounded out within "an endlesse, and perfect Circle." The Seer and the Geometer joined hands and drew the circle of Infinity, for "immortality, and eternity is a Circle too" (*Sermons* II, 199–200).

In the Brunonian mind, the ever-filling power of love impregnated a universe "in which the sun's rays penetrate in the Earth's bosom. The Earth in fact continually unites itself with the Sun, conceiving and giving birth from every part of its body" (*Opere,* 708). He could only reiterate his faith in the boundlessness of life: "There are no ends, boundaries, limits or walls which can defraud or deprive us of the infinite multitude of things. Therefore the earth and the ocean thereof are fecund; therefore the sun's blaze is everlasting, so that eternally fuel is provided for the voracious fires, and moisture replenisheth the attenuated seas. For from infinity is born an ever fresh abundance of matter" (*Infinite,* 145).

In the wake of the discovery of new stars and planets (Tycho Brahe 1572, Kepler 1604, Galileo 1610), Milton wrote about a universe wherein

> other Suns perhaps
> With their attendant Moons thou wilt descry
> Communicating Male and Female Light,
> Which two great Sexes animate the World.
> (*Paradise Lost,* VIII, 149–51)

On English shores, belief in panspermatism and the "vitalistic" school of biology, taught that, at creation, seminal particles were diffused through the world, causing generation by direct entry into the organism. After death, such a "seminal principle" makes itself available once more; it is a kind of indestructible *élan vital.*[50] And there were some who wrote that, in the beginning, there was Chaos, which was not yet "impregnate by the voice of God" (Thomas Browne, *Religio Medici,* I, 16). The baroque mind therefore linked the very emergence of cosmos to an act of interstellar generation.

Although history and his own tragic destiny could have instigated despair, Bruno never faltered in his beliefs, and did not make Tasso's mistake. As a man and an artist, the Nolan nurtured his poetics in a spirit of immeasurable abundance, which, in Donne's words, cherished the "endless increase" of "all plural things" (*Devotions*, 30–31).[51]

PART II

The Formative Unity of the Arts

The Challenge of the Seashell and the Chronotope of Formation

> *The only thing that is given to us and that is when there is human life is the having to make it, each one for himself. Life is a gerundive, not a participle: a* faciendum, *not a* factum.
>
> —*José Ortega y Gasset*

I

Inclined, as he was, toward an ever-expanding concept of life, Giordano Bruno envisioned a cosmos in which each thing "must be subject in all its parts to all forms, so that in all its parts (as far as capable) it might become all, be all, if not at the same time and instant of eternity, successively and vicissitudinously" (*Ash,* 156–57). To sustain that transformational condition, a "formative principle" is "always present—*è sempre presente il principio formatore*" (*Opere,* 460)—in space, nature, and the creative mind.

In the fifteenth-century spirit of Florentine Humanism, Alberti presumed that art alone could give a higher unity to the shapeless variety of things; the stability of form stood above nature.

At the other side of mythic timelessness, Neoplatonism also endorsed dynamic notions of beauty, since "form is an act"[1] and "there is no thing which is all it can be. Man is what he can be, but not all he can be" (Bruno, *Cause,* 112). At the turn of the seventeenth century, many believed that stability was "nothing but a more languid motion" (Montaigne, *Essays,* 610); in fact, "our nature consists in motion" (Pascal, *Pensées,* 129). Once permanence itself was taken to be transitional, process fixed and unraveled form in the same breath of life. Baroque art at large thrived on tensions between definition and mutation. Instability was innate to form, which always tended to carry itself toward another form.[2]

Reflecting on formation in his study of sea shells, Paul Valéry noted that we "can conceive of the structure of these objects, and this is what intrigues us. Although we ourselves were formed by imperceptible growth, we do not know how to create anything in that way."[3] Art was called upon to "stage" the development of form. Answers to his challenging remark could be found at both ends of the seventeenth century, when the unfolding of the creative act led artists (Velázquez, Vermeer) and writers (Montaigne, Cervantes) to face the task of representing formation, the heartbeat of baroque poetics.

Perhaps by a happy coincidence, the twofold meaning of formation captures the "concordant diversity" of baroque forms. As a noun, formation points to geological layers of rocks with common characteristics. The word therefore is past-oriented, bearing out a completed growth. On artistic grounds, we can see that process in stages of sculptural and pictorial "finish" (Michelangelo, Velázquez), literary additions (Montaigne), and older manuscripts (Cid Hamete) vis-à-vis more recent texts (Cervantes) or imitations thereof (Avellaneda).

As the act of shaping or giving form, formation is a future-oriented gerundive that best captures the forward thrust of creative activity. In its gerundive mode, the term could be taken as, or traded with, formativeness, which gives a better sense of the tentative nature of sculptural form (Michelangelo's late works) and essayistic attempts (Montaigne and his readers).

Often, formation and formativeness coexisted in baroque art at its best. Bruno himself set out to avoid "*formabilità finita,*" that is to say, any finite development—or completed formation (*Opere,* 453). What was needed instead was formativeness without boundaries. Cervantes found a manuscript, wrote a text, inspired imposters, finished the second part of the book, but could not stop Tordelliscan scribes from plagiarizing him again. Likewise, Velázquez showed older pictures on the walls of *Las Meninas,* which is the painting we are looking at; at the same time, the artist in it is yet to finish—or to begin—the one we cannot see. Through the "artist at work," the formative process was caught at its source.

II

Flawless as they were, humanist artworks thrived in the ethereal realm of hypothetical images (The Courtier and The Prince). Once it was restored to the empirical coordinates of baroque time and space, form had to inhale the breath of life. Such an invigorating experience made it possible for Bruno to declare that man's task is to "*inumanire* (inhumanize)" (*Dialoghi,* 922). Verbal forms of that kind touched on processes of incarnation whereby literary and pictorial characters embodied chivalric ideals (Cervantes's Don Quixote), Christian humility (Caravaggio's peasants), and pagan mythology (Velázquez's drunkards).

It need only be mentioned that the Ignatian culture of the Counter-Reformation called for the exercising of the *Exercises.* The Saint's own words are a call to activism: "What have I done for Christ? What am I now doing for Christ? What ought I do for Christ?" (*Spiritual Exercises* I, note). Sermons first were to be preached and then experienced, since "the subsequent life is the best printing, and the most useful and profitable publishing of a Sermon" (Donne, *Sermons,* VI, 264).

Between 1580 and 1585, the verb "ingraft" shifted its botanical reference (insertion of a shoot or graft from one plant into another) to the implantation of virtue, and Donne applied the metaphorical transfer to the Church: "When she baptizes a child, that action concerns me; for that child is thereby connected to that body which is my head too, and ingrafted into that body whereof I am a member" (*Devotions*, 108).

The "organic connection" favored metaphors compatible with doctrines of rebirth. The issue was not "being mimetic" but "thinking mimetically," and art was to link mimesis to the reproductive strategies of natural change.[4] The very death of Christ was interpreted as an act of "hand-writing" that would call for "practice." In the Christological nomenclature, writing was meant to inspire acts of reincarnation that would make of our life "the perfect sentence" (Donne, *Sermons*, X, 196; 3, 188).

On the subject of God's presence in the Holy Shroud, Giambattista Marino resorted to the verb *medesimarsi*.[5] Its meaning, "to physically become oneself," (or "to enter one's own self"), echoed the Spanish *ensimismarse* (a kind of threefold "selving" vortex). Both of them uttered the incarnational sense of much Catholic ritual.

Ingrained as it was in the Spanish language, the incarnation of concepts set *honor* (the objective concept) against *honra* (the living experience), and *ser* (the absolute dimension of what one is) against *estar* (as being situated in relation to time, space, or a particular living experience). Words were indeed "living powers" by means of which the things of most importance to mankind could be humanized. In the logological realm of "god-terms," verbs became more pregnant than ever with "potency" and "act." John Donne exuded a Brunonian enthusiasm when he pinned the process of knowledge turning into action to the most protean of verbs: "Joy is peace for having done that which we ought to have done. . . . To have something is doe, to doe it, and then to Rejoyce in having done it, to embrace a calling, to performe the Duties of that calling, to joy and rest in the peaceful testominy of having done so; this is Christianly done, Christ did it; Angelically done, Angels do it; Godly done, God does it."[6]

Whereas Humanism celebrated nouns (*virtù, grazia, sprezzatura*) as definitionally elusive as the literary figures they were associated with, the Baroque favored an energetic use of language. Whether assertive (Bruno's "*inumanire*" or Marino's "*medesimarsi*"), relational (Donne's "interinanimate"), expressive (Thomas Browne's "incurvate" or Quevedo's "*metamorfoseando*"), or dubitative (Shakespeare's "to be or not to be," Montaigne's "*Que scay-je?*"), the transitive activity of verbal forms gained strength from its own dynamics. And Bruno proved the case: "Should Hercules be attacked by unheard-of monsters, let him turn them away, reform, expel, persecute, imprison, subdue, despoil, scatter, break, tear, shatter, abase, submerge, burn, destroy, kill, and annihilate them" (*Expulsion,* 128). As the most active form of linguistic "becoming," the verb expanded within its infinitive mode.

In the smallest unity, the vital "seed" contained the "capacity-to-be" with "its being-in-act" (*Cause,* 111), which made it possible for "*self-formation*" to lead to "*other-formation.*"[7] Because of its propulsive tendency to relate and vivify all things, Bruno's *minimo* is simultaneously means and end ("*integrat omnia,*" *Opere,* 96).[8] His "formative principle" in fact "forms matter and shapes it from within, and from within the seed or root is sent forth and unfolded the trunk, from within the trunk are thrust out the branches" (*Cause,* 82).

Just as seeds potentially contain trees, so did artists generate nuclear forms such as essays (Montaigne, Bacon), *pensées* (Pascal), aphorisms, maxims (La Rochefoucauld), and *minuzie* (Sarpi). Likewise, *luminismo* in the visual arts (from Caravaggio to Rembrandt) intensified details that became symbolic of reality at large. Fragments of the seashell, Valéry wrote, engage the imagination "to think further; they call for a whole."[9] The axiom that often less is more was as significant to the baroque mind as its counterpart, that of cornucopian abundance.

In its developmental mode, formation can sort out what grows, is growing, and what is grown. Whereas the humanists put forward static constructs (treatises and the system of linear perspective), Bruno moved toward events and functions. For him, unity meant process; it was to be thought of as "unifying" rather than as "unity."[10] With an eye to organic transfers, forms were more likely to be born than made, and to grow instead of being built.

Amidst a Copernican universe that was challenging its man-measured bearings, the classical (Protagoras) and humanist (Alberti) heritage was shaken. Form was set against a largely unknown and unknowable cosmos in which "you do not come any nearer to proportion, likeness, union, and identity with the infinite by being a man than by being an ant" (Bruno, *Cause*, 136). The formative mode brought movement to the concept of order. Unfolding as they did in time and space, baroque forms emerged amid what Mikhail Bakhtin would call chronotopic interactions. Meaning literally "time-space," *chronotope* qualifies "the intrinsic connectedness of temporal and spatial relationships that are artistically expressed in literature" and the arts. The mathematical character of the concept (as part of Einstein's theory of relativity) was transferred to literary criticism "almost as a metaphor" with "an intrinsic generic significance."[11]

For Bernini, "a person who poses, fixed and immoble, never is as much himself as he is when he is in motion, when those qualities which are his alone and not of a general nature appear." His bust of Cardinal Scipione Borghese (1632) grew out of rapid sketches of the subject in action.[12]

To borrow from Bakhtin's chronotropic language, time in Bernini's *Apollo and Daphne* (1622–25; Fig. 9) "thickens, takes on flesh, becomes artistically visible" once metamorphosis "ingrafts" the human body into roots, bark, and leaves.

Whereas the humanist David either claimed victory (Donatello, Verrocchio) or was ready for it in the static *contrapposto* of Michelangelo's ideal nude (Fig. 10), the *David* of Bernini (1623; Fig. 11) is engaged in the chronotopic undertaking of a shepherd whose action disregards any outcome. In that broader perspective, formation as a metaphor of spatiotemporal processes was indeed central to baroque art.[13]

III

Applied to man, the "formative principle" spurred on the growth of the human personality. After Michelangelo added

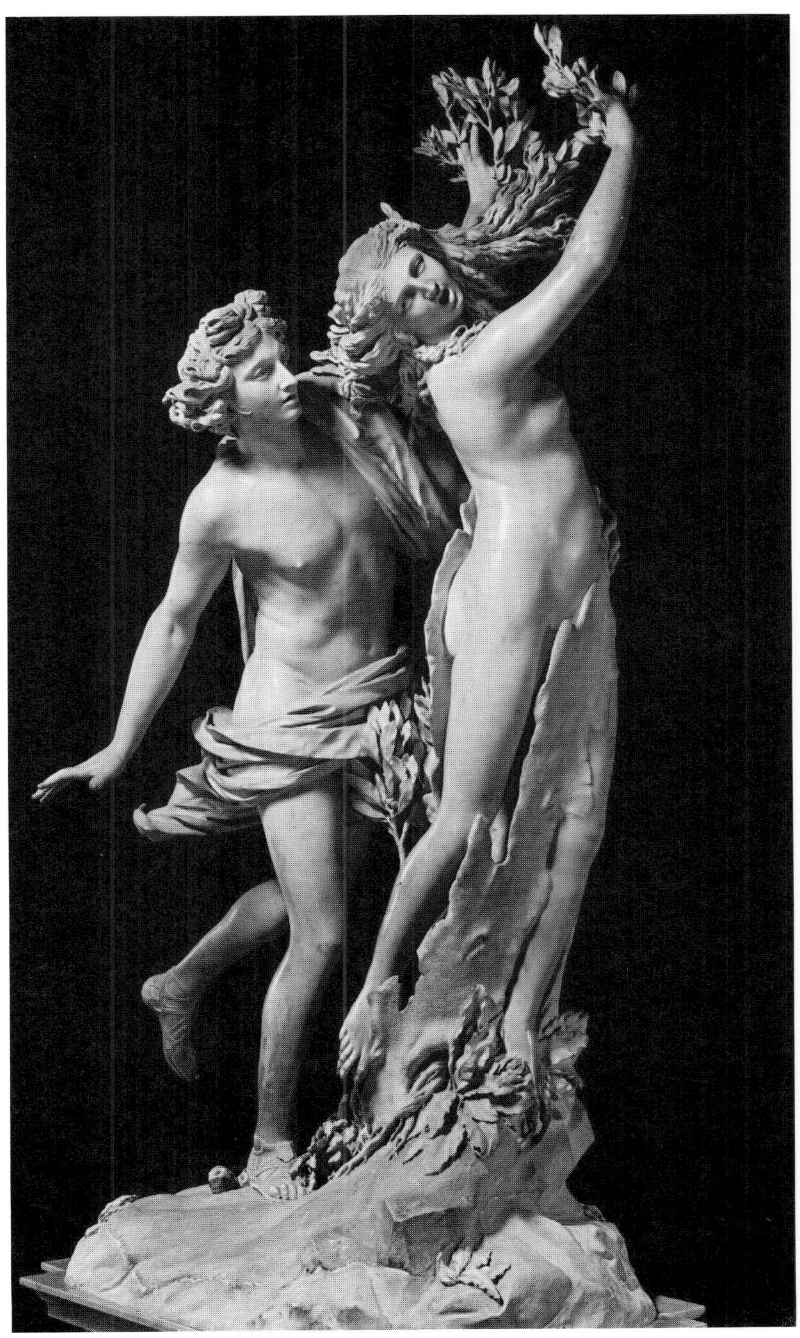

Fig. 9. Bernini, *Apollo and Daphne*, 1622–25. Galleria Borghese, Rome

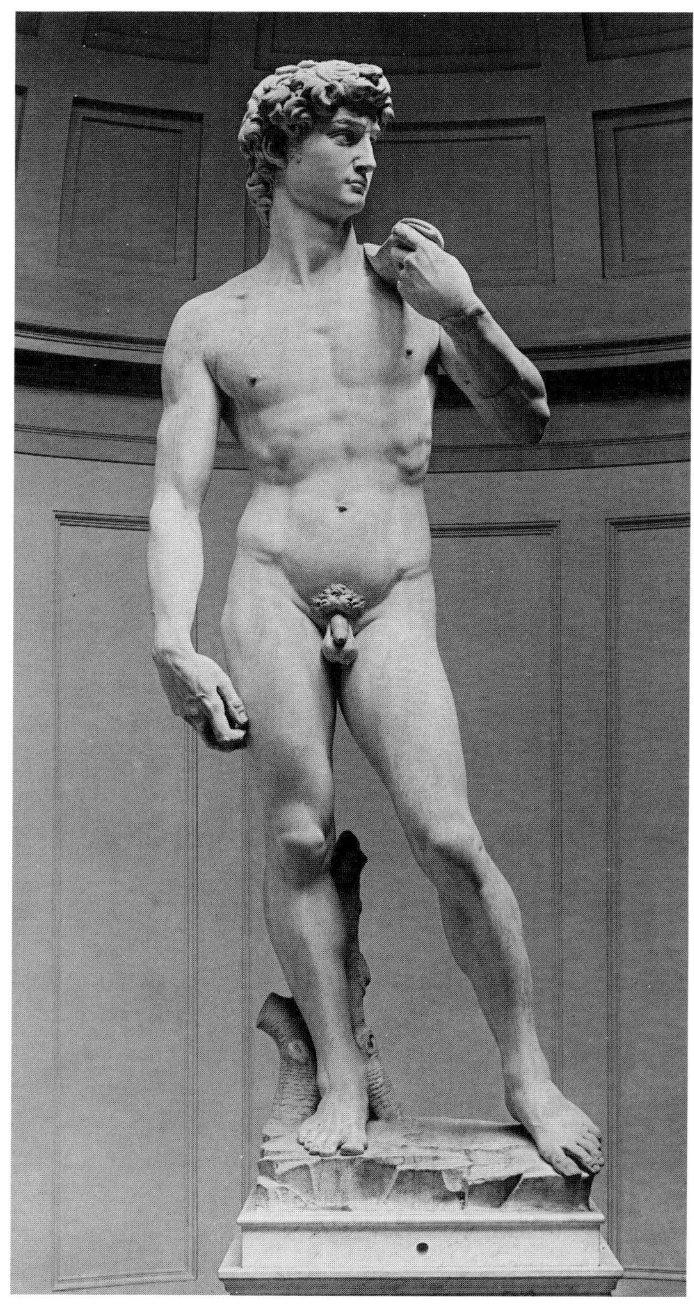

Fig. 10. Michelangelo, *David*, 1501–3. Accademia, Florence

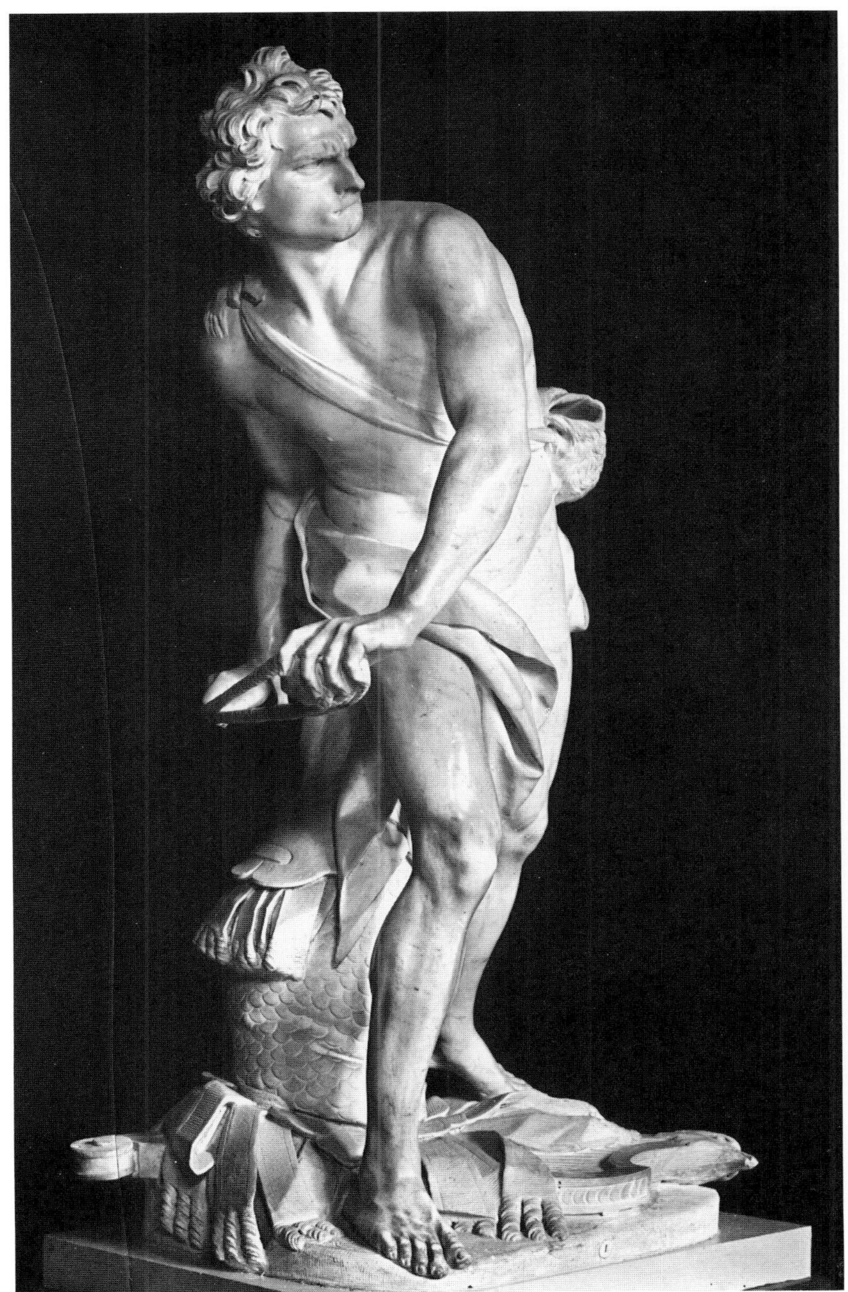

Fig. 11. Bernini, *David*, 1623. Galleria Borghese, Rome

youth (Magdalen) and old age (Nicodemus) to the *Florence Pietà*, Bernini's *Aeneas, Anchises, and Ascanius Fleeing Troy* (1619) drew attention to human growth at a time when picaresque fictions thrived on characters developing through maximal contact with the present in all its open-endedness.[14] After humanist treatises and panegyrics had outlined figures as hypothetical as the utopian environments they were meant to inhabit, essays and novels emerged as genres in the making rooted in the process of human experience.

From the fourteenth to the seventeenth century, prose narrative largely dealt with chivalric matters of the sunny day before yesterday. Parallel to it, there stood a more prosaic world of profit and survival.[15]

In "formative" terms, Boccaccio's *novelle* present characters who have achieved maturity. Ciappelletto is the wickedest man on earth, and Fra' Cipolla the greatest rogue in the world. Since the superlative itself denies development, the stories enact established traits.

As the sixteenth century unfolded, episodes (short stories) grew to encompass picaresque lives. One day in the life of Andreuccio da Perugia (*Decameron* II, 5) was prolonged into Lazarillo's growth. Although some picaresque tableaux (*buldero*) echoed *The Decameron*, each chapter of *La Vida de Lazarillo de Tormes* (1550?) adds to the *pícaro*'s march toward adulthood. As the title implies, individual episodes grow into a lifetime; in Spanish the key word is *vida*.[16]

Insofar as the *pícaro* has to fend for himself in a reality either unfamiliar or inhospitable, the prototypical novel unlocked a formative process already completed in the *novella*.

The acquisition of cunning skills in the tactics of survival (first *tratado*) beefs up Lazarillo's *buena fortuna*, which comes to a halt when churchmen set up traps. Even before the *pícaro*'s education gets under way, the basic unity-duality of the mousegrain finds an archetypal precedent in his father, who was caught "bleeding the sacks belonging to the people . . . they arrested him, and he confessed, denied nothing and was punished by law." Later, he served as a mule driver for a *caballero* in an expedition against the Moors, and "ended his life with his master like a loyal servant."[17] Thievery leads to jail and loyalty to the grave; paternal legacies therefore spell trouble.

As an ironic symbol controlling much of the entire narrative, the mouse trap triggers twice in the first *tratado*, where both characters fall for the same bait: a stone bull and a stone column. One gets the *pícaro*'s growth under way, and the other marks his emancipation from the blind man. Crushing punishments again follow the enjoyment of a delicious bite in the second *tratado*. Heaven becomes hell, since results are inconsistent with expectations. Like a trap, life will take more than it would ever give, and Lazarillo is destined never to shake himself free of corrupted priests.

Actions mark Lazarillo's growth in the elementary world of the first two *tratados*, where God and the devil are as interchangeable as alms and eucharist on the altar. While the *pícaro* sees God in the loaves of bread (*paraíso panal*), the priest finds "the mice and snakes that were destroying him." Having spent "three days in the belly of the whale" (47), the boy does not die; the ritual bread (*bodigos*) is not eaten in remembrance.[18]

In the ensuing narrative (third *tratado*), the *pícaro* is afraid of a funeral cortege heading toward "the sad and accursed place, the gloomy and dark dwelling, the domain where there is no food or drink" (60), which he identifies with the *escudero*'s dwelling—"the entrance was dark and so dim that it would freighten anybody entering it" (50). At that point in the story, Lazarillo's intelligence is still literal. He could not quite cope with metaphorical meanings, and it was the *escudero*'s task to introduce him, however unwittingly, to a new world of ideas.

Once growth affected the inner self, Lazarillo left things unspoken in the much underestimated fourth *tratado*, where reticence to judge others marked a turning point. References to shoes worn out in a week (and needing replacement) keeps his cleverness sharp. At the same time, the literal gives way to the conceptual. Having already said enough about priests, Lazarillo refuses to explain "one or two things" (66). His discreet silence turns action into reflection, thus forcing experience to come to terms with ideology (or compromises thereof).

Later, four short paragraphs (sixth *tratado*) contain the lessons, rather than the deeds, of Lazaro's life as a waterseller. Survival has given way to the pursuit of social status. Although self-sufficient as a water-seller, the young man sets out to become a more legitimate member—*hombre de bien*—of the community; "The moment I saw myself properly dressed, I told my employer to take his donkey, since I no longer wanted to continue in that job" (54). Speech introduces a professional milieu wherein the future holds promises of a better life.

Somehow, the *escudero*'s ideas have caught up with Lazaro. Unfortunately, one's language of chivalry falls on deaf ears in the commercial world of Toledo, and so does the discourse of life mute the other's words of hope. In the end, Lazaro enters society through the back door, in secondhand clothes, married to a secondhand girl, and invested with a second-rate sense of honor. Dishonorable means seem to have earned him a place under the sun. Even though the blind man's prophecies have come true, Lazaro has outgrown the wits of an existence on trial. While his wife offers her services next door, he waits alone at home. Time comes to a standstill, and the novelistic chronotope finally comes to rest.

If one were to test Boccaccio's *novelle* against E. M. Forster's standards of "life by values" and "life by time,"[19] it could be suggested that the former—or parodic treatments thereof—guides mankind in *The Decameron*. With an eye to novelistic potential, the day was yet to come when the narrative chronotope would yield "picaresque" and "educational" formation. We do not know whether Andreuccio ever became Andrea, but we do know that Lazarillo outgrew his onomastic diminutive.

IV

Lazaro's self-formative experience stood at pace with autobiographical forms of humanist writing (epistles, reflections). In the *Essays,* Montaigne proudly declared: "I have no more made my book than my book has made me—a book consubstantial with its author" (300). An identification indeed formative: "I do not portray being: I portray passing. . . . My history needs to be adapted to the moment—*Je ne peints pas l'estre. Je peints le passage . . . Il faut accomoder mon histoire à l'heure*" (611). Like the Spanish narrator, he is author and character within a literary structure akin to a *Bildung*. Actually, the *Essays* are novelistic insofar as they outline the history of the formation of a personality.[20]

For Montaigne, "a spirited mind" is always "aspiring and going beyond its strength; it has impulses beyond its powers of achievement" (818). As continuous and meandering as thought itself, the essay is a judgment and its testing.[21] Mental turbulence produced ever-shifting forms: "I give my soul now one face, now another, according to which direction I turn it . . . whoever studies himself really attentively finds in himself, yes, even in his judgment, this gyration and discord" (242).

To unveil the mind's unrelenting activity, Montaigne often shaped thought into adverbial molds, and spoke of knowledge "meagerly and piteously, the latter secondarily and accidentally, the former expressly and principally" (809). Since they bear on function rather than definition, adverbs sustain ever-expanding modes of behavior in which memory and experience link formation to formativeness.[22]

With a passion, the baroque mind gave literary form to the thinking process. For Montaigne, "it is a thorny undertaking, and more so than it seems, to follow a movement so wandering as that of our mind" (273). The essay is not simply *a* test, *an* experiment, but a method of intellectual growth voiced in the emblematic question: "When I declare 'I do not know' or 'I doubt' they say that this proposition carries itself with the rest. . . . This is more firmly grasped in the form of interrogation: 'What do I know?'—the words I bear as a motto" (392–93). Doubt became an inquisitive tool, and even Bruno recommended that "whoever wants to philosophize should initially doubt everything" (*Opere*, 94). As vehicles of epistemological inquiry, doubt and persuasion turned into baroque cornerstones.[23]

Between the Shakespearean extremes of "a piece of work" and a "quintessence of dust," of "to be or not to be," Montaigne's "What do I know?" explored the inexhaustible—and untragic—range of man's commitment to forward his own becomingness. In the tradition of ancient legacies (Heraclitus's "I searched out myself" or the Socratic "know thyself"), the baroque mind "selved" (to quote a more recent verb-noun coined by Gerard Manley Hopkins) itself unrelentingly. In Montaigne's own words, Heraclitus maintained that "one could not advance so far toward the understanding of the soul as to attain it" (406). Search replaced accomplishment. Since "attempts well exceed performances," "infallible experiments," and "assured determinations" (Thomas Browne, *Pseudodoxia Epidemica*, "To the Reader"), "the struggle alone pleases us, not the victory" (Pascal, *Pensées*, 135).

Although bending to the wind, man was a thinking reed. Fear of the world *without* strengthened faith in the world *within;* growth tested the depths of the human soul. For some, "all our dignity consists, then, in thought" (Pascal, *Pensées*, 305), while others believed that "our creatures are our thoughts, creatures that are born giants; that reach from east to west, from earth to heaven . . . thoughts reach all, comprehend all" (Donne, *Devotions*, 23). When poetry asked:

> Did I prosper or decay?
> When I so
> From *Things* to Thoughts did go?
> (Thomas Traherne, *The Review*)

The answer was unequivocal: thoughts

> Know no Bar, Denial, Limit, Wall:
> But have a Liberty to look on All.
> (Thomas Traherne, *Thoughts*)

Thoughts could indeed be epic wanderers leaping through the universe.

At the baroque juncture, Claudio Guillén would point out, the novelist raised the question: "How does one shape a life?" In a more meditative form, Austin Warren found that Thomas Browne's *Religio Medici* sought to express "the movement of ordering the mind in the process of thinking."[24] Likewise, the essayist tackled a kindred problem when he set out to shape thought. In the formative mode, they all met their challenge.

V

Marking stages of the formative process, the *Essays* bear evidence of three editions. Not only the "made" but the "making." Hence, the famous directive: "I add, I do not correct" (376). "To get more in," Montaigne piled up "only the headings of subjects." In fact, "were I to add on their consequences, I would multiply this volume many times over" (185). Written words were the tip of the iceberg, the fragmentary signposts of intuitions that overwhelmed literary discourse. The essay therefore draws on a wealth of thoughts whose very abundance is marginally captured on paper. Language was on trial and thought struggled to vindicate its rights against writing.[25]

Inevitably, "process" took up the representation of its own formal "making." At first, the sculptor uncovered layers of formation (Michelangelo's *Captives* and *Rondanini Pietà;* see chapter 1). Later, the essayist suggested work-in-progress; the novelist wrote prologues about the writing of prologues (Cervantes's *Pròlogo*); the poet wrote sonnets on the composition of sonnets (Lope de Vega's *Soneto de repente*); the painter painted different stages of completion (Velázquez's *Waterseller* [1620] and *Las Meninas* [1656], Figs. 12 and 13); and the playwright first took care of the "staging" and then sat down to write the plot of the comedy at the beginning of the second act in Bernini's unfinished *The Impresario* (also known as *Fontana di Trevi* [1643?]).[26] As Donald Beecher writes, the play consists of "dramatic process, fulfilled in its becoming rather than in its ending." Art represented its own chronotopic duration.[27]

Often, the baroque chronotope unraveled sequential representations. Viewers may have looked at the paintings behind the artist; they are looking at *Las Meninas* and are yet to see the canvas Velázquez is working on. As to the painter in the painting, the canvas presents what he is about to do or has been doing; a portraitist is portraying the portrayal.[28]

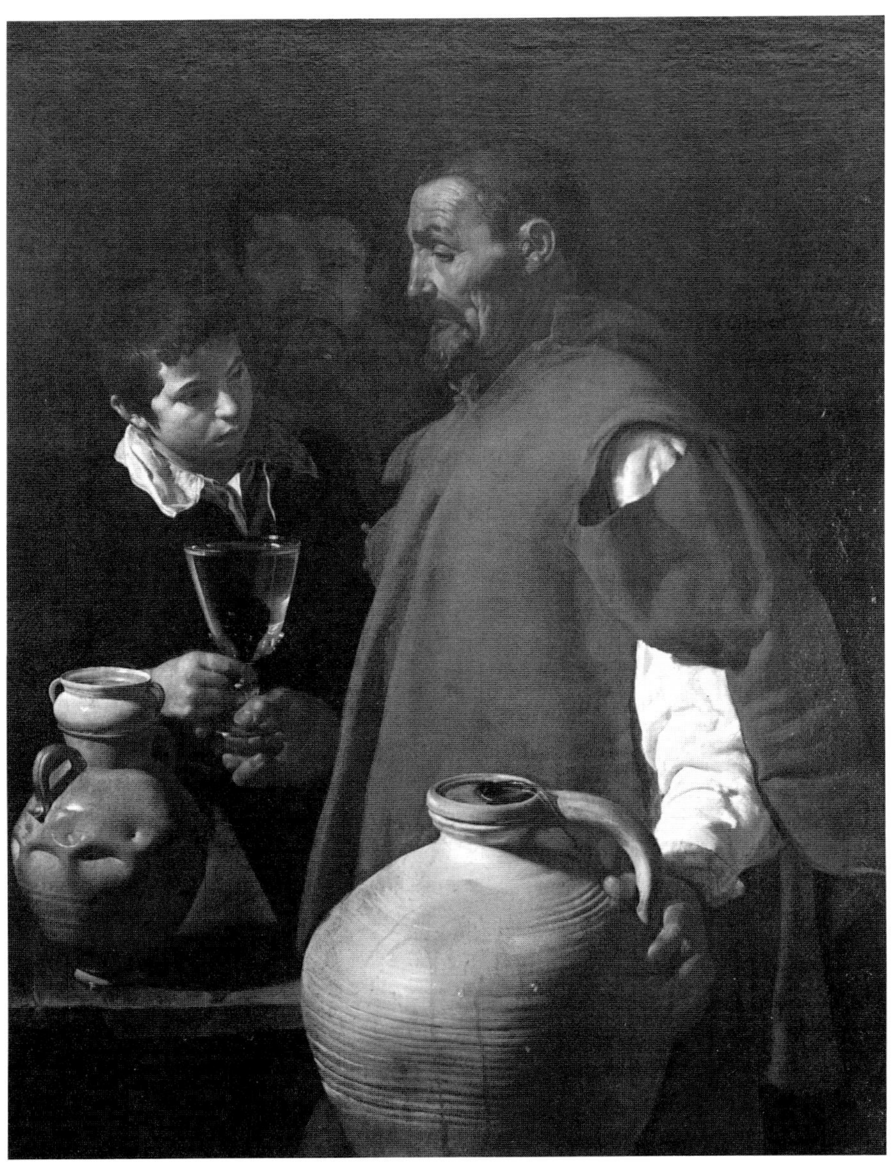

Fig. 12. Velázquez, *The Waterseller*, 1619–20. Wellington Museum, London

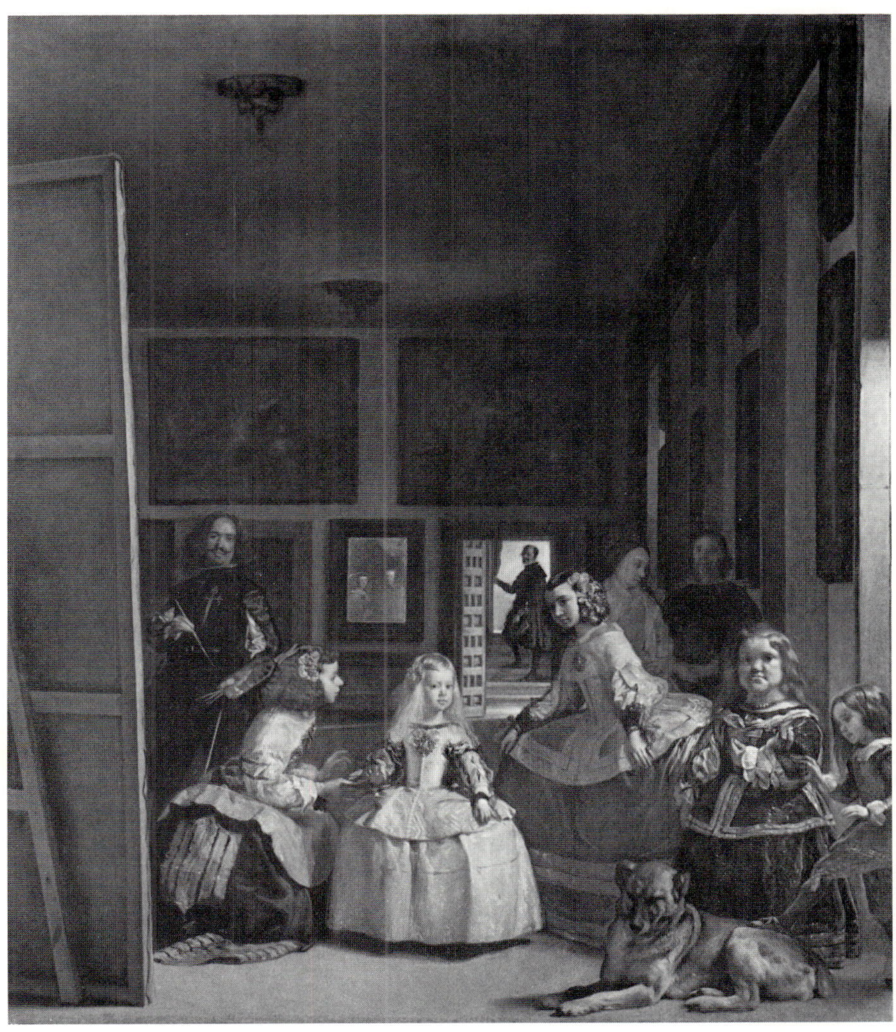

Fig. 13. Velázquez, *Las Meninas*, 1656. Prado, Madrid

Likewise, narration makes its way through the old Arab manuscript, the two parts of *Don Quixote,* and the authorial impasse in the *Pròlogo.* While Don Quixote discovers (Part II) that his deeds are already circulating in apocryphal versions, "spin-offs" alert the reader to conclusions which the main narrative is yet to reach (or about to contradict). Amid a maze of texts, the priest requests a death certificate to discourage further writings. Yet, insistence on the "completedness" of the story in the final paragraph would not stop the "fictitious and Tordellis-can scribe [to] pen again" (940) the *hidalgo*'s feats.[29] In concentric circles, the translated text opens up to translated language and translated authorship. Within a book midway between the old (romance) and the new (novel), the chronotope parodies itself.[30]

At the other side of high artifice, the process of art was nestled in the familiarity of the home, where Vermeer's insistence on the same window by the same corner of the same room seems to pace the recurrence of daily existence. While framing episodic sequences, such chambers are enclaves of being that body forth the evolving consciousness of its personae.[31]

I would like to suggest that, if one only looks at *The Lacemaker* (1669–70), *The Milkmaid* (1658–60), or *Young Woman with a Water Jug* (1664–65; Fig. 14), not to mention musical lessons in other rooms where the same chairs, table-cloths, and rugs weave a textural unity, we do grow accustomed to the process of life in much the same way as Velázquez and many a novelist have made us familiar with picaresque existence. While growing into a kind of novelistic intimacy with people and things, we also become more aware of similar objects and gestures in our own space. On this side of the table, even more familiar girls read letters, pour milk, and fall asleep without having to become Judiths who must cut off Holofernes' head to be noticed. While looking into the house next door, we become protagonists in ours; we have written the letter, and we are listening to the clavecin. The little corner of our house has become the great theater of the world. If we could let ourselves be surprised by the magic of normal lives, the spectacle of reality would open up to the "revealed vision" of our own actions. At

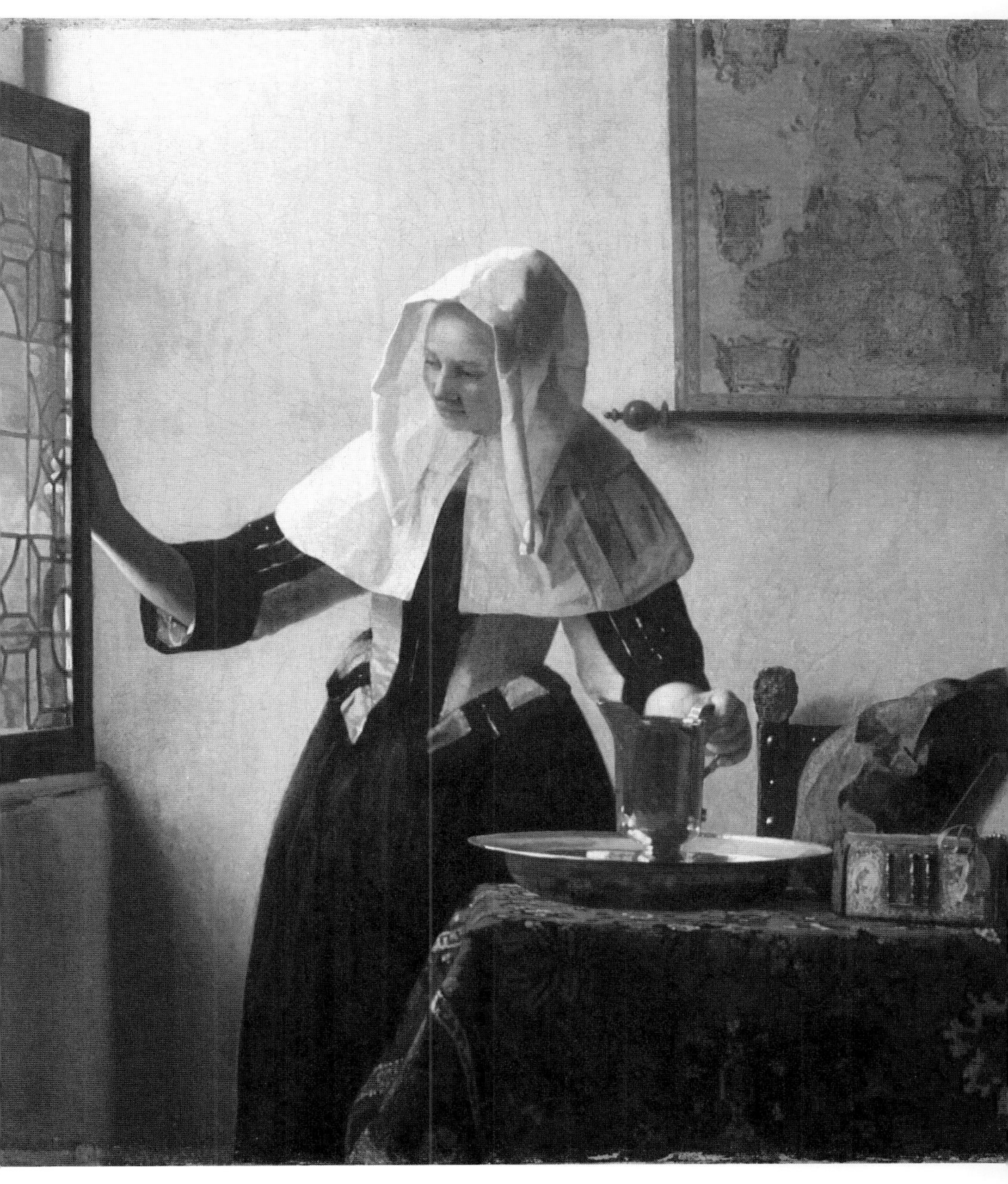

Fig. 14. Vermeer, *Young Woman with a Water Jug*, 1664–65. The Metropolitan Museum of Art, New York

that point, the baroque chronotope was about to keep at pace with the pulse of life.

Because he refused to delimit his artifact, the artist could control neither his nor his audience's freedom. Although inconclusiveness often replaced completion, chaos did not settle in; writers and readers, artists and viewers, were partners, not foes. Relationships between text, public, and author became central to the formative core of baroque art.[32]

When they commented on art, classical philosophers employed the strategy of mimesis to describe how the audience thought about the process toward wholeness that the artist revealed.[33] The "implied" reader-participant played an equally active role in the formative experience of art at a time when Counter-Reformation propaganda took a strong hold of people's minds. For Bruno, "each one [should] gather from this medium the fruits that he can, according to the capacity of his own bowl" (*Expulsion,* 74). To find common grounds for debate and consensus, baroque art dramatized its nearness-to-life.

Montaigne challenged readers to follow, and even compete with him, along a path he had never traced to its end. By the time each essay is completed in its literary form, readers are encouraged to undertake their own trials: "And how many stories have I spread around which say nothing of themselves, but from which anyone who troubles to pluck them with a little ingenuity will produce numberless essays" (115).[34] Since an active mind "has impulses beyond its powers of achievement," and its pursuits "are boundless and without form" (818), the essay might mature in other chronotopic dimensions. Actually, "an able reader often discovers in other men's writings perfections beyond those that the author put in or perceived, and lends them richer meanings and aspects" (93).

Similar claims could be made with regard to essays (Bacon) in which discourse invites inquiry beyond the written page; paradoxes (Donne) reaching out toward readers who might resolve them beyond the text;[35] fairy tales (G. B. Basile's *fiabe* of his *Pentamerone,* published posthumously in 1634–36) ending with proverbs that often call for reinterpretations of the whole story. Whether "*suffisant*" (Montaigne), "gentle" (Burton), or

"*desocupado*" (Cervantes), readers stretched the literary chronotope to new lengths.[36]

Whereas humanist systems of literary and spatial representation presumed fixed (linear perspective) and passive (treatise, panegyric) viewers-readers, baroque art called for involve-
ment. In the visual arts, baskets and stools about to tilt over
urged viewers to grab them (Caravaggio's first versions of the
Supper at Emmaus [1598–99] and second version of *St. Matthew with the Angel* [1602–3]). At times, backdrops, animals,
and deep chiaroscuro pushed the composition toward the foreground and into the spectator's space (Caravaggio, Rembrandt).
In a significant way, art had become a technique of persuasion
calling on bilateral relationships.[37]

VI

Even language kept abreast of the formative mode. In the flow
of baroque discourse, metaphoric words grew into metamor-
phic expressions. Bruno was convinced that "it is possible to
convert any fable, romance, dream or prophetic enigma, and to
signify all that pleases him who is skillful at tugging at the sense,
and is thus adept at making everything of everything—*e far
cossì tutto di tutto*" (*Frenzies*, 63). As a cornucopian copula, the
Brunonian *fare* (to make) enacts the process of changing proper
terms into metaphors.[38] Donne found "infinite latitude in every
Metaphor" (*Sermons*, II, 130) and gave free range to the resources of language. At the same time, *vero, verosimile, fantas-
tico,* and *meraviglioso* opened the gates to a metaphorical realm
(*Bildfeld*)[39] in which "the intellect understands more than language can verbalize, and the *concetto* supplies what words fail
to convey."[40]

As Philip Wheelwright points out, metaphors are based
on "semantic motion; the idea of which is implicit in the very
word 'metaphor,' since the motion that the word connotes is a
semantic motion—the double imaginative act of outreaching
and combining that essentially marks the metaphorical pro-

cess."[41] Tesauro would have linked outreaching and combining to *perspicacia* and *versabilità,* by means of which the intellect "rapidly compares such circumstances among themselves . . . it ties and divides them; increases and diminishes them; deduces one from the other, and with marvelous dexterity puts one in place of the other. And this is the metaphor."[42] Metaphoric outreaching could grow into all possible forms.

Basile's *fiabe* offer vivid images of the metaphorical expansion of language. Entrusted with taking care of the hen during his mother's absence, Vardiello, "who was the stupidest idiot in the village," accidentally killed the bird:

> Misfortune had now indeed come, and Vardiello tried to think how he could remedy the evil done. Making a virtue of necessity and in order to keep the eggs warm, he quickly took off his breeches and sat himself down on the nest, but he squashed them with his behind so that they were all reduced to an omelet. Seeing that he had made a double figure he was ready to dash his head against the wall. But at last, since every worry comes back to the mouth, he became aware of an empty feeling in his stomach and made up his mind to fill it with the hen.

Awkward attempts at substitution shatter the eggs. In Italian, the metaphorical phrase *ridusse a frittata* ("to make a double figure") fosters ambivalence; while pointing to a mishap, it also turns the eggs into an omelet. Having stirred Vardiello's appetite, the edible item foreshadows the lad's disheartening quest for a meal. The cooked fowl, however, is stolen by a cat and then forgotten amid greater mischiefs. Vardiello's ensuing actions betray fear and despair:

> So he took down out of the cupboard the jar of preserved walnuts, which she had told him was poison; he began to eat them and never stopped till he saw the shining bottom of the jar. Then with his stomach well filled he got right into the oven.

Through metaphoric inversions, food still affects behavior. Whereas Vardiello expects to die from harmless walnuts, Grannonia's initial guile leads to a downpour of figs and raisins. Although unable to protect eggs and hen, the lad survives lethal walnuts. Having decided to become omelet and fowl, he sticks his head into the oven; self-punishment takes on a culinary guise.

By flashing out images linked to a disastrous sequence (*ridusse a frittata* also means "to make a mess"), language confirms Vardiello's stupidity, his responsiveness to hunger, and his naive attempt to take an advantageous course of action. The effect is comical with regard to expectations, directional in terms of plot, and circumstantially plausible. After all, what can one do with broken eggs other than make an omelet? Such a pivotal phrase therefore grows to affect character, action, and meaning. The artist could manipulate words and objects at will, for their identity was contingent on as many functions as they could be suited for.

Forced to leave Naples, Cienzo stopped at the Capuan gate in another *fiaba:*

> Ah, my beautiful Naples, behold, I am leaving you, and who knows if it will be my lot ever to see you again: you whose bricks are of sugar, whose walls are of sweet pastry; where the stones are manna, the rafters are sugar-canes and the doors and windows are wafer-cakes. . . . Where another Gelsi, where the silkworms of love continually weave cocoons of pleasure? . . . Farewell, parsnips and beetroots, farewell fritters and cakes; farewell, cauliflowers and pickled tunny fish; farewell tripe and liver; farewell minced meat and grated cheese! Farewell, flowers of cities, glory of Italy, painted egg of Europe, mirror of the world![43]

Sadness is drowned amidst a gingerbread landscape where bricks are made of sugar and walls of sweet pastry. Nostalgia feeds on the metaphorical sweets of a synaesthetic banquet of odors, colors, shapes, and flavors. Long before a single *madeleine* recaptured times past for Marcel Proust, Basile transubstantiated remembrance into succulent forms of gastronomical beatitude.[44]

At at time when few acorns prompted quixotic images of the Golden Age, Cervantine language exploited its own metaphoric potential. For Sancho, a *cosa que relumbra* at first calls for literal distinctions (basin versus helmet) in the episode of Mambrino's helmet (I:21). Upon reflection, however, he later shifted toward compromise. The *bacia* and the *yelmo* were soldered together into a verbal *baciayelmo.* At least in its literary form, the magic of language could resolve contradictions.[45] The baroque imagination became a cornucopian horn of plenty once experience and memory set up metaphorical processes that by far exceeded the initial words or objects.[46]

The formative process exploited polysemy, allusiveness, and semantic expansion. Its aim was to reach for a universal *concinnitas* whereby man became "that amphibious piece between a corporeal and a natural essence, that middle frame that links those two together . . . that jumps not from extremes, but unites the incompatible distances by some middle and participating natures" (Thomas Browne, *Religio Medici,* I, 34). Human nature was outreaching and combining at heart, and it thrived on a metaphorical mode that Aristotle had found at once artistic and philosophical (*Rhetoric* III, 11).

As a shapeless matter, metaphoric reality was always prone to let the potential live its future out.[47] At the top of the spiritual ladder, Donne saw God as a "figurative, a metaphorical God . . . in whose words there is such a height of figures, such voyages, such perigrinations to fetch remote and precious metaphors . . . the style of thy works, the phrase of thine actions, is metaphorical" (*Devotions,* 125). Such an inclination was born of a spirit of semantic plenitude symbolic of the baroque *Weltanschauung.*[48]

VII

By bringing together what is apparently dissimilar, the metaphoric process depends on latitude and depth ("outreaching"), so much so that "combining" often involves polarity, antithesis, and contradiction. Since Heraclitus, paradox at its most constructive has linked the tactics of "either-or" to deeper insights into "both-and." Exclusion was a means for setting up convergence. Because "nothing is exclusively this or that," something can "be *both* of two disparates or two contraries, leaving the reader to contemplate the paradox." As a matter of fact, "if metaphor is employed without a touch of paradox, it loses its radically metaphoric character and turns out to be virtually no more than a tabloid simile. If paradox is employed without metaphor, it is no more than a witticism or sophism."[49] From an ontological standpoint, paradox is a formative structure that mocks clarity and defies resolution. Such a posture was central to the unity of the arts throughout the Baroque.

In the visual language of architecture, Borromini's *prospettiva* (1632–36; Fig. 15) in Palazzo Spada (1632–36, Rome) lengthens space to the extent that the gallery, actually 8.60 meters long, is "represented" as if it were 37 meters long. The result is that a little statue placed on a pedestal in the adjacent courtyard appears to be almost lifesize. As one proceeds to walk through the colonnade, distance and size are altered. Depth transforms position into function, which unsettles near and far, focused and blurred, before and after. Expectation yields to confusion, and uncertainty to discovery. While testing its illusionistic range, the perspectival construct is metaphoric inasmuch as it pulls in opposite directions, which are at once complementary and antagonistic.

Phrased in the more admonitory tone of a sermon, a similar mechanism is operative in Donne's understanding of— and warnings against—"the way of Rhetorique," which first troubles "the understanding, to displace, and to discompose, and disorder the judgment, to smother and bury in it, or to empty it of former apprehensions and opinions, and to shake that beliefe . . . and then when it is thus melted, to powre it into new molds, when it is thus mollified, to stamp and imprint new forms, new images, new opinions in it" (*Sermons*, II, 282). Art therefore performs a deconstructive and permutational function that could be either deceptive (at worst) or pedagogical (at best). As a result, it was hoped that human judgment would be alerted

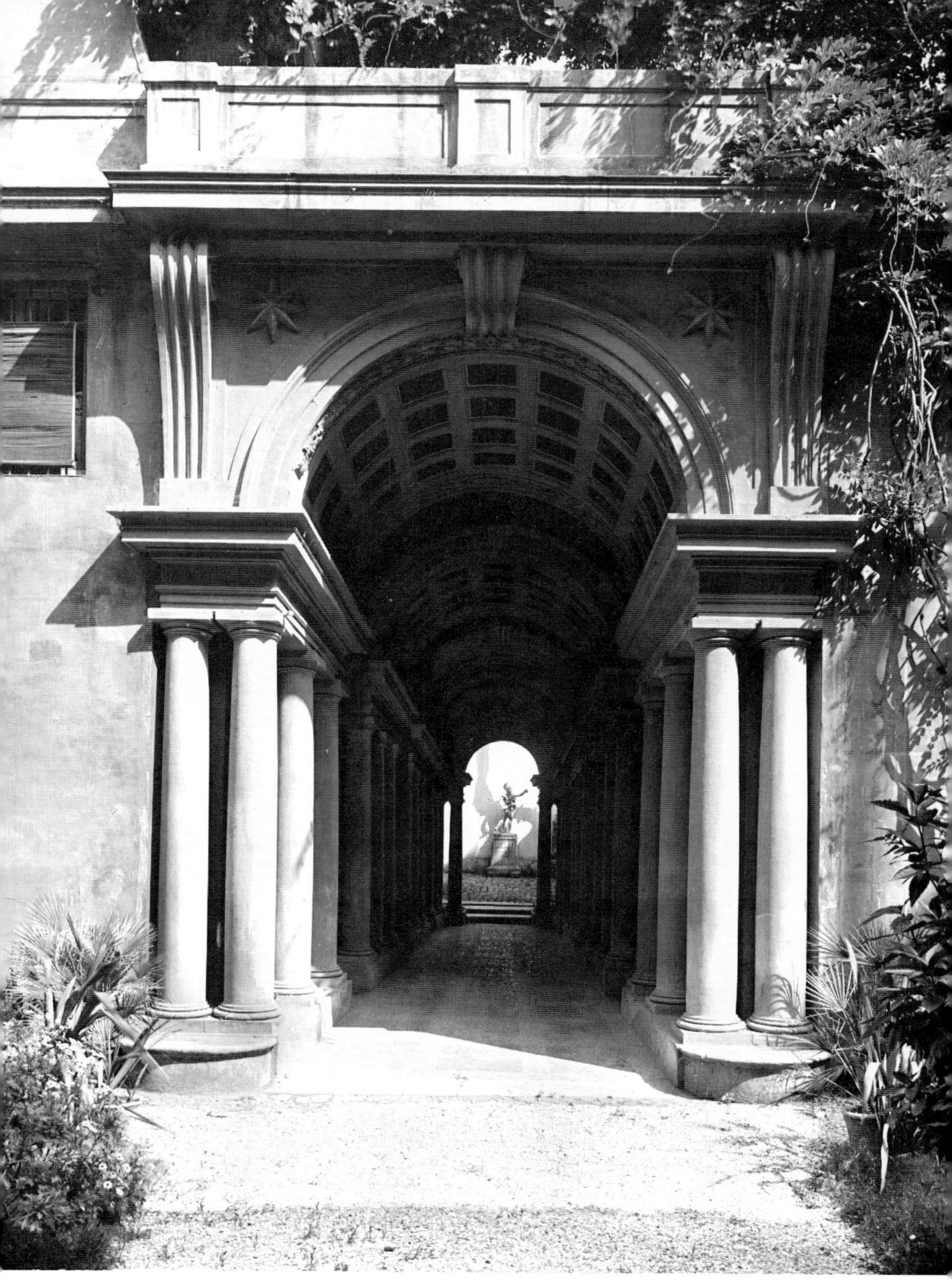

Fig. 15. Borromini, *Prospettiva* di Palazzo Spada, 1632–36. Palazzo Spada, Rome

to the volatility of both illusion (visual) and opinion (conceptual). In the process, certitude had to face the indeterminacy of fleeting perceptions.

It is in the literary perspective of *verosimile* that Cardinal Paleotti was reminded of Aristotle's phrase: "Often a lie resembles truth more than truth itself."[50] As it unveils and renews its deception, the *prospettiva* develops a kind of blurring for the sake of deeper insights. What ultimately counts is the viewer's understanding of clarity in relation to its opposite, and their intermediate combinations. He "incarnates" the artifact, which otherwise would be both incomplete and meaningless.

By undermining reasonable assumptions on sight and size, the Borrominian *prospettiva* forces viewers to become simultaneously real and fictive. Art made room for eccentric and articulate minds alike. We could guess that Montaigne would have walked through the colonnade aware that his question ("What do I know?") was echoed in a place where certainty and incredulity are intertwined, and where questioning is a matter of epistemology.

The Frenchman admired the paradoxical bent of the Pyrrhonians, who used "their reason to inquire and debate, but not to conclude and choose . . . they do not fear contradiction in their discussion. . . . They advance their propositions only to combat those they think we believe in" (374, 372). As such, paradoxes establish a perspective on their own technique.[51] While Hamlet would walk through the *prospettiva* weighing alternatives, Don Quixote would have cherished experiences of that sort. In the process, the parody of mimesis shed a brighter light on man's perception of reality.

Fiction's attack on itself produced inversions and double mirroring. Throughout the arts, reversals of roles were flaunted with a passion, and one need only mention actors turning into spectators in plays within plays (*Hamlet*), or Cervantine characters who become readers of stories written about them. To the Duke and the Duchess who have read the first part of the book, Don Quixote becomes "real" when they meet him. For us, however, the encounter makes the couple more fictitious. Such unthought-of manipulations of time, space, and identity could be disturbing, for "*l'autre*" could become "*un état paradoxal du*

Même.[52] Paradoxical forms of that kind were germane to those compatible incompatibilities of life that make of paradox a function of thought.[53]

To see clearly no longer meant to know with certainty, and Pascal's reflection is an apt commentary on the shift in the symbolism of perspective from Humanism to the Baroque:

> If one considers one's work immediately after having done it, one is entirely presupposed in its favor; by delaying too long, one can no longer enter into the spirit of it. So with pictures seen from too far or too near; there is but one exact point which is the true place wherefrom to look at them: the rest are too near, too far, too high, or too low. Perspective determines that point in the art of painting. But who shall determine it in truth and morality? (*Pensées* 381)

The certainty of axioms and fixed distances (perspective) gave way to the testing of knowledge and experience (perspectivism). Borromini therefore offered a visual construct pivoting on the clash between form and function. At all levels, his *prospettiva* exploited stylistic and psychological "telescoping."[54]

Because it teases the intellect the way optical illusion teases the eye, paradox calls on the reader-spectator to expose its deception, leading him to find better reasons against it. Since "by discord things increase, " Donne maintained that "we are ascertained of all disputable doubts, only by arguing, and differing in opinion, and if formal disputation which is not a painted, counterfeit, and dissembled Discord, can worke us this benefitt, what shall not a full and maine discord accomplish?" In the paradox *That All Things Kill Themselves,* Donne's emphasis on the preposition "if" undermines certainty:

> And if
> these things kill themselves, they do it in their best
> and supreme perfection: for after perfection immediately
> follows excess, which changes the natures and the names,
> and makes them not the same things.[55]

Repeatedly, the hypothetical "if" shifts language toward grounds on which statements can collapse the moment they are made. Although expectations are not met, deception is short-lived; paradox presents a direction only to confront it with a counterdirection, or, with Shakespearean flair, "by indirections find directions out" (*Hamlet* II.1). Whether visual or literary, perspectivism frustrates perception, discredits truth, exposes the blind side of belief, but ultimately instigates the growth of knowledge.

From architecture to literature, meaning could be undone as fast as it was produced. Because they were determined to make readers stop and think, artists often bluffed. For Tesauro, metaphors of deception lead the intellect to "find a secret and innate pleasure in realizing that it has been pleasantly deceived (*scherzosamente ingannato*); to cause movement from deceit to truth is a method of learning that is unexpected and, therefore, pleasing."[56] Baroque forms tended to enact their own problems.

VIII

In nature, growth can shift through different orders of life; seeds become trees and worms turn into butterflies. Likewise, metaphorical language presented "vegetable gold," "liquid pearl" (Milton), and "painted words" (Shakespeare), much as poetry imitated birds and musical instruments emulating each other (Marino, Crashaw).

Metaphorical transformations turned marble, feet, and hair into wood, roots, and leaves in Bernini's *Apollo and Daphne,* just as one of the spouts of his *Fontana dei quattro fiumi* (Piazza Navona, Rome, 1648–51) ejected (as it still does) a kind of transparent sheet of water. And whenever the *piazza* was flooded on festive occasions (*festa del lago,* beginning in 1652), water liquified the facade of Borromini's St. Agnese into undulating reflections. With a passion, artists played solidity against fluidity, while motion melted matter away.

The bee's wings in Bernini's *Fontana delle api* (Piazza

Barberini, Rome, 1644) spread out into the ridges of a marble seashell lifted into the air. By contrast, water expands into floating ridges in the basin below. Throughout the city, *tritoni, barcaccie, terrine,* and *mascheroni* uttered ebullient voices.

Sculpture borrowed from dance and theater (Bernini's *Apollo and Daphne,* the Cornaro chapel in Santa Maria della Vittoria, 1645–52), while architecture became pictorial (Borromini's Cappella Spada, 1662, San Gerolamo della Carità, Rome; Pietro da Cortona's ceiling in Palazzo Barberini, 1633–39, Rome). In the painted glass of Bernini's *Gloria (Cathedra Petri,* 1657–66, Saint Peter's, Rome) clouds turn into cherubs and light into pictorial forms.[57] Visual images relinquished generic separations, and the idea of unifying the arts came of age.

Sculpture and architecture blended together in Bernini's *Baldacchino* (1624–33; Fig. 16). Placed at the heart of Saint Peter's, it combined religious pageantry, visual designs, ritual gestures, the incense odor of Christian rites, single voices, choral chants, organ music, the reading of books, and the preaching of words. Indeed, an appropriate setting for Crashaw's verses on inner life at its mystical intensity. Expression edged on the intersense analogies of synesthesia. Walter Pater would have found such a "metaphor of the senses"[58] central to the "divine services" of early Christianity, when his aesthetic hero saw the mass as "a sort of dramatic action, and with the unity of a single appeal to eye and ear" (*Marius the Epicurean,* IV, 23).

Bernini's baldachin and Calderón's *gran teatro del mundo* were the signposts of a culture that favored complex (non-Aristotelian) artforms like melodrama, opera, and "shaped poems" (Herbert's *Easter Wings*). European courts invested large sums of money in festivities, and the English masque integrated poetry, painting, music, and dance. Often, theatrical works (Calderón, Lope de Vega) anchored the scenic center to paintings of sacred images. The stage itself was conceived as a metaphor merging art, artist, and audience into indistinguishable parts of a single experience.

One of the most important services in Counter-Reformation Rome was the Devotion of the Forty-Eight Hours, which included processions of religious companies, special sermons,

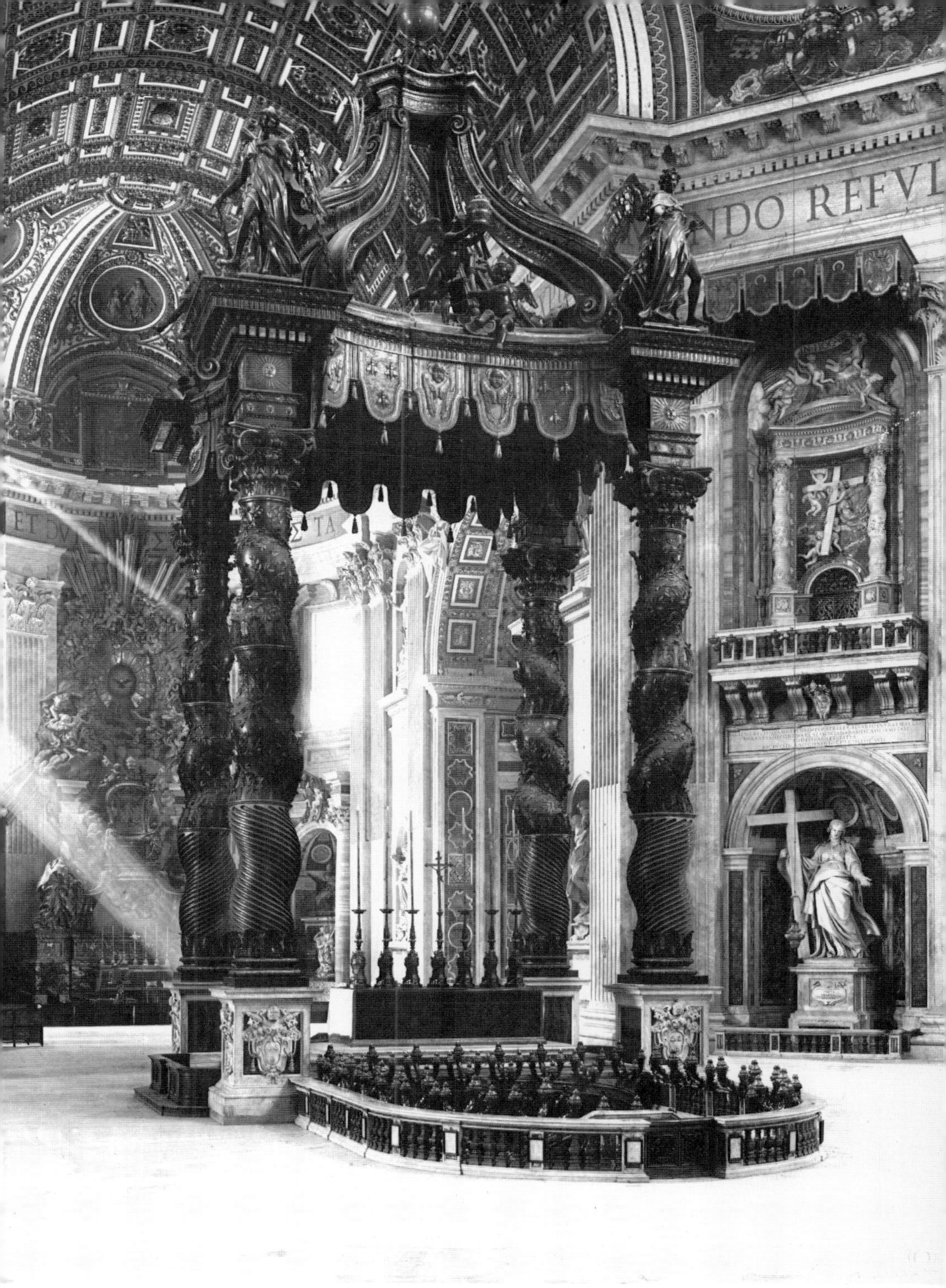

Fig. 16. Bernini, *Baldacchino*, 1624–33. Saint Peter's Basilica, Rome

and hymns. Inside the church, theatrical *apparati* (some de-
signed by Bernini himself) enhanced the illusion of stage set-
tings. Artforms grew into each other and out into the open,
where devotional functions moved along the new streets that
connected the Christian basilicas. With the mobil chair (apse)
and the transient *baldacchino* (high altar) as their symbols, all
processions, Bernini well understood, came to rest in Saint Peter's. In 1928, Leo Spitzer emphasized the incarnational nature
of a similar experience during the processions of Holy Week in
Seville, "when the cathedral spills out into the street, when the
religious confraternities carry through the streets superhuman
Virgins. . . . I saw the image of the spirit's descent into the
flesh. . . . I understood then all the abstractness of Judeo-
Protestant moral teachings and all the carnality of Mediterranean Catholicism."[59]

Such a gargantuan eclecticism pointed to the baroque
idea of artistic growth toward the total work of art. Along the
southern shores of the Mediterranean experience, art combined
architectural motives, figure sculpture, and painting into a unified interplay of forms on altars (José Churriguera's high altar
in the church of San Estebán, 1693–96, Salamanca) and *Ora-
tori* (Giacomo Serpotta's "*teatrino prospettico*" of the Battle of
Lepanto, begun 1686–88, in the Church of S. Cita, Palermo;
Fig. 17).

An astounding example of the integration of the arts is
the "Sacro Monte" in the alpine region of northern Italy (Fig.
18). Since the early seventeenth century, environment, architecture, and the visual arts began to map out Christian mythology
in the lifesize scale of a utopian *locus*.

It was Bernardino Caini who, at the end of the *Quattrocento*, put forward the idea of re-creating Mount Zion and the
Holy Places—his New Jerusalem—in Varallo (Lombardy). From
Guadenzio Ferrari's *Calvario* to Giovanni d'Enrico's *Ecce
Homo,* a series of chapels (forty-three were planned) mark way
stations—*via sacra*—that lead to the Piazzale del Tempio. In each
of them, painting and lifesize sculptures (in wood, plaster, or
terra-cotta) of a naturalistic realism akin to that of *presepi* figu-
rines guide the faithful to scenes (from Adam to Christ's sepul-
chre) whose emotional pathos is discharged into ritual events.

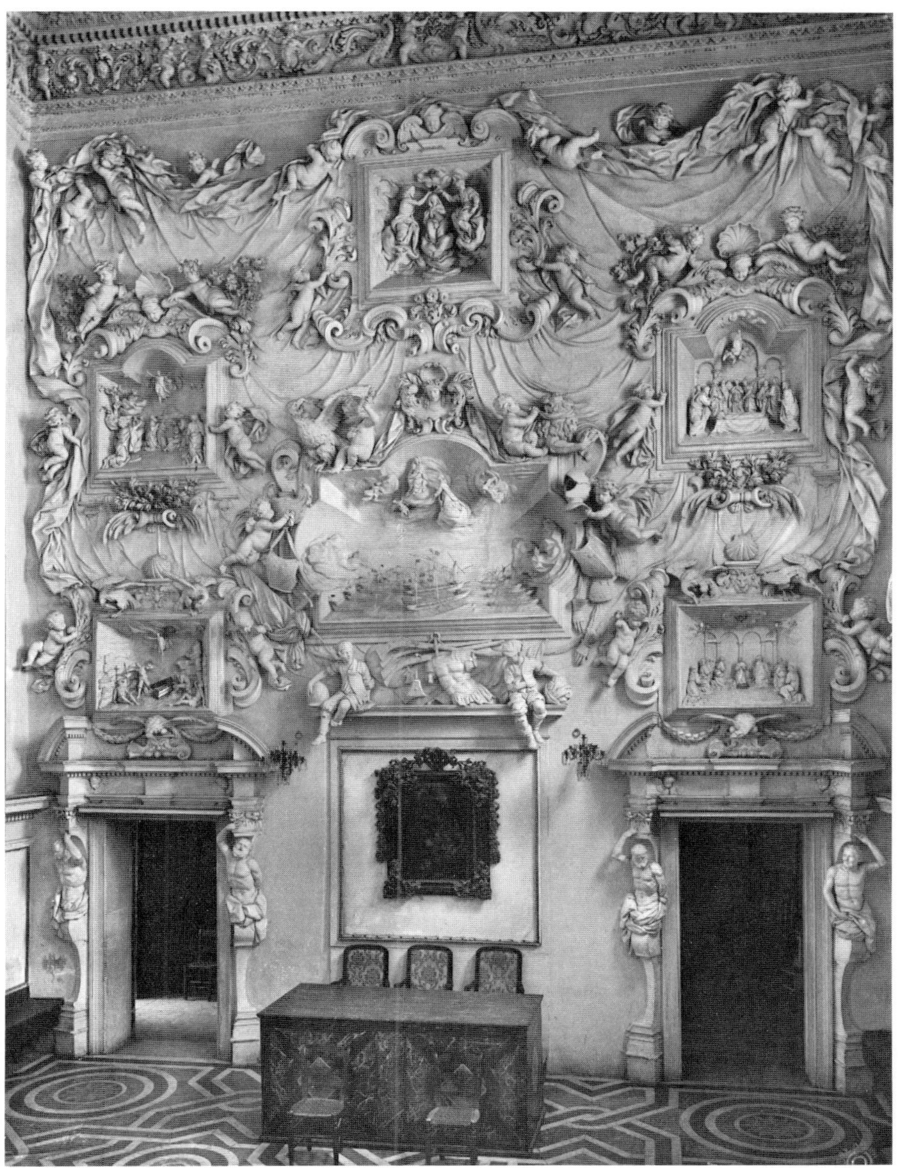

Fig. 17. Giacomo Serpotta, *The Battle of Lepanto*, begun 1686–88. Oratorio, Church of S. Cita, Palermo

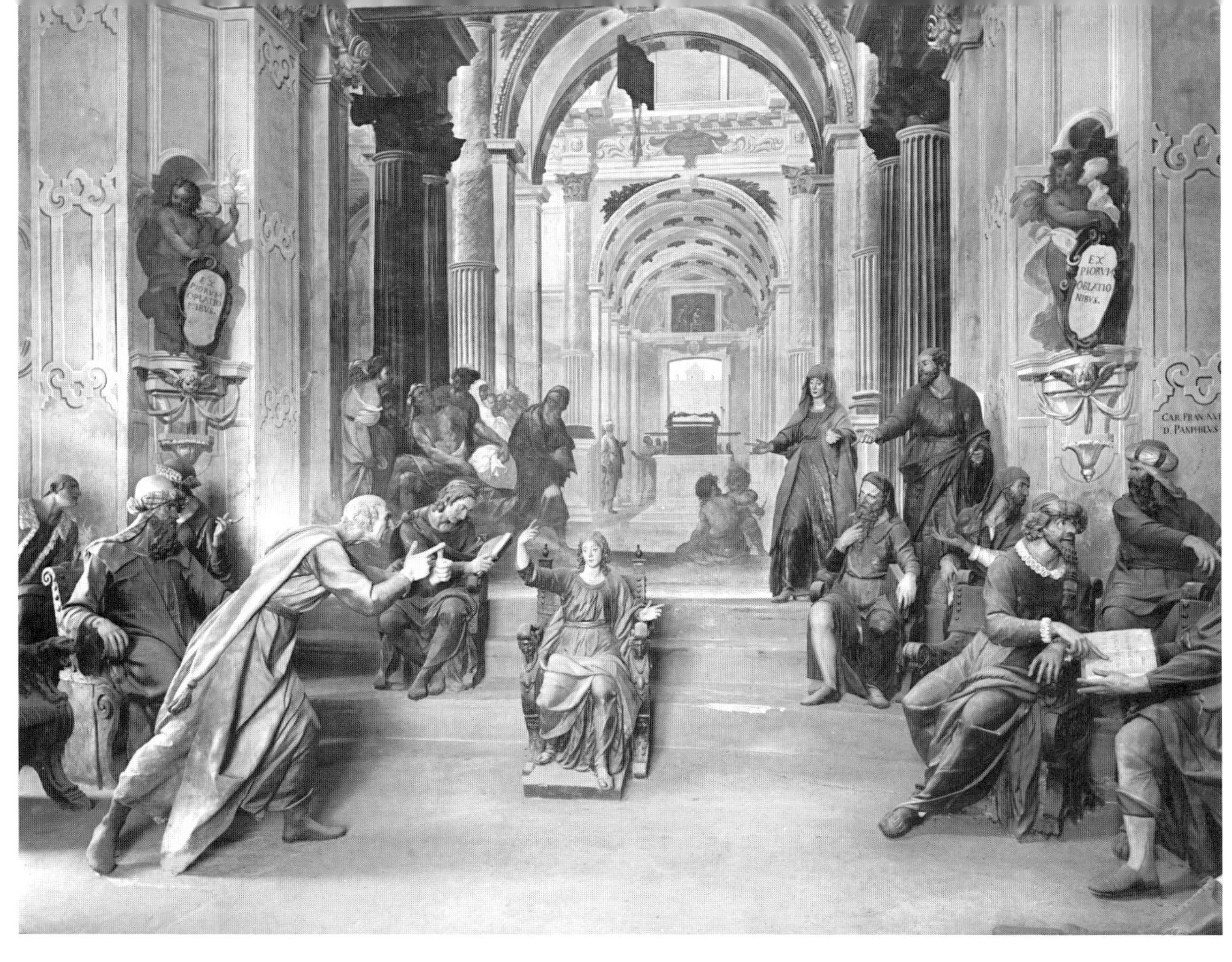

Fig. 18. Chapel 5, *Disputa di Gesù coi dottori*. Sacro Monte, Varese

In the tradition of devotional pilgrimages, mimesis staged live experiences on the *gran teatro montano*. From the sixteenth to the eighteenth centuries, a number of *sacri monti* emerged in northern Italy (Ossuccio, Varese, Arona, Orta, Oropa, Crea, Monta), and they all thrived on a "discoursive architecture" that sheltered the visual arts in "processional prayers" toward the city of the spirit.[60]

Theoretical discussions on the visual arts (Marino's *Dicerie sacre*) featured the artist as poet, painter, composer, orator, preacher, concert master, and stage director—a match for the Wagnerian ego. In the mid-seventeenth century, John Evelyn called Bernini "Sculptor, Architect, Painter and Poet: who a little before my coming to the City, gave a Publique Opera (for so they called those shows of that kind) wherein he painted the scenes, cut the statues, invented the Engines, composed the Musique, writ the Comedy, and built the Theater all himselfe."[61] His spellbinding optimism spurred on the creation of churches, bridges, chapels, sculptures, fountains, parades, festivals, and colonnades that made of Rome an outdoor *Gesamtkunstwerk* whose construction spanned the artist's lifetime.

In ways that today would appear odd, public anatomies in the Netherlands combined justice, science, and spectacle into a sort of forensic-medical multimedia event. As iconological studies of Rembrandt's *Doctor Tulp's Anatomy Lesson* (1632; Fig. 19) inform us, such ensembles proceeded in three acts. First, the solemn public execution of the "patient." Second, the formal public anatomy of the criminal, which also elicited thoughts about death redeemed for knowledge's sake. And finally, the semiprivate guild banquet and torch parade in honor of justice revindicated. In the process, the Anatomy Theater must have made hefty profits if it commissioned Rembrandt in 1656 to paint an even larger canvas, *Dr. Deyman's Anatomy Lesson* (lost in a fire, except for a fragment now in the Rijksmuseum, Amsterdam).[62]

Beyond forms of perceptible size, formativeness reached nonrepresentational levels at which truth and beauty could be experienced "in silence" (Bruno, *Frenzies*, 191). While humanist art was meant to have "nothing to do with things that are not visible" (Alberti), its baroque counterpart made room for "that

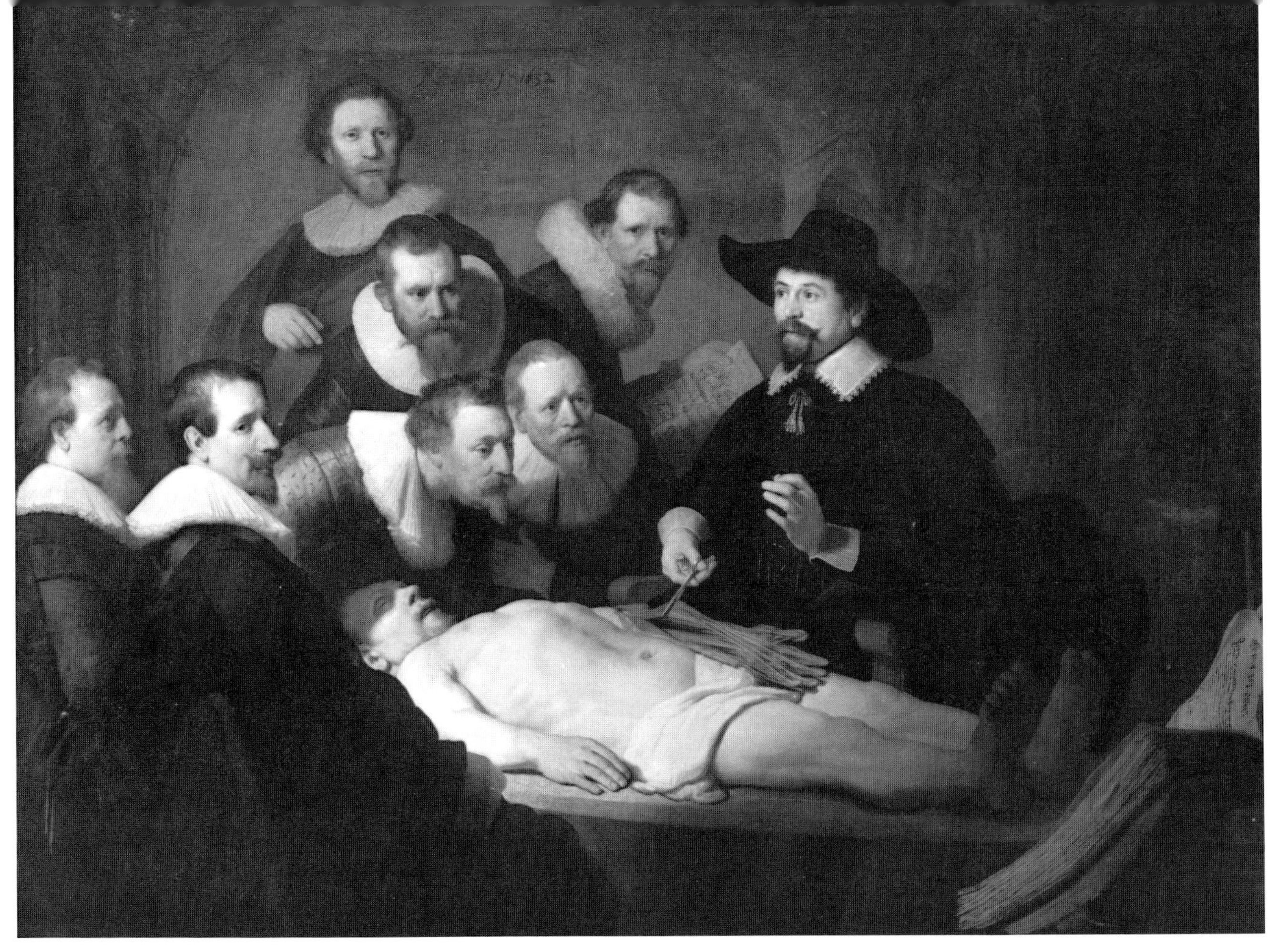

Fig. 19. Rembrandt, *The Anatomy Lesson of Dr. Tulp*, 1632. Mauritshuis, Amsterdam

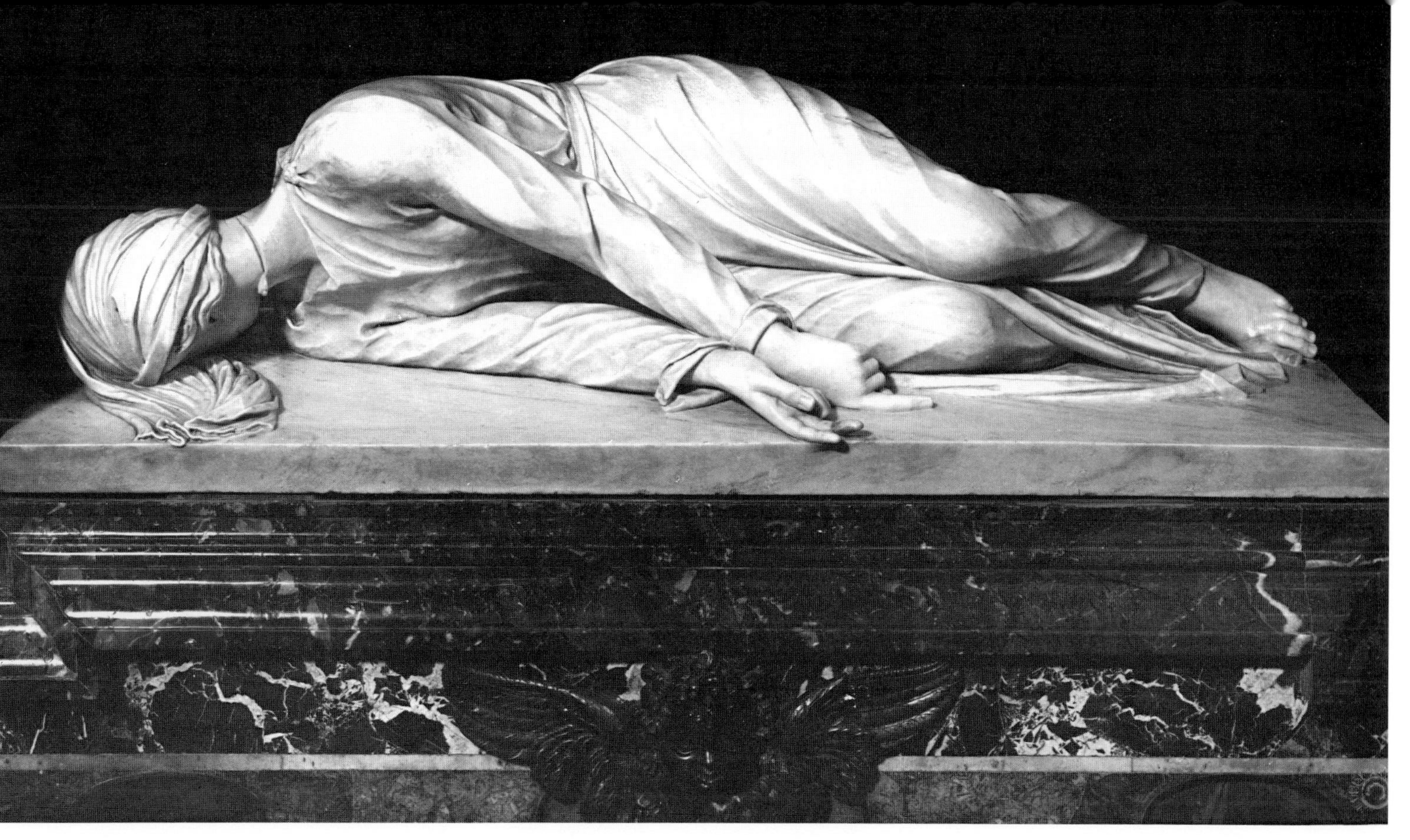

Fig. 20. Stefano Maderno, *Santa Cecilia*, 1600. Santa Cecilia in Trastevere, Rome

which is not corporeal, and therefore invisible" (Salvator Rosa). Actually, "the intellect understands more than language can verbalize, and the *concetto* supplies what words fail to convey" (Tesauro).[63]

At the edge of its outreaching mode, the formative *élan* bordered on the unspoken and the unpainted. Pictures in which more is intended than demonstrated (Caravaggio, Rembrandt) were popular, and it was enough for the painter to show "only the head of this, the horn of that, the hind quarters of another, the ears of this . . . so that one would with greater satisfaction wonder, guess and spin a story about the picture" (Bruno, *Ash*, 45). Language could only intimate heroic frenzies for Bruno, while cloth disintegrated amid clouds and pure light in Bernini's *Ecstasy of Saint Theresa* (1647–52). The creative process defied figurative boundaries.

On sculptural grounds, Stefano Maderno presented *S. Cecilia* (1599–1600, Santa Cecilia in Trastevere, Rome; Fig. 20) lying on her side with her face totally hidden. Since time, expression, and spatial realism have been denied, the artwork thrives on its psychological impact on the viewer. Although he represented the body the way Cardinal Sfrondati had found it in 1599, the artist let the saint's white robe draw a rhythmic outline (arching from head to feet) that seems to call for responses of a musical order. At the same time, the stillness of the figure translates sculptural language into a metaphysical silence that Christianity has always linked to eternity. Whereas Bernini was to tie spiritual expressions to the action-word of death and ecstasy (Ludovica Albertoni, 1671–74, Saint Teresa), Maderno sculpted a nonverbal condition of supernal feelings. The nonrhetorical character of his artwork vibrates with intimations of transcendence, as if the black niche housed the muteness of the divinely unspeakable.[64]

IX

At its most representative, baroque art foregrounded the "making," the "made," and the development leading from one to the other; creation as a *faciendum* rather than a *factum*.

Because they exist as characters in their own fictions, Cervantes and Velázquez somehow relinquish authorial privileges and become functions of a creative activity enacted by pens and paintbrushes.

Beyond literary legacies, the power of writing survives dead chroniclers (Cid Hamete), live novelists (Cervantes), and unwelcomed impostors, who turn into markers of an inexhaustible continuum. At the very end, authorial voices are silenced, and the pen (*la pluma*) makes its ultimate claim: "For me alone Don Quixote was born and I for him. His was the power of action, mine of writing—*Para mí sóla nació Don Quijote, y yo para él; él supo obrar, y yo escribir.*" The feminine ending of *sóla* cannot refer to Cid Hamete but to the pen, which "shall live long ages." Warning scoundrels of all sorts that writing is a deed "reserved for me alone" (939–40), the pen transforms the creator himself into a metaphorical *faciendum*.

The "medium" asserted itself as pure process even on English shores, where Shakespeare was confident that his pen would shelter the ever-growing mortality of the vernacular:

> When all the breathers of this world are dead
> You still shall live—such virtue hath my pen
> (Sonnet 81)

Destiny itself unraveled as a graphic line, which is "drawne by night, and the various effects therein by a pencill that is invisible; wherein though we confesse our ignorance, I am sure we doe not erre, if we say, it is the hand of God" (Thomas Browne, *Religio Medici*, I, 43).

Writing outlasted writers, and the pen replaced names. "The Art of Writing" flaunted its nomenclature through drawings of wise men sharpening their pencils (Gerrit Dou, *An Elderly Man Sharpening His Pen*, Amsterdam Historisch Museum, Collection Fodor) and canvases with angels teaching apostles to write (Caravaggio's first version of *St. Matthew*). At its most professional, Caravaggio presented *St. Jerome Writing*.

In the writer's own description of his craft, Cervantes has just finished his master work, and the writing of the preface leads him to an impasse. There are moments of indecision:

"Many times I took up my pen to write it, and many times I put it down, not knowing what to say." The pen sketches out the very rhythm of his thinking process, outlining in a most intimate space the ups and downs of an instrument that sustains creation from the volatility of fleeting thoughts to the safety of a scriptural gesture. The act of writing falters at first, and then stops altogether: "With the paper before me, my pen in my ear, my elbow on the desk and my hand on my cheek, thinking what to write" (26). The mind is running idle, and the pen seems to be posted by its source of motion. Lodged between brain and ear, it stands as a graphic organ ready to register the thinking process. Cervantes is lost in doubts. As if held hostage to the entrapments of learning, the pen waits, ready to shift from behind the ear (perception) to a hand still weighed down by indecision (expression).

The problems of one yielded to the pride of a whole tradition when Luis de Góngora celebrated Cordova:

> Oh siempre gloriosa patria mia,
>   tanto por plumas cuanto por espadas!

In a humanist spirit, Michel Butor writes, Cordovan pens referred back to Lucan and Seneca.[65] The pen could speak in the first person, or as the collective marker of an unbroken heritage. Italo Calvino dates such a "transfiguration of the artist in the practice of his art" back to Guido Cavalcanti,[66] who wrote a sonnet in which pens—along with the instruments used for cutting and sharpening them—speak in the first person:

> Noi siàn le triste penne isbigottite,
>   le cesoiuzze e 'l coltellin dolente . . .

> (We are the sad, dismayed pens,
>   the scissors and the sorrowing knife . . .)

Such verses opened up much of modern poetry inasmuch as they presented a writer aware of his own act of writing. Between

Cavalcanti and Mallarmé, Cervantes took a stand at once critical and sympathetic toward the fact that written words were
indeed written words.

Pens and words cemented traditions through epochs and
across the oceans. It was the age of geographical discoveries and
typographical inventions. At once a writer, a scientist, and an
inventor, Galileo wrote:

> But surpassing all stupendous inventions, what sublim-
> ity of mind was his who dreamed of finding means to
> communicate his deepest thoughts to any other person,
> though distant by mighty intervals of place and time! Of
> talking with those who are in India; of speaking to those
> who are not yet born and will not be born for a thou-
> sand years; and with what facility, by the different ar-
> rangements of twenty characters upon a page![67]

At once outreaching and combining, *"venti caratteruzzi sopra
una carta"* made of the alphabet the ultimate instrument of
communication.

In the arts, the Florence *Captives* proclaimed Michelangelo's "willing" captivity to a sculptural *non-finito* that was to
remain forever in progress. Likewise, the paintbrush in the artist's hand overcame all ambiguities in *Las Meninas.* If its subject
is only a reflection, if representation borders on parody and the
painter is unwilling to explain its content, "painting" has none-
theless executed its autonomous task. And so it did with
Adriaen van Ostade (*A Painter's Studio,* 1660s), Vermeer (*The
Painter's Studio*), and Rembrandt, who also leads us to *Artist in
His Studio* (Museum of Fine Arts, Boston) through the back of
a canvas whose subject we shall never see. Unlike Velázquez, the
Dutch master is not carrying out an appointed task under royal
patronage, even though the rather large size of the frame on the
easel suggests a historical subject. As in the case of *Las
Meninas,* he has just finished or is about to begin painting. In a
room where poverty and desolation are offset only by the instruments of his art, he is alone with painting. The large easel
guides our attention toward the left, where the paintbrush in

the artist's hand holds pictorial "making" hostage to a pause of creative intensity by far more valuable than any "represented" subject.[68] With a passion, the "Art of Painting" paraded its medium.

Centuries later, baroque referentiality caught up with Dali, whose hand leads us into the very act of painting *The Chair* (1975). On matters of origination, we cannot but notice that Dali's paintbrush drives our eye right into the "painted" holograph of his own *Las Meninas*.

Poems that rewrite themselves (Tansillo and Bruno, Marino and Crashaw), dialogues that "have been set down and developed only as the material and subject" of future works (Bruno, *Expulsion,* 73), Shakespearean plays in which characters finally promise to tell each other the story they have just heard, unfinished nudes (Michelangelo), canvases that we are yet to see (Velázquez), and promises (or fears) of essays and books to come (Montaigne, Cervantes) project art beyond the very last forms it has produced. In Velázquez's *The Spinners* (Fig. 21), Ariachne flaunts her craft in the foreground. Behind her, other women admire the finished tapestry. Yet, the process of completion draws from the unfolding tradition of art. The tapestry in the background represents Titian's *Rape of Europe,* which is placed at the dead center of the perspectival construct. Craft "makes" art, which renews its greatest achievements; referentiality is classical and modern, prosaic (weaving the tapestry) and poetic (the pictorial image). We cannot but agree with Leonard Barkan that "the highest point of sublimation—beyond craft, beyond connoisseurship, even beyond the drama of mortal and divine artist—is the work of art itself."[69]

At its most daring, the very concept of representation edged on memory and hope; while Donne wrote his own funeral sermon (*Death's Duel*), Rembrandt painted a portrait of his wife Saskia (*Portrait of Saskia,* Berlin, Staatliche Museen, Gemäldegalerie) in 1643, a year after her death. At the height of the baroque experience, the artist stepped aside and let the authorless continuity of pens and paintbrushes declare art's undying *persona*.

When he measured formativeness—*formabilità*—against the infinite, Bruno brought home the idea of creation as a pro-

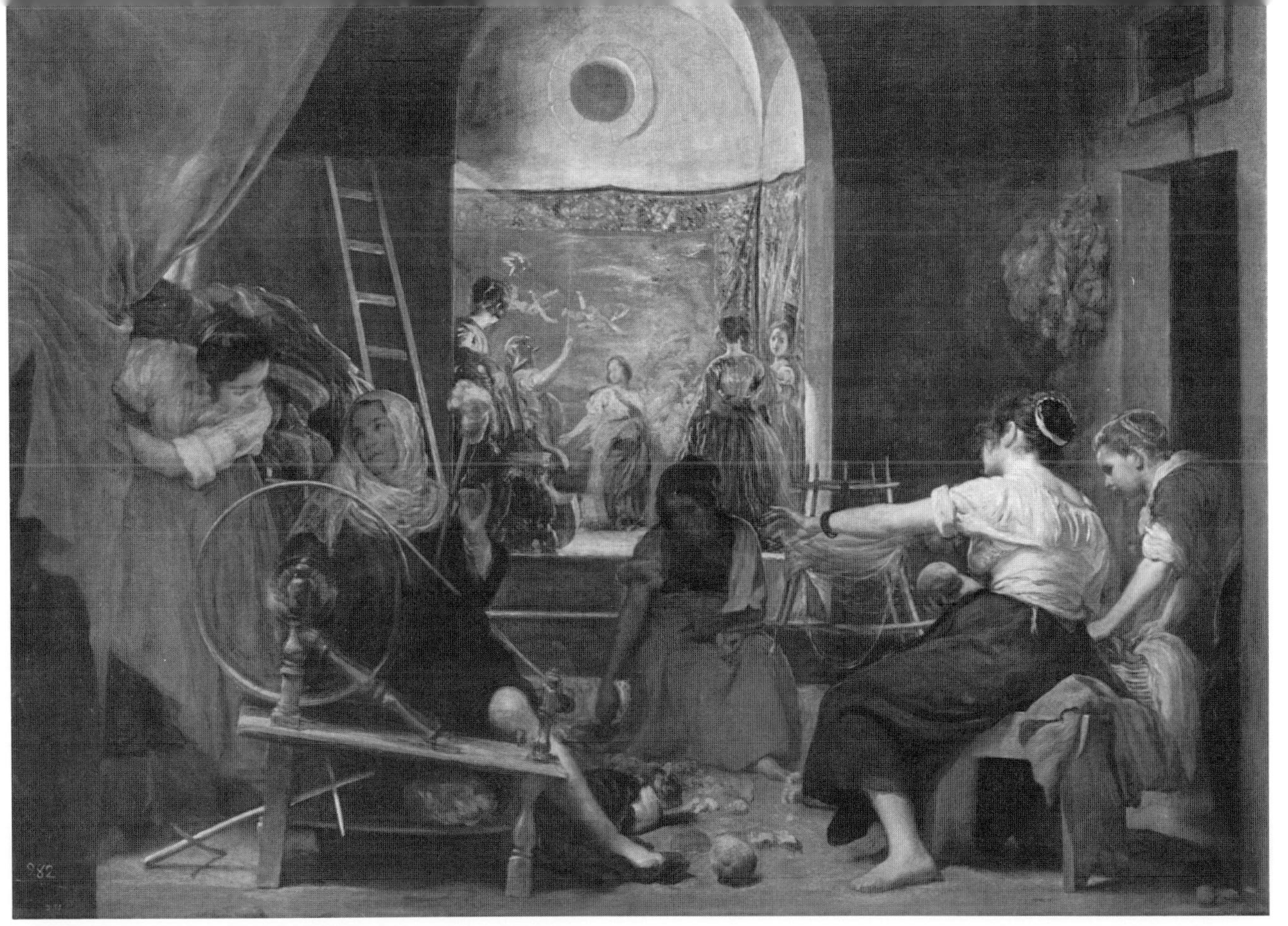

Fig. 21. Velázquez, *The Spinners*, 1657? Prado, Madrid

cess without beginning. Beyond the perfect stasis of either the classical Being of Beings or humanist plenitude, his generative principle defied "founders," "origins," and "bests." As such, formativeness did not set cosmos against chaos, but it did set form against its own dynamic potential.

On strictly artistic grounds, therefore, baroque referentiality is neither a matter of imitation (classicism) nor emulation (humanism), but a necessary component of what Henri Focillon calls "the life of forms." The "maker" (Tansillo and Bruno, Ariosto and Cervantes) is subservient to the "made" (lyric poetry, chivalric poetry-prose), which in turn overcomes "formation" by keeping the "making" alive. As a result, formativeness is immune to the death of geniuses, the mediocrity of impostors, and the misunderstandings of either ignorance or prejudice (Bruno, Copernicus, Galileo).

X

To a substantial extent, the historical fortunes that the seashell has undergone do bear on the poetics of formation. When William Hogarth delivered a blow against the impenetrability of objective forms, shells served his critical undertaking:

> Let every object under our consideration be imagined to have its inward contents scooped out so nicely as to have nothing of it left but a thin shell, exactly the shape of the object itself. . . . the imagination will naturally enter into the vacant space within the shell, and mark the opposite corresponding parts so strongly, as to retain the idea of the whole, and make us masters of the meaning of every view of the object, as we walk round it, and view it from without.[67]

To provide a total view of the object, artists and viewers were to break its surface open. The notion of the eye placed within the shell implied a knowledge of the inner workings, if not the vitality, of form.

Hogarth's concerns surfaced again in Kant's distinction between free (natural) and dependent (human) beauty. While purposiveness is a constituent part of the latter, the former presupposes "a concept of what the object ought to be. . . . Many birds (such as the parrot, the hummingbird, the bird of paradise) and many seashells are beauties in themselves, which do not belong to any object determined in respect of its purpose by concepts, but please freely and in themselves." The constituent parts of the free (natural) whole are independent of human apperception, for they find a *raison d'être*, if there need be one, in their cohesiveness. Accordingly, "beauty is the form of the purposiveness of an object, so far as this is perceived in it without any representation of a purpose" (*Critique of Judgment*, 16–17). The natural beauty of flowers and seashells, as they appear in themselves, justifies a judgment of taste involving our sensory perception of the object.[68]

After Kant, the romantics exposed the inadequacy of objective forms (appearance) to express their creative principle (essence). As the "indwelling spirit of nature," formativeness stands above form. Art therefore should reproduce the vitality rather than the inanity of things: "The life of the plant consists in silent receptiveness. . . . Only with the animal kingdom does the struggle between life and form seem really to commence: its first works it conceals in hard shells, and where these are laid aside the inanimate world reunites with the realm of crystallization through the act impulse."[69] As a challenge to the completeness of natural beauty, the seashell ought to steer eye and mind to seek power of expression beneath the beauty of form. And it was by "stretching forth the shell, so beautiful in shape," that "a loud prophetic blast of harmony" could be heard (Wordsworth, *The Prelude*, V, 90, 95). By combining animate and inanimate orders of nature, "*corals* and *conchylia*" met the challenge of growth, for "the whole act and purpose of their existence seems to be that of connecting the animal with the inorganic world by the perpetual formation of calcareous earth." In romantic imagery, the stone was a symbol of geometric truth, and the shell stood "for life-giving power,"[70] what Bruno called "an efficient and formative principle from within—*un principio efficiente ed informativo da dentro*" (*Expulsion*, 76).

Set against that historical trajectory, Valéry put forth his own concept of formation, which he based on the alliance

> of a form, a material, an idea, an action, and a passion; the absence of any clearly determined aim or of any result that might be expressed in finite terms; a desire and its recompense, each regenerating the other; a desire that creates and hence causes itself; something breaking away from all particular creation and ultimate satisfaction, thus revealing itself to be a desire to create for the sake of creating.

Given those conditions, "there is no such thing as an *idée fixe*." As a matter of fact, an idea is "a transformation sign, which more or less affects the system as a whole . . . whatever its nature, a thought that becomes fixed assumes the characteristics of a hypnosis and is called, in the language of logic, an idol; in the domain of art and poetic construction, it becomes a sterile monotony."[74]

XI

Because of its integrative mode, baroque formativeness did not affect a reality in which unity had broken down. If romantic minds found at the very core of life the diasparactive triad of ruin, incompleteness, and fragmentation,[75] their baroque ancestors would have sought ways for mending the pieces.

Although the Copernican lesson had taught that there could be no real center, the baroque mind thought of immensity as "nothing else than a center one can find everywhere" (Bruno, *Opere,* 111). The center—or any center—was only a point of departure for, or a way station within, the progress of life. Actually, "God has made this whole world in such a uniformity, such a correspondence, such a concinnity of parts that it was an Instrument, perfectly in tune" (Donne, *Sermons,* II, 170). Since it made possible the shift from one picture to the other, the Christian poetics of kaleidoscopic transformation of symbols "tuned" all forms of human experience into a world harmony.[76]

Formation could not freeze art in the humanist vacuum of hypothetical perfection, for each form expresses *a* condition, not *the* ideal condition of life, which demands otherness instead of sameness. In front of seashells, there can be neither indifference nor bewilderment;[77] if one only dared to look beneath the surface of things, it would be possible to make everything of everything else. As a conceptual and artistic mode predominant in the culture of the Baroque, formation linked islands to continents and estrangement to togetherness. Life as a whole came to be viewed in a state of becoming pointed toward an endless "furtherance of life" (Kant, *Critique of Judgment*, 23).[78]

Art at the Threshold:
Boundary Forms and
Fictions of Denial

*After all, the boundaries between fiction and
nonfiction, between literature and nonlitera-
ture and so forth are not laid up in heaven.*
—Mikhail Bakhtin

I

A creative paradox lies at the heart of the transformational nature of baroque art, which thrived on what
Bruno called an "efficient and formative principle" that could
not "eternally nestle among the same temperaments, perpetuat-
ing the same threads, and preserving those same arrangements,
in one and the same composite" (*Expulsion,* 75). Because of its
own dynamics, therefore, form constantly verged on renewal
and destruction; its capacity-to-be waged war on its being-in-
act.

At that threshold, art challenged its achievements,[1] and

so did Copernicanism vis-à-vis the Ptolemaic worldview. From the discovery of the circulation of the blood (Harvey) to that of new stars (Galileo), much anxiety beset the age. Once science unveiled the illusion of an "unmoved" universe of fixed stars, human and heavenly bodies proved to be more mutable than could be imagined. Yet, the process of becoming cut through appearance and reality alike; form became much like a phoenix rising from its own ashes.

Bruno believed that all forms "incur innumerable vicissitudes and a kind of mutation" (*Expulsion*, 75–76) pointed toward higher levels of unity. The instability of such an overreaching process often nurtured doubts rather than hope. For some, the past was obsolete, and many believed that the future foreshadowed doom. Art was caught in between, and often begot fictions of denial that set existence against utopia.

The boundaries between art and life were tested, and so were genre and authorship. Because criticism took on invention, works of art began to nestle a critique of creation within the created work itself.[2] The very concept of representation at times neared collapse, and form bore the scars of that conflict. At arm's length from the extremes of artifice institutionalized (Tesauro, Marino) and ridiculed (Cervantes, Tassoni), Montaigne wrote: "I would naturalize art as much as they artify nature" (666). His belligerent precept edged on the watershed between life and fiction.

In the realm of "boundary genres" and "boundary works," baroque artists courted parody. In fact, they could create entire texts of uncertain status, and exploit the resonance between kinds of reading. Heraclitian rather than Platonic, such a threshold literature, Gary Saul Morson would suggest, is anti-utopian, for it accepts "the possibility of continual progress of hypotheses and new hypotheses, with no final determination— no "last number." In short, utopia claims to know, anti-utopia asks why we think we know. . . . When it affirms the existence of universals of human nature, those universals are, characteristically, humanity's unchanging need for growth, creativity, and change itself."[3] By the turn of the seventeenth century, art "de-artified" its classical, chivalric, and humanist heritage. In the anti-utopian realm of essays and novels, knowledge rested with the testing of knowledge itself. At the boundary, the artist put himself on trial.

II

Because of their criticism of authoritative stands, Bruno, Montaigne, and Cervantes could not legitimize countergeneric claims without edging on normative postures of the kind they had just rejected. To a significant extent, parody and paradox allowed them to create forms by somehow denying them. At a time when heliocentrism was called the Copernican paradox even by those who accepted it, Copernicus himself called the wandering stars *errantium syderum,* which meant to "wander" as well as to "err" and to "deviate" from the correct path of traditional astronomy. For Kepler, the elliptical trajectory of planets was a "declining" form of circular perfection. Once displacement and eccentricity entered the syntax of art and science, error became part of the baroque worldview, which kept the Copernican revolution at the periphery of the geocentric tradition that official theology had sanctioned. As a matter of fact, the preface that Andreas Osiander added to Copernicus's *De revolutionibus orbium caelestium* turned its thesis into a hypothesis about a "metaphorical reading" of celestial appearances. That strategy got the book published, but charged the reader with hermeneutical responsibility; he had to interpret a text whose content was incompatible with its subtext.[4]

From stars to books, we accept Montaigne's essay even though it often demands that readers venture beyond the text. Since an active mind can outgrow "its powers of achievement," and its pursuits are "boundless and without form" (818), that better trial may belong to life rather than art: "Fie on the eloquence that leaves us craving itself, not things . . . life, soul, devotion, adoration, serf slave, all these words have such vulgar currency that when letter writers want to convey a more sincere and respectful feeling, they have no way left to express it" (185–87). Once they have reached a place of communication, words should burst open the abundance of meaning.

Montaigne hoped that the substance could so "fill the imagination of the listener" that he would "have no memory of the words" (127). Art shaped mental forms in a way that they could be made communicable beyond its own reach. Where can one draw a line between *essai* and *pensée* as literature or personal utterance? Often, forms vacillated between genre and anti-genre, art and the brew of life.[5] Many feared that the boundary could become the center, for they knew that myths of innovation were liable to abuses as easily as myths of continuity.[6] The challenge was to revise canons without becoming canonical.

III

At the threshold of the world "within," the process of literary creation never tired of unearthing forms of the inner self. Accordingly, generic modes had to stretch their expressive range to take in the mimesis of thought itself.[7] At the surface, however, form often appeared illegitimate to its own creator.

From sermons and spare-minutes to prayers and conduct-manuals, much seventeenth-century prose met devotional needs before it would fulfill artistic requirements. At the boundary of intrageneric modes, utilitarian function and artistic form could not be set apart. Religious meditations aimed at exciting the will "to heavenly things, not to learne but to love them" (Saint Francis de Sales). By "assimilating" the written page (Joseph Hall) to the living self,[8] hope could turn into experience.

Essays and thoughts readily shifted from written fiction to straight discursive writing, and hatched as many variants as their novelistic counterparts. Sermons could be generic or extra-generic, as their authors wrote and preached the text. Much of the literature drawn after Ignatian models and Anglican piety was part of daily life, and its unrhetorical—though not structureless—style was effective in kitchens and throne rooms alike. In Counter-Reformation Spain, Ignatius's *Spiritual Exercises* was less than a didactic treatise on meditation, since the text was not available to the public during the early days. In fact, the Jesuits "gave" the Exercises not as readings but as instructions to be practiced. Form therefore thrived on what Stanley Fish calls a "dialectical presentation," which "succeeds at its own expense; for by conveying those who experience it to a point where they are beyond the aid that discursive or rational forms can offer, it becomes the vehicle of its own abandonment." The self-consuming nature of such texts is not demonstrative but therapeutic. Like a medicine, the artwork is consumed "in the workings of its own best effects"; and it "signifies most successfully when it fails, when it points away from itself to something forms cannot capture." In the Augustinian tradition, baroque art updated the "good-physician aesthetic," which actually is an "anti-aesthetic."[9]

Alongside the novel, there were prose forms that one could hardly set apart from mental utterances in which the literary or hypothetical intention is peripheral.[10] Almost all the words derived from the term "prose"—prosaic, prosy, prosiness, prosify, and so on—are derogatory insofar as they suggest an unwillingness to accept prose for its own sake: prose is not poetry.[11] Ambiguity could be affirmative, while the weaving and unweaving of form called for the denial of any foreclosed system.[12]

At the boundary, conventions were on trial and novelty was challenged. Prevalent was the belief that any written text is somehow canonical. Robert Burton did not "amend" style and could not lick confused lumps "into form" (*The Anatomy of Melancholy,* "Democritus to the Reader"). Cervantes moved to grounds unfamiliar to both epic and romance. From Sancho's proverbs to Don Alonso Quijano's will, "inserted genres" were incorporated into the Spanish novel for the sake of their very extraliterariness.[13] Without ignoring epistles, treatises, and commentaries, Montaigne settled with grotesque sketches that sought out "change indiscriminately and tumultuously" (761). His literary attempts colonized nonfictive prose, which stretched from the narrower boundaries of literature to the larger ones of "writing"—from the language of rhetoric to that of truth.[14]

Writers had to be mentors and foes. Often, they stepped back and let those ripples of literary possibilities edge on unwritten matters of taste, tradition, and folklore. Actually, extrageneric mixtures found new energy in what Thomas Browne called a pervasive condition of "unavoidable paradoxology" (*Pseudodoxia Epidemica,* "To the Reader"). Tensions between written and unwritten poetics tested the diachronic resilience of genres.[15]

IV

At its paradoxical peak, boundary art marked yet another threshold, for the inherent dynamics of growth had to sacrifice product to process. Michelangelo had taught (*Florence* and *Rondanini Pietàs,* see chapter 1) that creation could come out of incompleteness, and baroque artists steered his lesson toward parody and denial.

As a novel, *Don Quixote* sets out to repudiate its anachronistic hero; the narrative neither begins nor ends with him. Cervantes thus anticipated the Pirandellian challenge: "Is it possible to represent a character by rejecting it?" Can art thrive on its own undoing? Whereas the six characters are still searching for an author at the end of the drama, Don Alonso Quijano regains sanity and casts off quixotic *valer* (to be worthwhile) for *ser* (to exist).[16] At that point, he has nothing left to live for.

As an author, Cervantes denied paternity to Don Quixote, while a forgotten manuscript downgraded his originality. An impostor then forced the writing of the second part of the novel, which was cut "from the same cloth as the first" and did nothing but present "the knight at greater length." Unwilling "to take the subject up again," the writer turned to the *Persiles,* which he was "just finishing, and the second part of *Galatea*" (470).

To complicate things, the Moorish translator warns that Cid Hamete ought to "be praised not for what he writes, but for what he has refrained from writing" (746). And the Arab chronicler has the last word in a narrative whose subtext obscures the text to the very end. Throughout, interruptions and deletions test credibility in what has been written. Part I obscures Part II, and both of them fade behind other works in progress.

Insofar as characters are concerned, Cervantes fathered the paradoxical dualism of Don Quixote–Don Alonso, each of whom lives by denying the other. Likewise, the book with wind-mills and basins cancels out the one with giants and helmets. At the end of the narrative, Don Quixote the Good is played against Don Quixote the Bad, and so is Sancho. "It's very sur-prising," Don Alvaro notes, "to see two Don Quixotes and two Sanchos at the same time, alike in their names yet how different in their deeds. Let me affirm once more that I didn't see what I did see, and that what happened to me didn't happen" (928). To various degrees, translators and impostors lock horns, just as the narrator stands up against the "first author" for having lost the pages of Quixote's duel with the Biscayan.

Early in the story, the priest burned all translations in Quijano's library because they could not be "as good as the original" (59). For that very reason, what credence could read-ers give to Spanish translations of Arab manuscripts? Cervantes seems to be in league with his reader as a commentator upon narrative inauthenticity.[17]

Omissions, gaps in manuscripts, and liberties taken by translators mark ominous interruptions in *Don Quixote*. In much the same way, we accept *Las Meninas* (see Fig. 11), even though Velázquez sits down to paint a royal portrait we shall never see. Likewise, the intrusion of life at court (children, dwarfs, dog) could easily distract painter and sitters, who might walk away through the open door in the background. The "rep-resented" seems to come in the way of "representing," much as clashes between plan and circumstance heighten uncertainty.

If the original title of the canvas was *The Royal Couple,* why has Velázquez presented a casual moment peripheral to the official picture he is (or should be) painting? Although the *in-fanta* is the only figure to pose, the artwork is named after maids of honor.[18] It seems that an ironic wedge has been drawn be-tween titles, roles, and pictures. In fact, we shall never know whether the artist was about to paint a portrait or change the original subject.

Likewise, Cervantes could have turned to autobiography when the Captive met Saavedra (355), that is to say, the author himself in the fiction he was writing. To favor generic shifts of that sort, Gines de Pasamonte made of his appearance in the novel an autobiographical episode (176–77).

Especially in Spain, humanist legacies (via Sannazzaro and Castiglione) stood against Erasmian clashes (via Juan López de Hoyos, Cervantes's tutor) between wisdom and folly. Estranged as it was from a leadership out to chase imperial dreams, much of society thrived on the coexistence of acceptance and refusal (*engaño* and *desengaño*). In *El peregrino en su patria* (1604), Lope de Vega echoed widespread criticism: "If it were possible for a man, he ought to be born in France, to live in Italy, and to die in Spain. To be born in France because of the French nobility, who have always had a king born in their own land and who have never brought in foreign blood." National bankruptcy was declared in 1595, and post-Armada Spain nurtured literary forms of despair.

Around 1600, the glory of Charles V had faded into a royal twilight. Five years later, Cervantes published his book. Perhaps less than unconsciously, the royal couple in *Las Meninas* is a tainted reflection of monarchic splendor. In 1644, Velázquez painted Philip II as a shallow icon and his dwarf Don Diego de Acedo as a real person. Since the king was a mere figurehead on a foundering ship of state, his court painter turned much of his attention to the sovereign's costume; fashion overwhelmed authority.

For certain, the royal sitters in *Las Meninas* have been divested of the symbols (crowns, scepters) associated with the genre (Rubens, Van Dyck). Suspicion of authority was ingrained in the Spanish character, whose long-standing aversion toward monarchic policies offered fertile soil for anti-utopianism. Even at court, history was scorned on the very occasion of its intended triumph. The early seventeenth century was not only a time of crisis but a time for the awareness of crisis.[19]

V

Wary of tradition and originality alike, Cervantes wove quixotic deeds through layers of the old which offered him an image he could not find in life. *Pícaros, hidalgos,* and modest country gentlemen aside, the shapelessness of existence resisted anachronistic quests shifting in and out of "quoted" narratives. After a few sallies, Sancho's appearance set up a kind of "dialogic protagonism" that kept chivalric clichés at bay but could not conceal signs of exhaustion.

During the ten-year interval between the two parts of the master work, the *Exemplary Novels* experimented with canine narrators (telling overlapping stories), picaresque thieves (Rinconete and Cortadillo), and Master Glass's brittle madness. Between the super and the subhuman, the writer must have foreseen the possibility of fathering a book with a protagonist of strictly human dimensions.[20]

Absence and rejection surrounded Cervantes at the doorstep of life in the making. In the Castilian tradition, he had to test time and again the possibility of the impossibility;[21] like his character, he turned to books. Cid Hamete retained Don Quixote's paternity to the end of the novel, where the narrator-stepfather (*padrastro*) might have claimed the birthright to an original story with a protagonist he could believe in. Yet, he would not draw an image out of a reality which had no images to offer. His experience did not lead him to foresee a future in which the educational growth of novelistic characters would raise hopes of a better life. As a result, he set his "true history" against the fabricated originality of Avellaneda's "new history" (853). *Novedad* (novelty) could not disrupt the Spaniard's deep-rooted commitment to keep existence within the frame of his own personality.[22] To the very end, Cervantes remained an author in search of a character closer to the chronotope of life.[23]

By the time Don Quixote appeared on the horizon of Western art, the baroque mind had settled with the idea that, whereas "previously seeing had been certain and believing confused, now seeing was confused and believing certain."[24] Cervantes's allegiance to imagination created a figure (Don Quixote) dedicated to what he longs to be, whereas the plain man (Sancho Panza) lives bound to what is necessary.

When friends found the *Galatea* in Quijano's library, they noted that the book set out "to do something" and concluded nothing; nevertheless, it was agreed to "wait for the second part" (62). If we were to turn expectation into conjecture, one may wonder whether Cervantes would have added

Part III to his great novel: the *History of Sancho Panza*. On utopian and anti-utopian grounds, promises remained unkept. But the compulsion was there, and Cervantes did bequeath to modern novelists at least the plight of the plain man, the man of human dimensions.[25]

To follow Don Quixote, Sancho left home and family. Like the people at the inn (276–82), he had been told enough about chivalry to find it attractive. In no uncertain terms, the squire confessed: "This master of mine is a raving lunatic who ought to be tied up—and me, I can't be much better, for since I follow him and serve him, I'm more of a fool than he" (527). Although he emerged as the unquestionable survivor, could Sancho be the alternative to old worlds of knighthood? Could a writer create a plain man out of a reality dominated by *parecer* and illusory *figuras?*

After a drawn-out dilemma, Cervantes was urged on by Avelleneda to write Part II, in which Don Quixote became ever more influenced by written stories, Don Alonso Quijano ran out of life, and Sancho probably would refuse to grow cabbages again. As promised, the writer did expose chivalry, even though he could not bring himself to confront the portrayal of reality.[26]

The fact is that depictions of "low life" gained little strength beyond the comic, the compassionate, and the extravagant. Scenes of popular life (from Van Leer's *Pastry Vendor,* 1630, to Bourdon's *Beggars,* 1640–45) often remained anecdotal. Like short stories, they lacked the ideological depth of a novelistic context, much as art theorists (Pacheco, Palomino) wavered amidst types (genre, comic scenes, *bodegones*) and mixtures thereof (comic genre scenes, *pitture ridicole*).[27] More dignified were Dutch interiors (Pieter De Hooch and Vermeer) of a middle class that sponsored images of its own achievements. But Holland was far from Spain.

On the literary front, Montaigne sought a middle-class audience, since his essays "might not be much liked by common and vulgar minds, or by singular and excellent ones; the former would not understand enough about them, the latter too much. But they might get by in the middle region" (227), where the "domestic and private" (2) commonness of the *homme suffisant* foregrounded the ordinary, not the exceptional, man.[28] Especially along Mediterranean shores, interest in the whole social spectrum stopped short of democratic concerns. Many believed that "wealth could not really be appreciated and properly measured in society without villanous and poor people. . . . Without contraries, there would be no act of nobility, virtue, and fortune" (Bruno, *Opere,* 304; see also *Frenzies,* 217). The common man may have appeared at center stage. As a sociopolitical creature, however, he could not have written his own script, even though some preached not to "think that mankind liveth but for a few, and that the rest are born to serve those ambitious" (Thomas Browne, *Christian Morals,* I, 19).

At once parodic and humorous, Don Quixote became a boundary image in reverse. Pointing toward the past rather than the present, solutions of that sort could preserve hope whenever the brew of life can offer nothing more than survival. How could a writer who had been part of the epic struggle of Christianity against the Turks at Lepanto (1571) produce forms of mere existence? It was inevitable that Cervantes would favor the heroic, and he so conceded in the Prologue to Part II: "I would still rather have taken part in that prodigious action than be at present whole of my wounds without ever having fought there" (467).

Even if he failed to convince Don Quixote that analogy is not identity on matters of imitation,[29] the stepfather would not have abandoned his stepson. Analogy was flawed, but identity would have been nothing at all.

Either unwilling or unable to be other than polemical toward the supporting structures of European culture, Cervantes ultimately turned to idealization in *Persiles y Sigismunda.* In spite of his humanizing vision, he could not abandon reading altogether. Likewise, Velázquez took on the validity of frames, framing, and framed in *Las Meninas.* Yet, he did not repudiate the traditional concept of representation under the aegis of royal patronage.[30]

With an eye to the future, the parodic layering of *Don Quixote* tests its own subject matter in the Prologue. Although the *hidalgo* "shall stay buried in the archives of La Mancha till Heaven provides someone to adorn him with all the jewels it lacks" (27), what the narration really needs is independence of authoritative texts. The impasse alerts readers to a confession: "I am too spiritless and lazy by nature to go about looking for authors to say for me what I can say myself without them" (27). The text is free of quotations at the margins, but it still follows and denies—among others—Amadis of Gaul, Ariosto, and Avellaneda. The original statement could thus be rephrased: "Could I say by myself what I can without them?"

I would guess that Cervantes foresaw the possibility of stretching episodes into whole lives, but did not create a protagonist who could carry out that project. Instead, he resorted to a *given* character, a subtext, and a stated goal that widened the gap between history and adventure. The very title of the novel (*El ingenioso hidalgo Don Quijote de la Mancha*) falls into a generic wedge. Is the book the imaginative biography of an ingenious figure, or the ingenious story of a historical character? Neither biography nor history, does the book thrive on the ambiguity between story and history, word and world? It would be just as difficult to pinpoint the beginning of the novel if we were to assume that such a point ought to be found where the writer steers clear of all other works, historians, and commentators. Is the antiheroic opening a departure from conventions, or is that moment marked by the introduction of madness, or of Sancho? Better yet, are we confronting a sequence of beginnings, or the testing of that very concept? Can we draw a line between orginality and origination?[31]

Although his masterpiece had survived older manuscripts and more recent novels, Cervantes could not fail to realize that he was yet to father a character free of quixotic insanity in a truly original and present-oriented work. He settled with formation but did not ignore formativeness.

Once again, the subjectless book to be written found a parallel in *Las Meninas*. It has been suggested that Velázquez could not be painting the royal couple, since no such double portrait of Philip IV and Queen Mariana exists or is known to have existed. Yet, what "plain" subject could an ambitious painter be free to paint at a court where he was determined to rise to the highest social rank?[32]

At the boundary of his creative experience, Cervantes probably felt the impotence of those few whose craft has led them to realize that any quest of an "image" would itself be a quixotic anachronism. He could not let characters guided by utopian dreams of old travel the time-bound roads of life. When he recommended Sancho to the reader at the end of the Prologue, however, sympathy must have clashed with a lingering preference for what Miguel de Unamuno later uttered: "No friend Sancho, no, there is no basin-helmet that is worth a straw. . . . what it can never be nor ought to be, however much be added to it or taken away from it, is a basin-helmet."[33]

At the end of *Don Quixote,* Cervantes found it futile "to make a third journey, or to embark on any new expedition" (940). To undertake that eventful trip, something new was needed. Since he had been *"el primero que he novelado en lengua castellana"* (Prologue to the *Exemplary Novels*), the language was there, but a new protagonist was still missing. A ray of hope filtered in when Don Diego de Miranda, who studied Latin and Greek for six years at Salamanca, brought to the novel an educated gentleman holding promises for the future. Unfortunately, he did not dedicate himself to law and theology but "soaked in poetry" and spent whole days in his "criticisms, whether Homer expressed himself well or ill in such a verse of the *Iliad;* whether Martial was indecent or not in some epigram." In fact, all his conversation was "about the books of these poets," with little regard for "modern writers in the vernacular." Once again, reading prevailed over action. Don Quixote justified those familiar symptoms, since children "should be allowed to follow that branch of learning to which they seem most inclined" (568). Even the new generations chased after the past, for history at times is not a passing dream, but the dream that lasts;[34] and that dream was buried deep in the Spanish soul.

Cervantes's fruitless search for a character also touched on authorial inadequacy. Unlike Pirandello, the Spaniard could not give "audience, every Sunday morning to the characters" of his "future stories." One of them, Dr. Fileno, chose to remain authorless rather than falling prey to an unworthy writer. His "extravagant ambition" disturbed the playwright, who feared that his authorial freedom could be in jeopardy.[35] Aware as he was that his deeds had to be recorded ("when the authentic story of my famous deeds comes to light, the sage who writes of them will say" [36]), Don Quixote doubted whether an Arab writer could do justice to his love for Dulcinea, since Moors were known to be "cheats, forgers, and schemers" (485). Nor could the dramatist offer support for a Cervantine quest not yet at ease with the "uncomposed and scattered" facts of life.

While he fulfilled—and even exceeded—Cid Hamete's expectations, Don Quixote was kept at arm's length by Cervantes, who eventually denied him. It seems as if the *hidalgo* had to carve an existence for himself between and against authorial interferences. By the end of the novel, Cid Hamete has grown to love him as a far better image of his own protagonist, for Don Quixote acted out the Moor's un-thought-of hopes.

In light of Dr. Fileno's complaint, the *hidalgo* deserved an author better than the Arab chronicler, and he got one. Pirandello's own comments on the chivalric knight point to a loftier reality: "Wherever a poet is really successful in giving life to an artistic creature, such a character lives independently of his creator."[36] If Cervantes was a stepfather, Don Quixote became a rebellious son who did not turn prodigal, but kept wandering over Machegan plains where he himself—Unamuno would agree—began "to visit" other writers.

At the outer margins of art, much sustenance was given to the modern novel. In that no-man's-land between literary and extraliterary genres, Cervantes could unearth no more than chivalric vestiges. By definition, a no-man's-land lies at the periphery of culture, at that restless province of human experience where sociocultural forms must emerge above sheer existence if the artist is ever to draw an image out of them. For that to happen, the praxis of the present is not enough. And what new demands could be made in a land where *"se está hoy del mismo modo que Dios la crió?"* (Baltasar Gracián, *El Criticón,* III, 9). *Novedad* had always been unwelcomed in Spain, where people had much to worry about the future.

Parody tested the concept of fiction, and process so favored authorial openness that Cervantes trusted his progeny with an idle reader whose experience would unfold beyond chronicles, impostors, and the artwork itself. It was hoped that the *desocupado lector* would part company with those who were reading the pseudo-Quixote without finding any difference between the two versions. His idleness was a kind of way station in the province of unwritten poetics, where his "strong reading" would decide whether the novel, or other boundary forms, could claim generic legitimacy.

The *lector* of the novel is at first idle; by the beginning of Part II, however, he has become illustrious, and at least primed for critical analysis in spite of influential contemporaries who saw the work as either extravagant (Lope de Vega) or burlesque (Calderón). I would like to think that Cervantes entrusted readers with the ultimate translation of art into reality, for each one of them was to weigh what share of madness and common sense (Don Quixote–Sancho Panza) could make life human.[37]

VI

Just at the surface of that no-man's-land, one could meet—part image and part raw existence—a woman frying eggs for a *pícaro* whose thirst would be quenched by an old waterseller. And if one decided to fill in the empty darkness in Velázquez's "picaresque" scenes (*Old Woman Frying Eggs*, 1618–20, Fig 22; *The Waterseller*), we may wonder whether such backgrounds ought to be painted or opened up to life itself.

In the foreground of *Christ in the House of Martha* (1619–20; Fig. 23), two women seem to be standing in front of a little picture of the subject hanging on the back wall. Yet, we might be looking into an adjacent room through a small window. It is even possible that we could be standing in front of a mirror that reflects an event taking place in our own space; "there" and "then" are juxtaposed to "here" and "now." Almost at the edge of fiction, the young woman leans out into our space, which is being filled with the smell of fish and garlic. Such a mounting response to boundary conditions stands out even more if we set the canvas against its staged treatment in an earlier version (1565–66). Representation thus moved closer to the presence of life, almost to the point that we intrude on Annibale Carracci's *Bean Eater* (1583–84). From butchers'

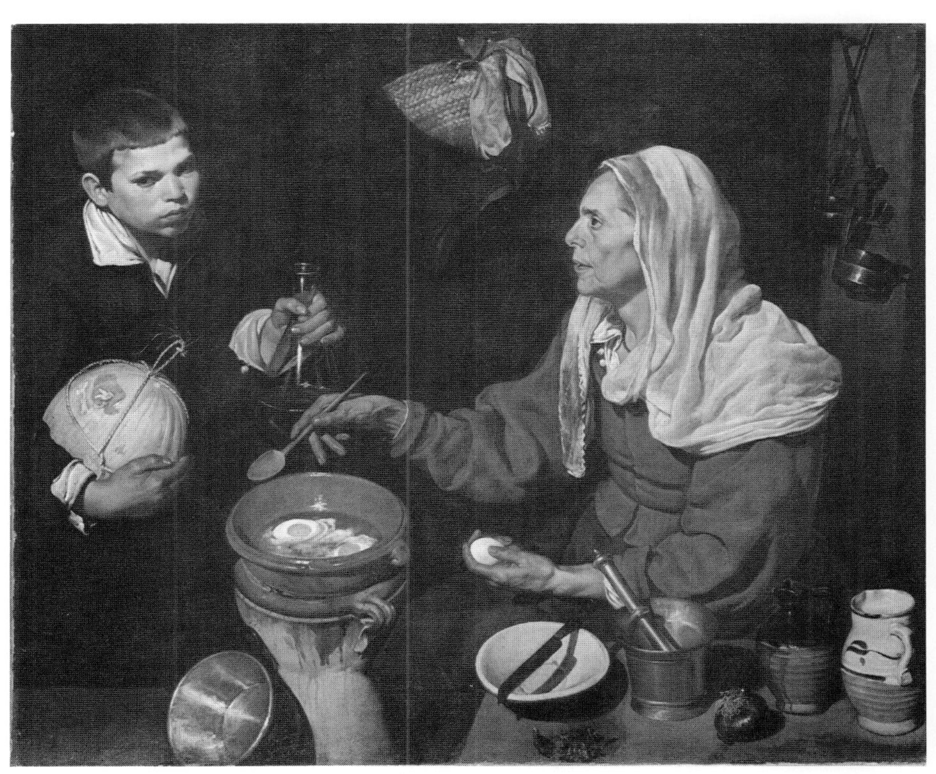

Fig. 22. Velázquez, *The Old Woman Frying Eggs*, 1618. National Galleries of Scotland, Edinburgh

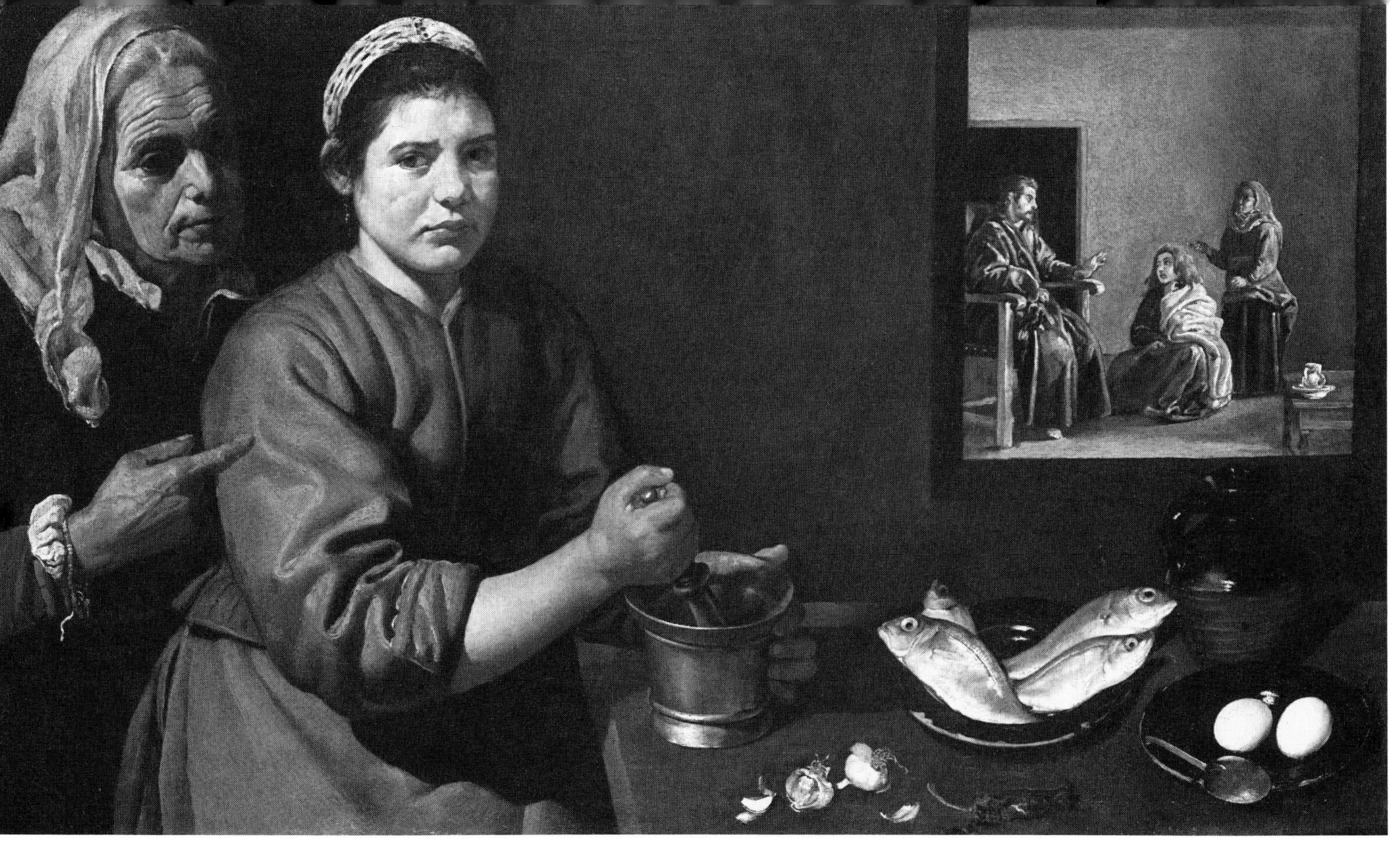

Fig. 23. Velázquez, *Christ in the House of Martha*, 1619–20. National Gallery, London

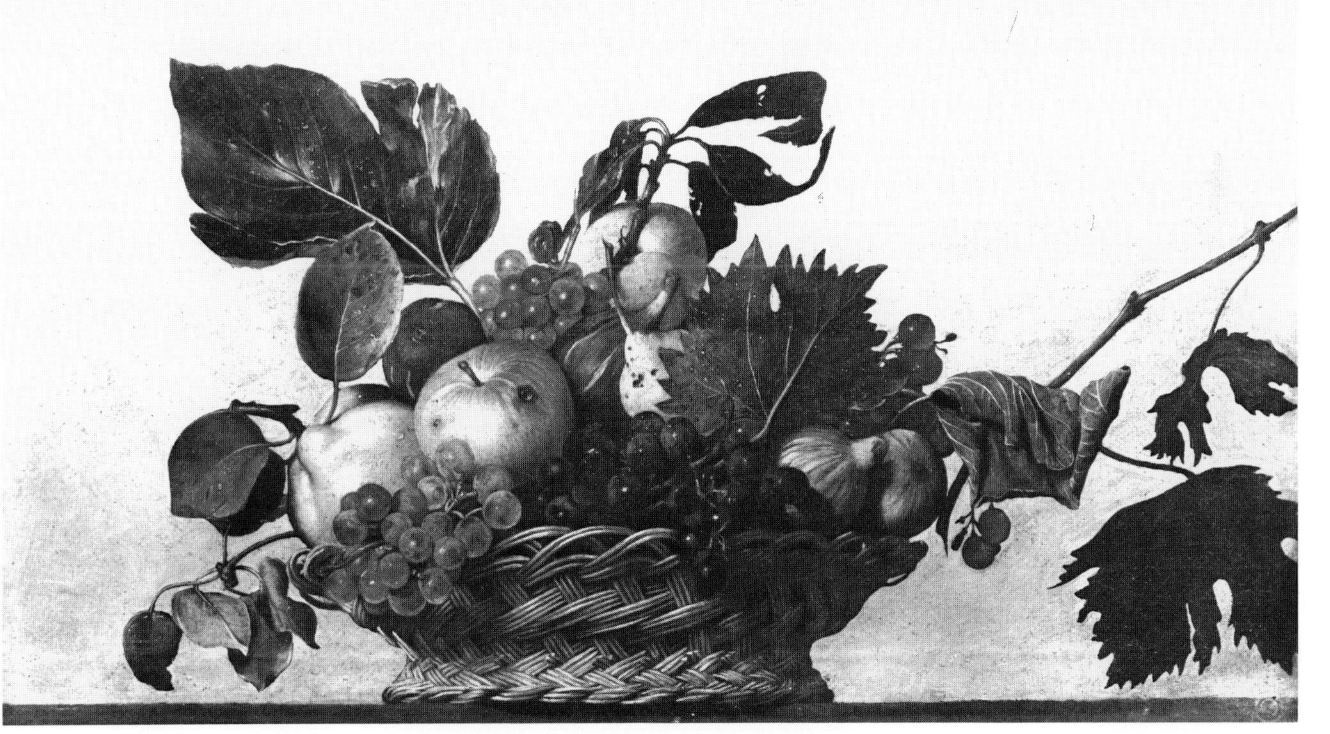

Fig. 24. Caravaggio, *Basket of Fruit*, 1596? Pinacoteca Ambrosiana, Milan

shops (Bartolommeo Passerotti, Annibale Carracci) to private homes, art brought out a range of incidental activities.[38]

At the boundary, a conflict developed between history and reality, narration and description. Gérard Genette has provided a succinct distinction on this matter: "Every narrative includes two types of representation, although they are blended together and always in varying proportions: representations of actions and events, which constitute the narration properly speaking, and representations of objects or people, which make up the art of what we today call 'description.' "[39] Humanist *istorie* (narration) gave way to unsequential representations of objects, people, places, and attitudes (description).

For the humanists, reality offered raw materials to be shaped into man-made forms. Perhaps mindful of Leonardo's lesson, baroque artists recognized that nature itself has form, and Tommaso Campanella took on humanist intellectualism in a letter written in 1607: "The difference between my philosophy and that of Pico is this: I learn more from the anatomy of an ant or a blade of grass . . . than from all the books."[40]

The proliferation of reality thus ensued. Caravaggio's *Basket of Fruit* (1596?; Fig. 24) stood as a baroque landmark; apples could be as legitimate as angels.[41] In Giovanni d'Enrico's *tavolo apparecchiato* (Sacro Monte di Varallo), three-dimensional objects on a dinner table are as real as fruit and vegetables could ever be; illusionism became complacently icastic.

Scenes of eating and drinking (*bodegones*) were popular amidst a culture that cherished images of low life in art and literature. As Barry Wind has recently written, water carriers appear in the *Lazarillo de Tormes*, Cervantes's *La ilustre fregona*, and Velázquez's *The Waterseller*. Even the frontispiece to the *Pícara Justina* proclaims wine, food, and music to be the baggage of picaresque life—*el aguar de la vida picaresca*.[42]

By contrast, Counter-Reformation precepts held that artworks without moral *istorie* were "vain and without any purpose, like all subjects that are not directed toward a clear goal, but are executed according to the painter's fancy (*capriccio*) in order to fill and adorn some areas of the canvas with inventions."[43] To find a clear goal, genre painters in Italy and Spain created *pittura ridicola* (Vincenzo Campi, *Cheese Eaters, Fruit*

Vendor; Juan Estaban de Ubeda, *Genre Scene;* Velázquez, *Three Men at Table, Three Musicians*), in which objects often carried moral symbolism.

However controversial, descriptive subjects gained credibility, especially among Dutch and Flemish artists, who had been accustomed to paint fish on a plate without treating it as food for the apostles. Some of them went to Rome, where Pieter Van Laer and the Bamboccianti created a style of "realistic" painting opened to the here-and-now of daily facts. It was hoped that images of poverty in the streets would stir appeasement and humility—if not guilt—in the wealthy.[44]

On French grounds, *peintres de la realité* brought an almost classical gravity to the rusticity of peasant life (Louis Le Nain's *The Peasants' Meal,* 1642; Fig. 25). Ribera's Neapolitan experience took on stark features in his canvases of drunkards and clubfooted boys. One step closer to the facts of human experience and we find Murillo's scenes of poor boys picking off fleas and sharing grapes or a watermelon (Figs. 26 and 27). Without past or future, without a road to follow or a home to return to, those adolescents are no more than breaths of life roaming somewhere between extraliterary grounds and humanity in the making. Matters of ideology are neither acknowledged nor refuted.

When children pick grapes in Italian canvases (Michelangelo Cerquozzi, *Picking Grapes*), they execute a chore. Bourgeois opulence stood against picaresque survival. In northern European art, middle-class children pursued the secular goals of a progressive society whose wealth could start the day with food and medicine even for household pets (Jan Steen's *The Pancake Maker, The Parrot Cage, The Cat's Medicine*).

On the other side of history, literary and pictorial scenes of picaresque life present acts of existence—"the mere facts of life" (Américo Castro), "*lo intranscendente*" (Ortega y Gasset)—a modern viewer can still witness amidst *scugnizzi* in the Spanish-filled soul of the Neapolitan landscape. Stricken and yet smiling, such urchins wore their happy mendacity with gusto. At the baroque boundary, it was indeed possible to conceive of purely descriptive artworks aimed at "representing objects solely in their spatial existence."[45]

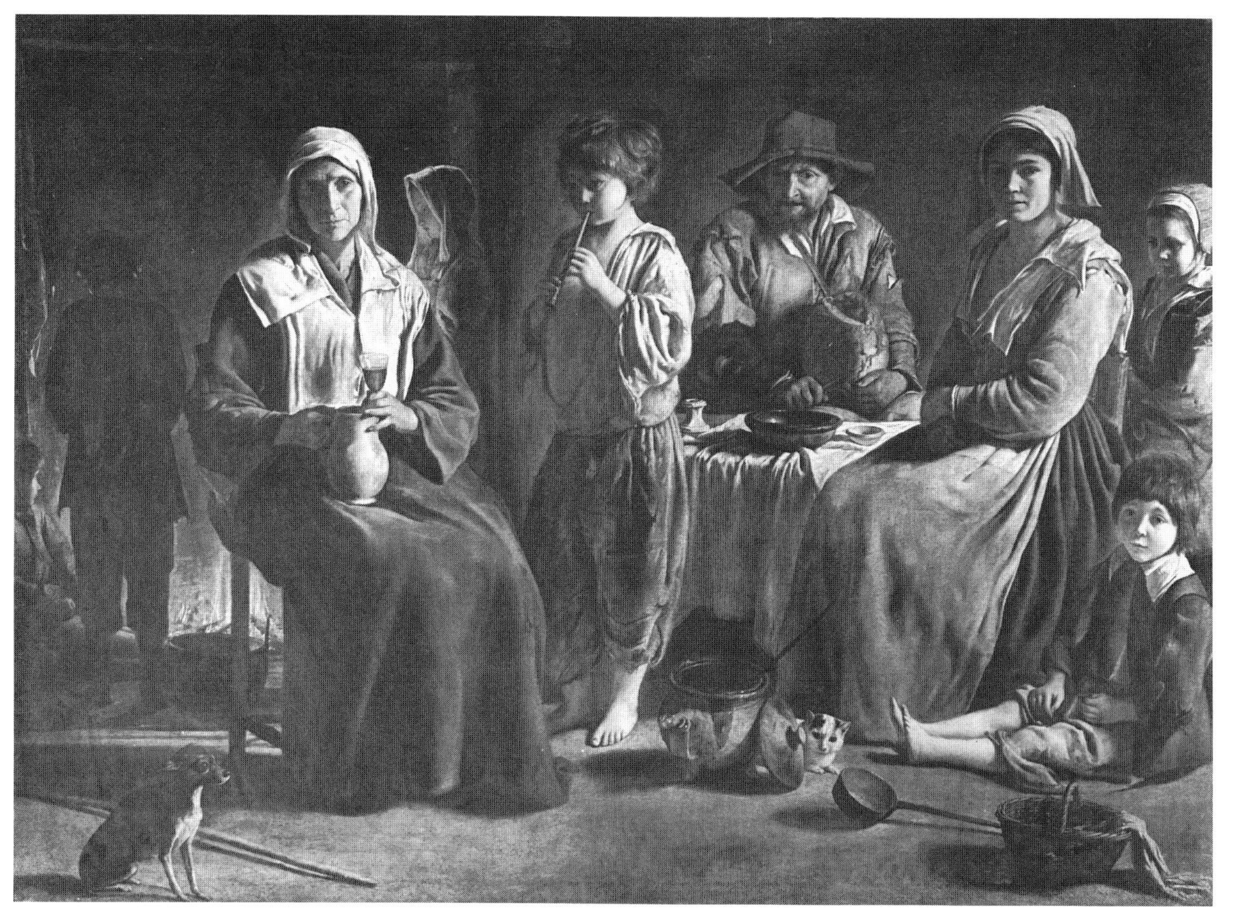

Fig. 25. Louis Le Nain, *The Peasants' Family*, 1643. Louvre, Paris

Through a paradoxical coexistence so typically baroque, life in the streets set unadorned survival next to social self-consciousness, not to mention the iconography of charity and beggary inspired by saints throwing gold coins to the poor. Under the skies of *Napoles hispanizada,* Castilian mores steered aristocrats and plebeians toward formalism, respectful etiquette in greetings, care for appearance, and gravity of manners. At the same time, the role-playing of "spagnolismo" influenced sacred oratory, drama, commedia dell'arte, melodrama, novel, lyric, and style in general.[46] Interest in, and display of, people's own awareness of role-playing in theaters, churches, and squares pointed to the recognition of life as patterned before art would touch it.

If one were to ask what formalized *el gran teatro del mundo* on both sides of the curtain, Lionel Abel would turn to myth, legend, and past literature, for they bring home the effects of dramatic imagination before the playwright could exercise his own.[47] As popular archetypes, comedic personages often have anticipated theatrical fictions. Back to back, or one within the other, people in the *piazza* and actors on stage could trade places. Theatrical doors swung both ways on the revolving stage of life.

> where men and women are
> merely players:
> They have their exits and their entrances.
> (Shakespeare, *As You Like It,* II.7)

Actually, the stage was just a corner of the square, and the two could hardly be set apart in Piazza San Marco (Venice), where life was almost as staged as in Bernini's Cornaro chapel. Born as a stadium for games under Domitian, the merry character of Piazza Navona (Rome) was ideally suited for feasts, fairs, markets, and processions. As Mario Praz comments, *"se dunque Roma è anagramma di Amor, questa è la piazza dell'Amore e di Roma."*[48]

To act, in fact, refers to theatrical and nontheatrical action, just as "role" can point to the stage or one's station in life. In the Spanish tradition of the *autos sacramentales,* history

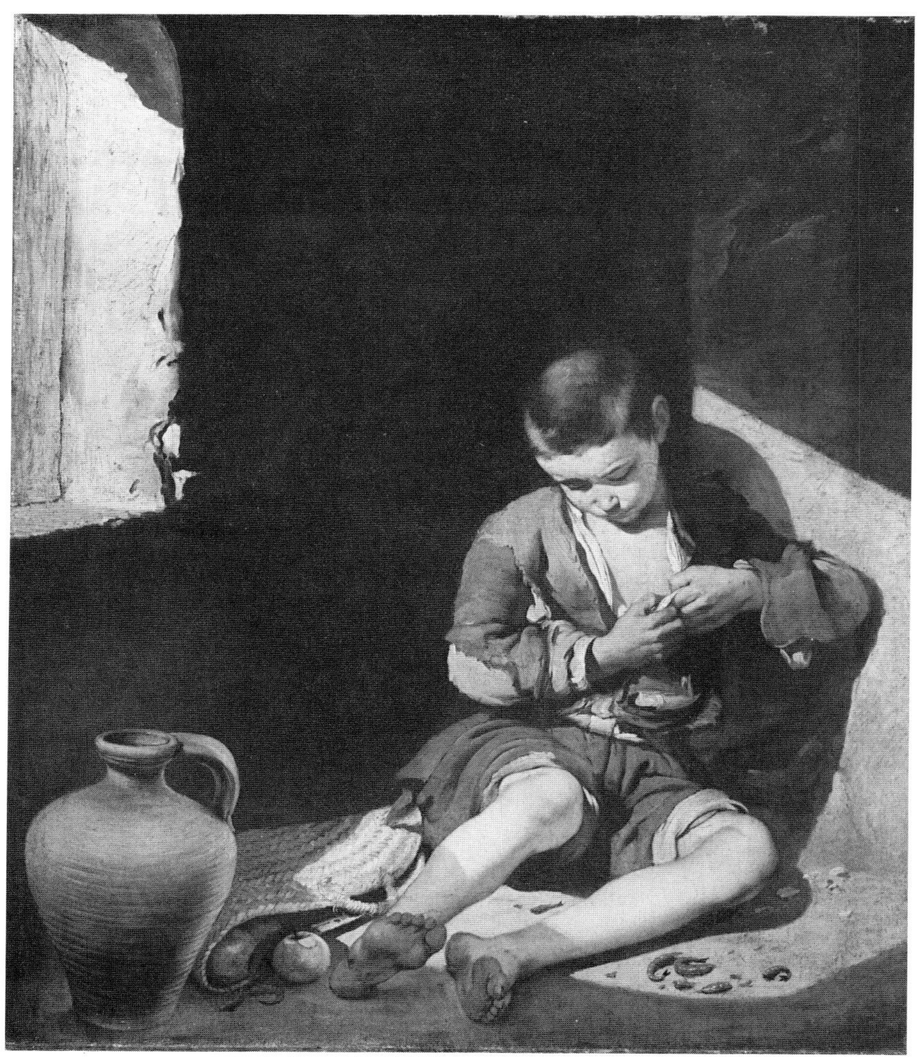

Fig. 26. Murillo, *Boy Picking Off Fleas*, c. 1645–50. Louvre, Paris

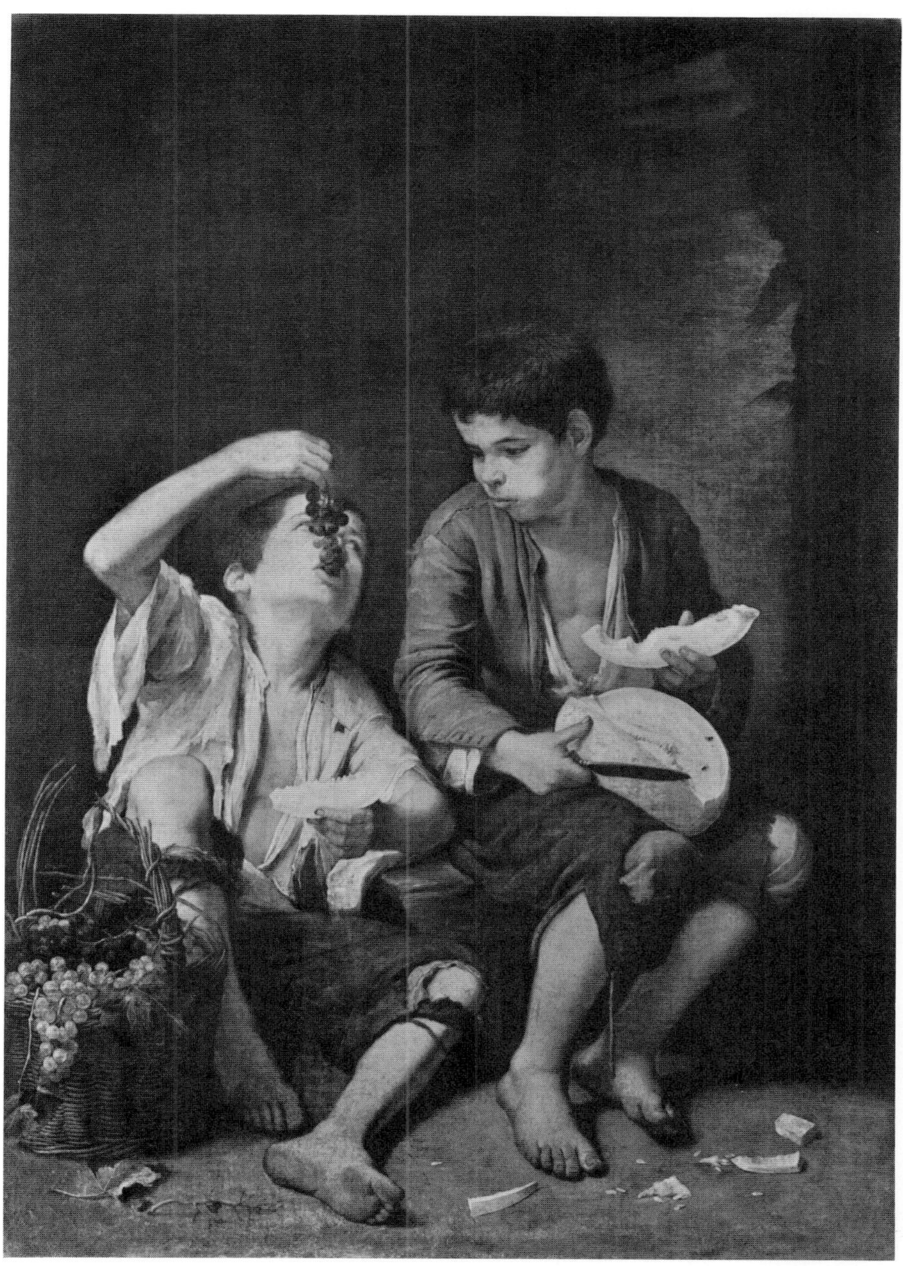

Fig. 27. Murillo, *Boys Eating a Watermelon*, 1670s. Alte Pinakothek, Munich

and society worked out a divine plan with assigned roles. The Spanish *Yo soy quien soy* does not define the self in itself (*ser sí mismo*) but demands that the self conform with *vividura,* that is to say, the traditional values of a people (their *moradas vitales*).[49]

Poets and scholars of the international Arcadia Academy took on pastoral names and met in bucolic gardens. While picaresque narratives borrowed from folkloristic sources familiar to Basile's fairy tales, the novel (both picaresque and Cervantine) explored the difference between literature and the other fictions by which we lead our daily lives. From an anthropological point of view, Victor Turner could call attention to carnivals, rituals, "anti" and "counter" patterns of the liminality of social experience.[50] To prove liminal transfers, Don Quixote and Sancho so caught the public imagination that they appeared at court festivities in Valladolid (1605), and at carnivals in Peru (1607) and Heidelberg (1613).

VII

At the baroque threshold, humanist distinctions between art and craftsmanship were blurred. Bernini's autobiographical artist-writer-director first prepares the scene and then sits down to write the text of *The Impresario.* Stagehands and actors gather for the arrival of the cloud machine, which, however, does not open (and is dumped down). The play is about the malfunction of the theatrical apparatus. With an eye to fictions of denial, nothing has been accomplished as the text breaks off; no machines have been made to work, and no play has been written.[51] Performance also seems to be on trial in the Prologue of Bruno's *The Candle Bearer.* In what appears to be a less-than-fictional backstage, some actors are late and others are too drunk to play their parts.

Ever more attractive, the display of preparatory stages and techniques invaded pictorial spaces. Velázquez set spinners weaving a precious tapestry in front of a room in which the finished product is proudly displayed (Fig. 21). Beyond fifteenth-century iconographic images of the spinning Virgin and the Three Fates, seventeenth-century Dutch artists were commissioned to do a series of paintings on the production of textiles from start to finish. Their endeavor was meant to honor the guild's pride in its industrial success, and they painted textile workers whose trade had brought prosperity to their cities.[52] While Don Quixote visited a printing press turning out a wealth of books in Barcelona, Dutch still-lifes paraded silverware and cut glass, which also made the Venetian glassblowers of Murano proud.

Once Velázquez (*Las Meninas*) and Cervantes (Prologue of *Don Quixote*) presented themselves at work, distinctions between art and craft disappeared. By the same token, craftsmanship had so gained in legitimacy that painting was finally accepted as a liberal art. In *Las Meninas*, as in Vermeer's *The Art of Painting*, the artist's contemplative moment captured the intellectual nobility of his profession.

We ought to remember that Alberti put forward the view of the learned artist as an *artifex*, a view upheld by Michelangelo and passed on to baroque painters from Velázquez to Poussin. Yet, there were too many unlettered artists whose reputation—and competence—did not exceed craftsmanship. Patronage in Spain neither demanded nor rewarded knowledge of letters. The first treatise on painting (Francisco Pacheco's *Arte de la pintura*) was published in 1649, at a time when painters still were the social equals of blacksmiths and carpenters. As the founder of an academy modeled after the Carracci's *Accademia del Disegno* in Bologna, Rembrandt had to break away from the guild rules of Amsterdam, where painting still was considered a craft rather than a liberal art.[53]

VIII

Within the living traditions of the Baroque, the magnificent *presepi napoletani* (Fig. 28) combined the craftsmanship and popular taste of figurine makers (*figurari*) with socioreligious rituals. During the fifteenth century, the Florentine workshop of

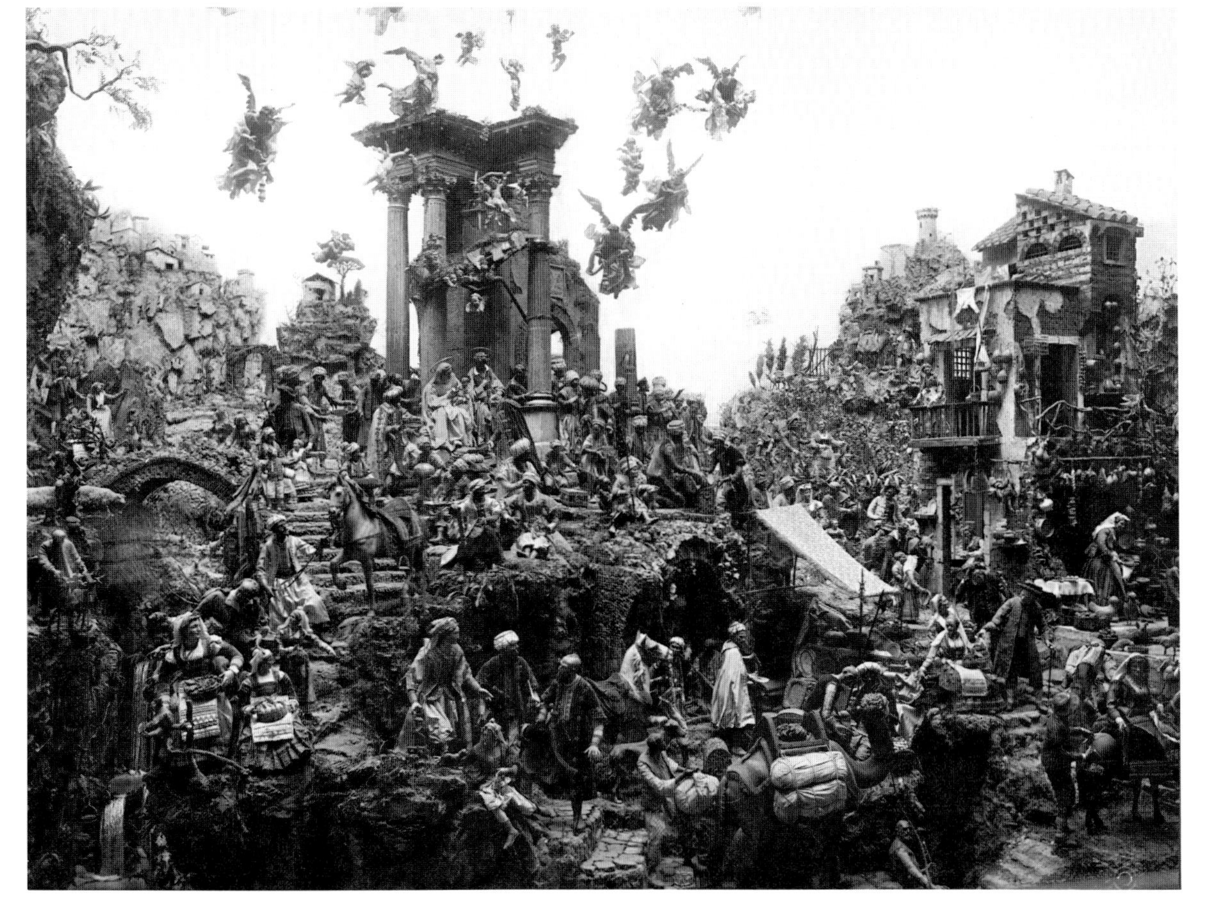

Fig. 28. *Il Presepio*, seventeenth century. Museo della Certosa di S. Martino, Naples

Antonio Rossellino produced a number of painted terra-cotta nativity scenes. Later, the genre peaked because of the southern Italian preference for episodic realism and naturalistic details. By the second quarter of the sixteenth century, *presepi* in Altamura and Matera (by Altobello di Persio and Sannazaro da Alessano, 1534) were renowned well beyond the Lucania region.

By convention, *presepi* displayed ruins symbolic of the triumph of Christianity over paganism; the tavern with typical activities; and a marketplace with gargantuan arrays of culinary items. The *presepi* borrowed from still-lifes, *bamboccianti*, *sacre rappresentazioni*, *tableaux vivants* and *quadri plastici*, much as they drew on the input of painters, sculptors, architects, tailors, and other craftsmen whose work was physical more than mental.

Often, *presepi* had movable parts that created stagelike effects in houses and churches. At times, such miniature *apparati* crossed antigeneric boundaries and developed the twin tradition of *presepi d'arte* and *presepi popolari*. Their visual language enacted the swarming life in the streets in much the same way as Basile depicted it in those *fiabe* which he wrote in the dialect for the entertainment of children—*trattenemiento de' peccerille*. Both artforms brought to light a heartwarming credulity through awkward metaphors, grotesques, and tropes.

Even the Neapolitan *maschera* Pulcinella (rooted in popular culture of Roman heritage) became part of the boundary complexity of *presepi* as a *figura straordinaria*. The *maschera* first appeared in G. C. Cortese's *Viaggio di Parnaso* (1621), in which he defends poetry written in dialect against the Tuscan. Such a posture could be expected from a figure of proletarian stock that Goethe found somewhat careless, lazy, and humorous. In 1628, Pulcinella appeared on stage in a comedy by Virgilio Verucci, *Colombina*. Thereafter, his presence in puppet shows, carnivals, and in the streets of Naples during ever-recurrent festivities has served as a kind of safety valve from everyday routine.

Like the black mask he wears on a white costume, Pulcinella is a creature of contradiction as elusive and ambiguous as his ghostly birdlike appearance. The fact that he often was caught in the act of digging his bare hands into enormous bowls of spaghetti hopelessly insufficient to satisfy his voracious appetite points to a shift in the eating habits of the Neapolitans. Pasta replaced vegetables as the staple food of the population toward the end of the sixteenth century, when building projects took over large farm areas. Moreover, great immigrations into the cities transformed "leaf-eaters" into "macaroni eaters."

Although canvases and frescoes (Tiepolo, Magnasco) kept on representing him, Pulcinella's popularity declined in the eighteenth century. Because it is still nestled in popular culture, however, the *maschera* could once again gain prominence. Until then, he shall continue to keep custody over unfailing instincts of survival, for his fatalistic mocking of both hope and despair is rooted in the Neapolitan ethos.[54]

IX

In a fundamental way, the baroque coexistence of invention and debate was more than a matter of ingenious emulation. At a time when it had become apparent that the discovery of a new continent stemmed from geographical misconceptions; when science (Ptolemaic-Copernican) and religion (Reformation–Counter-Reformation) were pulling away from, and often against, each other; when Bruno and Galileo had to pay for their convictions, while Descartes was grateful to faith for his rational method; when the telescope revealed new stars which Galileo's skeptical critics soon believed to be delusions generated by that very instrument; when the mind had inherited orations on human dignity (Pico della Mirandola) and praises of folly (Erasmus), it was inevitable that doubt, and Montaigne's testing question, would shape mental habits prone to exploit contradiction. The old circle of universal harmony was breaking down, and art contested its fundamental character; in the process, it was never more anxiously artistic. Whatever the aim, it was generally agreed that to doubt "well" (Pascal) and "wisely" (Donne) was not to stray.

At the very core of art, language faltered and the world of words became as unreliable as that of things. Montaigne warned that "the name is not a part of the thing or of the substance," but an "extraneous piece attached to the thing, and outside of it" (468); Donne recommended that "language must waite upon matter, and words upon things" (*Sermons*, X, 112); and Herbert kept writing poems even though he could not "spell." Keeping educational concerns in mind, Bacon believed that "the first distemper of learning occurs when men study words and not matter" (*The Advancement of Learning*, I).

Disjunctions between *signifiant* and *signifié* became predominant, and poetry uttered:

> Out, idle words, servants to shallow fools!
> Unprofitable sounds, weak arbitrators!
> (Shakespeare, *The Rape of Lucrece*, I, 1016)

Language was caught in a self-defeating predicament; it could correct itself only through its own mechanism. Montaigne unveiled the paradox:

> Our disputes are purely verbal. I ask what is "nature," "pleasure," "circle," "substitution." The question is one of words, and is answered in the same way. "A stone is a body." But if you pressed on: "And what is a body?"—"Substance."—"And what is substance?" and so on, you would finally drive the respondent to the end of his lexicon. We exchange one word for another word, often more unknown. I know better what is man than I know what is animal, or mortal, or rational. To satisfy one doubt, they give me three; it is the Hydra's head (818–19).

To overcome doubts, "I should testify about myself by works and deeds, not by bare words. . . . what my words express does an injustice to my thought" (274, 186).

At the threshold, body language challenged verbal means: "What of the hands? We beg, we promise, call. . . . With the head: we invite, send away. . . . There is no movement that does not speak" a language (Montaigne, 332). Nature itself gave man word (*"grammatica"*) and gesture (*"l'arte dei cenni,"* Tesauro). Lavinia's inability to communicate led Titus Andronicus to meet a new challenge:

> Thou shalt not sigh, nor hold thy stumps to heaven,
>> Nor wink, nor nod, nor kneel, nor make a sign,
>> But I of these will wrest an alphabet
>> And by still practice learn to know thy meaning.
>>   (III.ii.42)

Still on the Shakespearean stage, it was hoped that "words be made of breath / And breath of life" (*Hamlet,* III.iv.197). Yet, essayist and playwright proceeded to "wrest" that alphabet through a paradoxical use of language, for they knew that even action could be deceptive.[55]

However critical, writers could not dispense with words; poison was part of the medicine. Since no cure was available, the patient could either keep the illness under control (Michel de Montaigne) or let it become terminal (Don Quixote).

Whatever the outcome, names no longer afforded certainty, and Sancho took the liberty of making up words. His *baciyelmo* (basin-helmet) betrayed a verbal compromise. Because it made possible what experience denied, language was at once cosmetic and constitutive with regard to meaning. Donne pinned his paradoxical bent of mind to puns on his own name through self-denying prose (Donne/Ann Donne/Undone) and poetry:[56]

> When thou hast done, thou hast not done
> (*A Hymne to God the Father*)

At the edge of relational semantics, Cervantes and Shakespeare agreed that words have meaning because they can create something that would not exist without them.

Against the humanist grain, the noun no longer defined an elusive and yet privileged unity (*sprezzatura, virtù*). Words such as "honesty," "nothing," "noble" (Shakespeare), and "humid" (Bacon) spread out into webs carrying a wealth of connotations that valued facts less than false appearances (Bacon, *The Advancement of Learning*, II, xiv, 11). In the baroque vocabulary, the word could be seed and plant, literal and metaphorical. To keep at pace with the transformational nature of reality, meaning itself became circumstantial.

In the ever-widening gap between identity and resemblance, Don Quixote shifted names into the onomastic language of old romances; action enacted words. Conversely, Coriolanus's name stemmed from his valorous deeds at Corioli:

> My surname, Coriolanus. The painful service,
>   The extreme dangers, and the drops of blood
>   Shed for my thankless country, are requited
>   But with that surname—a good memory.
>   (IV.v.68)

Montaigne criticized those who, favored by fortune, took on "new genealogical titles" unknown to their ancestors. Concerned with the vanity of words as early as 1572, the Frenchman spoke out against those Italians who abused classical surnames to the point of bestowing the epithet "divine" on Aretino (223). By contrast, readers were encouraged to settle "with what contented our fathers," for "coats or arms have no more security than surnames" (202–3).

At best, language could function as a working hypothesis for comprehending reality. Monoglossia yielded to polyglossia; correspondence made room for transference, and analogical parallels gave way to metaphorical substitutions. The God-given status of language faltered. Meaning was not enshrined but manufactured; it was made, remade, and unmade by the competing wills of independent minds who also favored the vernacular. Shakespeare, Montaigne, and Cervantes cherished the protean fluidity of signifiers "doomed never to find peace in a signified." At the end of the lexicon, the unknown justified confusion, and language bore out the directions and indirections of an age prone to share a modern concern: "How thoroughly the human condition is a verbal condition!"[57]

X

Copernicus inspired Bruno to fly through the heavens, whereas
Pascal saw in the new cosmology a sign of man's fall from the
providential scheme of things. Between invention and insanity,
man had to find a point of balance where fear of the unknown
would not frustrate his thirst for discovery. It was becoming
clear that the mind's own epiphanies could turn into a curse. To
gain equilibrium, ingenuity had to be kept under control.

By the turn of the seventeenth century, it was quite apparent that Columbus's voyage had deceived Mediterranean na-
tions. The Italians lost economic power because of the commercial shift toward Atlantic waters. And the Spaniards realized
that imperial dreams were turning into nightmares. With the
exception of few pilgrims or scattered delusions of grandeur,
people understood that there was no pot of gold at the end of
the rainbow. Since well-meaning intentions hatched disaster, in-
quiries into the nature of those very intentions touched on
method, expectation, and ideology itself.

Although Leonardo da Vinci had foreseen the dreadful
impact that military technology could unleash, mankind built
means of destruction more harmful than ever. While gunpowder
blasted away lives on old and new continents, the printing
press—"instrument of instruments, and artifice of artifices"[58]—
that Don Quixote visited in Barcelona put our more chivalric
lies than enlightened truths.

The invention of the telescope altered the way man inves-
tigated reality, and the time had come when the earth could be

> clearly observed without impediment,
>> thanks to a marvelous instrument
>> through which things distant can appear close by;
>> and one surveying the bright lunar orb,
>> with one eye closed and with the other fixed,
>> will shorten the tremendous interval
>> by a small cannon with two crystals set
> (Marino, *Adonis*, X, 42; trans. H. M. Priest)

Because of a small cannon with two crystals, people could see
what they thought did not exist before.

To paraphrase Pirandello, man invented the telescope not to be inferior to nature. "While one eye looks from below through the smaller lens, and sees as big all that nature had providentially wanted for us to see small, what does our soul do? It jumps up to look from above through the longer lens, and as a consequence the telescope becomes a terrible instrument, which sinks the earth and man and all our glories and greatness."[59] Man's ability to explore the world through means other than his natural eye enhanced hopes and fears.[60] Because of what telescopes (and microscopes shortly thereafter) had revealed, the poetic and religious imagination of the age wavered between optimism and pessimism.[61]

Beyond quixotic nostalgia, Donne and Pascal could share their dim view of the future-oriented present with people who found neither Cicero nor Erasmus as intimidating as Copernicus and Galileo. By walking a tight rope between confidence and confusion, the baroque mind was in fact emulating itself.

XI

At the end of his remarks on the essence of humor, Pirandello refers to the old saying: "If Cleopatra's nose had been longer, who knows what other events the world might have experienced. This *if*—the minute particle which can be pinned to, and inserted like a wedge into, all events—can produce many different disruptions and disarrangements."[62] If we take Cleopatra's profile as the canon of flawless beauty, that "baroque" *if* of a longer nose shed a parodic shadow over the isolation of perfect forms, and by so doing it found faults with Cleopatra so that all women could claim individual measures of beauty.

A cohesive and articulate convergence of art, language, and philosophy made it possible for artists to produce mature forms representative of a mature age:

> The Baroque brings to an epoch of European culture a
> light all of its own . . . foregrounding an image of man
> that was inconstant and multiform, which was worked

out with thoroughness and originality into a contradictory dosage.[63]

The indeterminate and metaverbal components of language were in tune with artworks whose shadows became part of their forms. So conceived, art carried an empty reflection of itself; its own parodic "other."

Between characters and readers, baroque artists denied themselves authority by wavering between creation and criticism, completion and inconclusiveness. With a passion, they foregrounded what they had not written (Cervantes, Montaigne), painted (Velázquez), sculpted (Michelangelo), or staged (Bernini). Yet, their attitude toward, and presence in, the artwork thrived on the enduring presence of a declared (or pretended) absence.

At the threshold, the artist took a confrontational stand toward his own craft. Often, the creative act seemed to collapse under its own parodic underpinning, but it never did. After all, fictions of denial could deny fiction only through fictive means which deny . . . And so the cornucopian paradox—like a Borrominian spiral (see Fig. 7) that forever recoils on itself—kept on dispensing its magical shower of baroque forms.

PART III

Conclusion: The Progress of Perfectibility

The Baroque Gesture: Rembrandt's *Aristotle Contemplating the Bust of Homer*

*Consider man with man, and you see human
life, dynamic, twofold, the giver and the re-
ceiver, he who does and he who endures . . .
the request begged and granted—and always
both together, completing one another in mutual contribution, together showing forth
man.*

—Martin Buber

I

As the Baroque grew to maturity by the turn of the
seventeenth century, analogues of perfection clashed
with chronotopic processes that had to accept gaps and breaks
as innate to any developmental system.[1]
Whether they would lodge uncertainty or circumstance,

"gaps" were not part of the humanist heritage, which linked distance to the fulfillment of ideal resemblances (Michelangelo's *Creation of Adam*). Even at its most innovative, *aemulatio* could not foster unlimited progress within the finite boundaries of classical imitation and Ptolemaic science.

The humanists had a "spatial" rather than a "temporal" view of reality. For them, space secured the immobility of perfection, which was further enhanced by a new mythology of unflawed excellence. Quickly, in fact, the *studiolo* became the symbolic *locus* where pursuits of divine-like analogues could be housed in the privileged isolation of a "learned space."[2]

At an early stage, Petrarch had taken up the insanity of excessive learning: "Books have led some to knowledge and some to madness, who drew from them more than they could hold."[3] Without edging on excess, the *studiolo* could become a holy island immune to the facts of life. And he hoped that death would find him "reading or writing."[4]

After a day of earthy altercations in the streets, Machiavelli would take off "the day's clothing, covered with mud and dust, and put on garments regal and courtly." Scholarly behavior took on ritualistic overtones, and the study became a temple of spiritual treasures: "And reclothed appropriately, I enter the ancient courts of ancient men, where, received by them with affection, I feed on that food which only is mine and which I was born for, where I am not ashamed to speak with them and to ask the reason for their actions; and they in their kindness answer me; and for four hours of time I do not feel boredom, I forget every trouble, I do not dread poverty, I am not frightened by death, entirely I give myself to them."[5] In the humanist mode, longings of that sort stirred literary exchanges in the form of epistles and commentaries.

The visual arts also added to the triumph of learning in humanist *studioli* (Botticelli, Carpaccio, Dürer, Antonello da Messina). Later, such secluded islands became windowless in Palazzo Vecchio (Florence), where only a candle could illuminate Francesco I's obscure visions.

At the turn of the seventeenth century, the reading of a book (Cicero, Cardanus, Montaigne?) set up Hamlet's troublesome doubt. While Marlowe let Doctor Faustus enter a study where a world of

> omnipotence
> Is promised to the studious artisan,
> (*Doctor Faustus*, I.i.52–53)

the literature of chivalry drove Don Alonso Quijano astray. Whether they be medieval or humanist, imitations of outdated models at times led to nightmares. Still under chivalric spells, Don Quixote became a hero in search of the Same.[6] Concerned friends therefore found it necessary to wall up "the room where he kept his books" (64). Because he had been deprived of that refuge, the provincial gentleman could either renounce knight errantry or try to revive it in the real world. Either way, art had to touch life.

While Machiavelli never thought of walking through the streets of Florence in a Roman toga, Don Quixote chose to incarnate chivalric texts. Outdated as it was, knowledge turned into madness when he set his adventurous quest on the road. Attempts at living the past into the present forced him to turn similarity into identity; the windmills had to become giants.[7]

On the other side of madness, sane alternatives emerged. Although he had been brought up in the humanist tradition, Montaigne left the tower-*studiolo* to plant cabbages. Unlike Petrarch, he would gladly meet death in his "unfinished garden" (62). Experience "naturalized" academic upbringing, much as identity accepted the risks of appearance, language, and growth.[8]

Amid more popular environments, *studioli* gave way to those drawing rooms of Vermeer where empty chairs, open windows, and the reading of letters (see Fig. 29) pointed to stories of warmth and love. Places of scholarship and learned dialogues across the ages yielded to homes where people acted out their lives. Dutch artists caught the educational process at its source when they painted ladies teaching children to read (Caspar Netscher) and night schools (Gerrit Dou, Adriaen van Ostade, Jan Miense Molenar, Adriaen Brower, Jan Steen) crowded with unruly pupils.

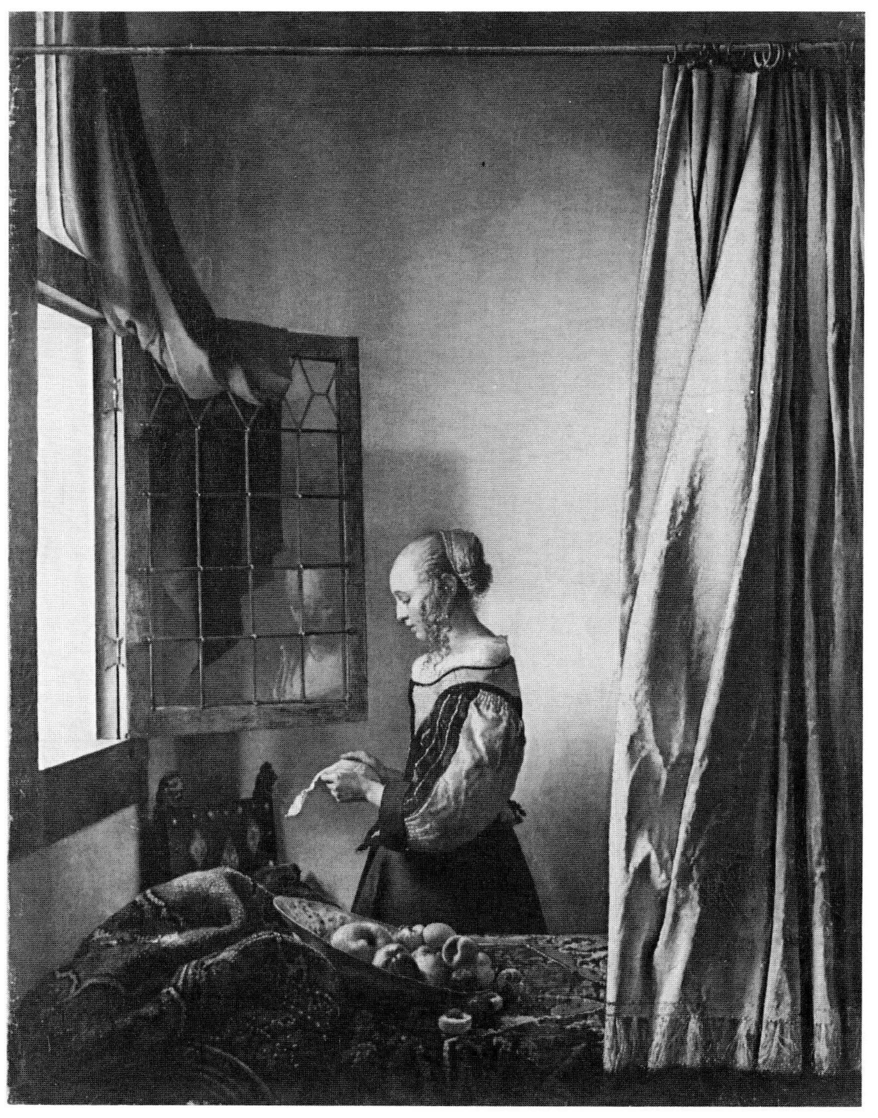

Fig. 29. Vermeer, *Woman Reading a Letter at an Open Window*, 1659–60? Gemäldegalerie Alte Meister, Dresden

II

Still in a humanist guise, Rubens joined company with Justus Lipsius in a canvas that honored the works of Seneca, whose bust is enthroned in a niche (*The Four Philosophers*, 1610).

Although less imbued with humanist culture, Rembrandt later painted *Aristotle Contemplating the Bust of Homer* (1653; Fig. 30), which presents a study with Homer's bust on a table and a few tomes hardly visible through a deep *chiaroscuro*. It is my contention that this canvas brought a baroque meaning to the *studiolo* theme.

It was common belief that Aristotle had been the first to form a library, which the Romans often decorated with sculptures of the great men of antiquity (above all, Homer). While preserving forms of eternity for the humanists, literature often pointed to boredom and decadence in seventeenth-century *studioli* (Frugoni's library of Gastrimargi), which also housed texts attributed to authors who had never written them (Thomas Browne's *Museum Clausum* or *Bibliotheca Abscondita*, Donne's *The Courtier's Library*). Within the tradition of Dutch still-lifes, books became symbols of the futility of all things.[9] One need only mention how suspect they were to Montaigne and Cervantes. Yet, they spent most of their lives writing books against books.

It seems to me that, in Rembrandt's *studiolo*, emphasis is placed on the scholar as teacher, a role indeed familiar to an artist whose school-academy had more students than any other in the Low Countries (except for that of Rubens). Also relevant to his sustained interest in, and familiarity with, that vocation are canvases of teachers of medicine (the anatomy lessons of Doctors Tulp, 1632, and Deyman, 1656) and religion (*Portrait of Anslo and a Disciple*, 1632–33?), not to mention many etchings of philosophers sharpening pencils and reading books.

Aristotle's attire well reflects the fashion of the day, to which the painter added a touch of "flashy" elegance. Earlier, Castiglione had recommended that clothes ought to tend "toward the grave and sober rather than the foppish. . . . black is more pleasing in clothing than any other color; and if not black, then at least some color on the dark side."[10] Such a description

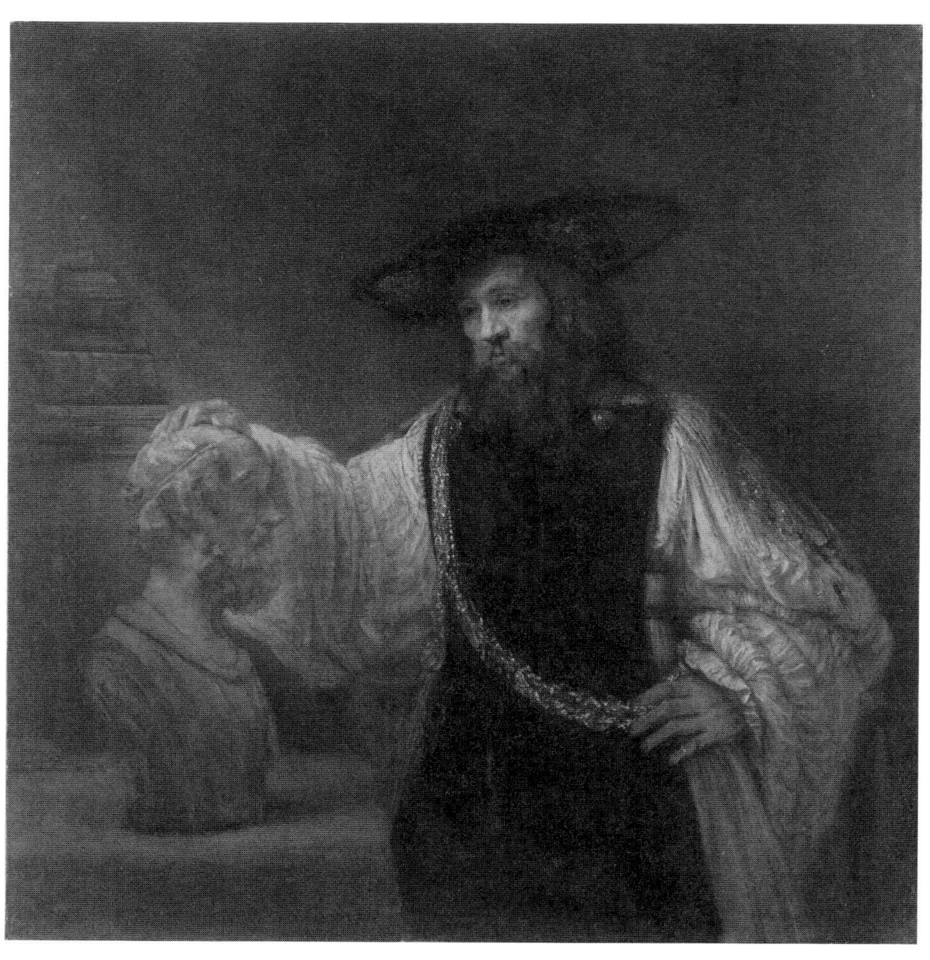

Fig. 30. Rembrandt, *Aristotle Contemplating the Bust of Homer*, 1653. The Metropolitan Museum of Art, New York

fitted Raphael's portrait of Castiglione, and it has been noted that the understated elegance of black was exemplary from the Spanish court to the Dutch regency.

Rembrandt had seen Raphael's portrait of Castiglione (which was put on sale in Amsterdam), and was quite bored by the sobriety of his first Amsterdam clients, many of whom were prudent merchants who wore black clothes (see *Portrait of a Man and a Woman in Black,* 1631; Isabella Stewart Gardner Museum, Boston). In the 1630s, a period of puritanism was in full swing, and black became the order of the day. Nevertheless, the artist was unrelenting in his love of rich fabrics, fur caps, gold chains, and splendid accoutrements that he collected at great expense. By 1653, his wealth had dwindled (for reasons as yet unclear). One factor was his purchase of ancient busts (of the kind Aristotle is looking at in our canvas).[11]

Amidst such misfortunes, however, Rembrandt still invested Aristotle with much of his own "kingly" elegance. Black hat and tunic set up the shining volumes and rich textures of the sleeves' fabric. The artist followed a liberal vogue whose "baroque abundance" stood out against puritan severity and humanist restraint. In light of Castiglione's negative measures of judgment, the philosopher's clothes tend to be "overample" (in the French manner) but are not "overscanty" (in the German manner). Furthermore, the symbolism of black clothing adds to the intellectual substance and moral probity of the ancient philosopher.[12]

Certainly, Rembrandt's portrait betrays taste and wealth, which echo autobiographical traits. Since it has been dated at about 1653, the canvas may refer back to the days when the artist was a successful teacher who also earned money through the sale of his pupils' drawings. His early prosperity was a matter of envy and admiration.[13] Fortunes changed, but the 1653 canvas shows no hint of the humbler station that the artist had taken up, even though he had known indigence quite early in his career (*Artist in His Studio,* 1628).

A medallion with Alexander's portrait hanging from a chain over Aristotle's black tunic points to human relationships. Petrarch and Castiglione had hoped that the man of learning would become an enlightened counselor to the prince. Their hypothesis, however, remained just that. Even the very paragon of reasonableness did not completely succeed in his tutorial experience with the Macedonian king, since his teachings were first praised and then disposed of.

Such a failure, however, was instrumental. In Montaigne's baroque voice, "Aristotle did not amuse his great pupil so much with the trick of constructing syllogisms or with the principles of geometry, as by instructing him in the good precepts concerning valor, prowess, magnanimity, and temperance, and the security of fearing nothing; and with this ammunition he sent him, still a child, to subjugate the empire" (121). By touching the bust of Homer in the foreground, I would like to suggest, the philosopher linked poetic constructs to the collective process of human experience. Asked by the Marchese Ruffo (who commissioned the canvas) about a companion piece, Guercino was struck by the gesture of the hand, which he read as a physiognomic expression of the way one can apprehend the world.[14]

Julius Held writes that "the melancholy reflections of Aristotle involve an awareness of the fickleness of princely favor. The prince who one day presents you with a chain of honor, may the next day look at you with suspicion and kill your friends and relatives. . . . it is hardly to be doubted that the picture is built upon the contrast between two sets of values, the more enduring one symbolized by the bust of Homer, and the more secular and transitory awards exemplified by the chain. That Rembrandt put his signature on the bust, may well assume a special significance as an act of identification with a higher moral principle."[15] To an extent, Rembrandt's own life would validate such an approach to the artwork. Unlike Velázquez, he was an artist without an Alexander. In his later life, guilds refused his work, nor was he commissioned by either the government of the United Provinces or the Reform Church. The Stadholder Frederic Henry and his son William II had no flair for Medician gestures, and they bought the five paintings on the Passion of Christ (1634) because of Constantijn Huygens's efforts on behalf of the artist.

However plausible on iconographic and biographical

grounds, Held's analysis does not do justice to the formal structure of the artwork. Placed at the dead center of the picture, the medallion stands as the compositional knot tying the figures together. Although he has established contact with Homer, Aristotle still is *chained* to the medallion, which he wears as a symbol of achievement.

Successful at first, Alexander's educational process came to a halt. At one point, he loved Aristotle more than his father (cf. Plutarch), but that kinship later dwindled. Even though Alexander's triumphs reflected no small measure of his teacher's talent, the cheerless mood of the picture bares out the instability of human fortunes. Homer's bust calls forth judgment, and the canvas betrays the evaluation of a relationship. Had it depended on a choice between the life of art and that of action,[16] the picture could have been less somber.

In terms of literary parallels, Montaigne set his portrait of Alexander against a criticism of public life. Like Caesar, the Macedonian leader always sought "unrest and difficulties" (42). By contrast, "private persons, says Aristotle, render higher and more difficult service to virtue than those who are in authority. We prepare ourselves for eminent occasions more for glory than for conscience" (614). The "we" functions as a bond for the shared belief that conscience ought to override glory. Alexander did not learn that lesson, and his tutor failed to teach it to him. "I can easily imagine Socrates," the Frenchman goes on, "in Alexander's place; Alexander in that of Socrates, I cannot. If you ask the former what he knows how to do, he will answer, 'Subdue the world'; if you ask the latter, he will say, 'Lead the life of man in conformity with its natural condition'; a knowledge much more general, more weighty, and more legitimate" (614). Heroism made room for normalcy, since "on the loftiest throne in the world we are still sitting on our own rump" (857). While the crown made the king for Don Quixote, the Frenchman found in the rump the common denominator of the human condition.

Aristotle could write poetics but not poetry; he could analyze, plan, and explain but not invent. Less than deferential, his friendly gesture in the Dutch canvas speaks for commitment to dialogue. In his own words, "no one is able to attain the truth adequately, which, on the other hand, no one fails entirely, but every one says something true about the nature of things, and while individually they contribute little or nothing to the truth, by the union of all a considerable amount is amassed" (*Metaphysics* II,1). It was typically Aristotelian to oppose one philosopher's solution of specific problems to those of other philosophers, just as older forms of investigation became dialectical starting points for new ones.[17]

Rembrandt captured that method, and his canvas foregrounds a frame of mind open to forms of human exchange. Consistent with that speculative bent, he did not portray an aloof scholar-theoretician holding one of the books (*Ethics*) that made him famous (as Raphael had done earlier in *The School of Athens*). Instead, he chose to stress the concordance between creation and its usage, Homeric invention and Aristotelian understanding. Aristotle's analysis of Homeric poetry aimed at a more accessible knowledge of art; above all, his gesture conveys a mental attitude open to a humanizing dialogue. Facing the medallion on this side of the canvas, the viewer's task is to capture an outreaching gesture that is conciliatory rather than peremptory.

In a baroque key, Homer and Aristotle link text to commentary, as Bruno did with his sonnets vis-à-vis prose narrative. Criticism updated creation, and analysis proved to be almost as important as the creative act itself. If the literary word is a crossroad of surfaces thriving on intertextuality and intersubjectivity, "history and morality can be read and written in the infrastructure of texts."[18] The dialogic composition of Rembrandt's canvas, I would like to suggest, wove antagonistic ideas into an unfolding experience that favored preferences over choices. On physiognomic grounds, in fact, the philosopher's left hand seems to touch the chain with affection. Emphasis is placed on a kind of circularity that brings forward an abstract of humanism as it was understood at the time: politics, poetry, and philosophy. We do know that the Marchese Ruffo asked Rembrandt for two more canvases of the same size, and the artist did paint *Homer* and the idealized *Alexander the Great* (also known as *Pallas Athena*).[19]

III

Since Macrobius, the golden chain of Homer has stood as a cosmic symbol extending without breaks from the Supreme God down to the last dregs of things.[20] In Proclus and later Neoplatonists, the chain linked men to specific gods, their patrons or patronymic deities. While symbolizing neither privilege nor choice, the chain reconciled ideas with conduct.

In 1600, Bruno chose to be burned for his faith; in 1633, Galileo, convinced that his survival was necessary for the progress of science, recanted; principle gave way to compromise. By the time Rembrandt's impact was felt, the baroque worldview had made up in depth of understanding what it had lost in ground-breaking intensity.[21] His canvas, in fact, seems to offer a visual image for Donne's steadfast conviction that man is never to quench his "desire of understanding," his "capacity of understanding," and his "means of understanding" (*Sermons*, IX, 357). The humanist emphasis on the order of things gave way to the baroque appreciation of, and reflections on, the complex world of human fellowship.

To borrow from Martin Buber's dialogic philosophy, Aristotle's open gesture builds up a twofold movement; "setting at a distance" and "entering into relation,"[22] which seem to stand as philosophical parallels to metaphoric "outreaching" and "combining." Humanism fixed distances and imposed exemplary models. The Baroque, instead, favored minds set "to rejoin with everybody, to discuss with everybody, befriend everybody, follow everybody, identify with everybody, lead everybody, be everything" (Bruno, *Dialoghi*, 923).

Such an inclusive view of life's plurality seems to verge here on *sensus communis,* that is to say, a sense common to all which Kant identifies with taste. The *Critique of Judgment* (40), in fact, links the discussion on artistic taste to a comparison of one's judgment "with the collective reason of humanity." We could "even define taste as the faculty of judging of that which makes 'universally communicable,' without the mediation of a concept, our feeling in a given representation." The baroque thirst for consensus was so rephrased in Kantian language: "The judgment of taste requires the agreement of everyone" (19).

Agreement is not postulated, for the judgment of taste "only imputes this agreement to everyone, as a case of the rule in respect of which it expects, not confirmation by concepts, but assent from others" (8). On human and artistic grounds alike, the very concept of the self became one of shared experiences between man and man—the dialogic I-Thou of Buber or the inter-individuality of Ortega y Gasset's *altruismo* and *nostridad*.[23]

At the very moment of creation, Donne wrote, God's own name proclaimed the value of relationship, for he notified himself to the world as *Elohim,* which "is a *plurall word* . . . so it hath no *singular;* they say we cannot name God, but plurally" (*Sermons,* VI, 152). The word *Elohim,* in fact, is said to be formed from *El* (strength), *alah* (to swear, to bind oneself), and *im,* which is grammatically plural.[24] As it moves from *Al* to *im,* the centrifugal activity of divine power is "outreaching," while the mediating role of the middle term *alan* states a commitment that is "combining." The baroque mind therefore read the very name of the deity as a metaphorical concept-mode. And Donne made the plural bond explicit: "Let us, us both together, you and we, make a man; join my Ordinance (you preaching) with my Spirit (says God to us) and so make man. . . . let us, us all, make man" (*Sermons,* IX, 58–91). Creation was envisioned as a process uniting God with man "metaphorically,"[25] in a spirit of collective interinanimation that would unfold forever.

For Donne, the metaphorical process of becoming bore on a future-oriented logology. Even God's name "is conceived in the future; it is there, *Qui ero, I that shall be.*" Whereas creatures " of an inferior nature are possest with the *present*"; man "is a *future Creature.* In a holy and usefull sense, we may say, that *God is a future God,*" since any consideration of him "is specially for the *future*" (*Sermons,* IX, 90). If the present is filled with the closures of failure and compromise, the future spurs amelioration. Knowledge set up an ever-fulfilling process of discovery that broke free of classical "remembrance."

Commitments to the communal nature of man went to the core of the baroque worldview, and the "outreaching" embrace of Bernini's colonnade of Saint Peter's (1656–67) stood as the architectural framework for people whose human nature demands that they "step into a living relation with other individuals."[26]

Because he was interested in man as a piece of work *and* a piece of the continent, Montaigne took his fellow man's faults upon himself, since "each part of us is less than ourselves. We are part of the world" (395). Just as no man is an island, so "each man bears the entire form of man's estate (*humaine condition*)" (611). And Donne was grateful to "him that *prayes* for me when my bell tolles, but I thank him much more that *cathechises mee,* or *preaches* to mee, or *instructs me how to live*" (*Sermons,* X, 241). Instructions in the art of living set baroque art at pace with social commitments.

Plurality was rooted at the core of baroque humanism. Since Ciceronian concerns with solitude (*On Duties*) were still in the air, Thomas Browne wrote that man cannot be alone, because "every man is a *Microcosme,* and carries the whole world about him." At the same time, the "heavenly and celestiall part within us" urges mankind's "heterogeneous parts" to long for a transcendent unity. Although embedded in feeble reeds and however distant in the future, such an overflowing vitality would not fail to steer human "dissimilarity" to seek spiritual "concourse" (*Religio Medici,* II, 10–11).

The Perfectibility of the Human Condition

The art of progress is to preserve order amid
change, and to preserve change amid order.
Life refuses to be embalmed alive.
—Alfred North Whitehead

I

To follow Hölderlin, poets are holy vessels that preserve the spirit of great men for posterity. Yet, teachers educate heroes, and only later on do their deeds become the
subject of poetry. For some (Don Quixote, Alexander), epic and
chivalric tales could stifle any firm grip on the present. For
others, "it was against the order of nature" that Homer "created the most excellent production that can be. For things in
nature are ordinarily imperfect; they gain in size and strength as
they grow. He made the infancy of poetry and of several other
sciences mature, perfect, and accomplished" (Montaigne, 570),
that is to say, immune to formativeness.

In a classical and humanist mode, Minerva and Adam

are new born and perfect, since they are ideal models rather than human beings. Homeric constructs and humanist prototypes of adult excellence (Courtier, Prince) crumbled once the baroque chronotope of formation linked knowledge to the world of experience. Since perfection could be neither given nor gained in real life, the growth of learning was traced back to infancy and lodged in Dutch schools or on Spanish roadsides.

As a way of drawing this study to an interpretative rather than synoptic conclusion, I would like to center on the way that scientific progress changed the twin concepts of finiteness and perfection when the Ptolemaic worldview met the Copernican challenge of an open universe. Either mythic or metahistorical, the completed formation of classical and humanist world order had to face the formativeness of the "New Science." And we have seen how that epoch-making clash affected the Baroque, as well as later concerns with evolution, relativity, and knowledge of man's outer frontiers.

By definition, perfection consists of fitness to purpose (Thomas Aquinas, *De Nom.* 1,31: "*Perfectio consistit in hoc quod pertingat ad finem*"), objective purposiveness (Kant, *Critique of Judgment,* 15), or "the conformity of a reality to its concept. Whenever a thing is found adequate to the idea which we have of it that thing is perfect."[1] Because it implies fulfillment, perfection bears on method instead of speculation. It can only cherish and display itself, which it did through humanist treatises, triumphs, and panegyrics. As a hypothetical point of arrival where any form of "process" comes to rest, perfection cannot lead beyond itself. In representational terms, it demands that human experience be fulfilled within a "known" reality that must be as spatially finite as the geometric figures that usually symbolize it.

II

We need only mention that, in a classical sense, knowledge was associated with "remembrance" and "unconcealedness" (*aletheia*); the growth of the mind amounted to no more than the bringing into light of what had always been there. Knowledge could not grow; it had to be rescued. Learning was a matter of movement in space (between surface and depth, clarity and obscurity), not in time. The Greek idea of the Supreme Being equated perfection with a hypostasis.

On the downside, perfection halts life into the mechanical order of a fixed cosmos secure within its own limits. In a Greek sense, being is perfection, which could be active only by aiming at self-thought. Any creative movement therefore had to be circular; *aemulatio* as a serpent biting its own tail. Greek thought was spatially cosmocentric, and Zeno's paradox about Achilles and the tortoise stemmed from a deep-rooted uneasiness with growth and motion. Form was a proportional construct, not a vital organism.

Once Christianity brought forth the idea of a "living" God whose main attribute was "*kabod*" (a Hebrew word meaning force, will, heart), intellectual concepts of perfection gave way to something which, though quite beyond our intellectual reach, lives in us and emerges into our consciousness through the life of action.[2] No longer theoretical, perfection was to be pursued through the experiences of life. Learning had to be sought after with a passion, and man was endowed with the power to discover—not to remember—knowledge. Adam's archetypal fall, Milton clearly understood, made a case for the educational process.

In his study of thought and action from Augustus to Augustine, Charles N. Cochrane writes that "to Christianity time is neither a 'thing' nor is it an illusion. As the 'order of becoming,' it is indeed as real as human life itself, and, in precisely the same way, quite as irreversible."[3] The dynamic thrust of the life of action marked stages instead of completions.

Since Augustine (*The City of God,* xii,18), Christianity turned away from the classical theory of historical circularity, whose *circuitus temporum* denied the Scriptural view of the *saeculum* as a creative and moving principle. Henry O. Taylor insists that the Greek saw the "dignity of life in the existent man who had attained to what he was." Yet, the severe outcome of pagan ethics, namely that man shall content himself within the self-poise of his will, brought discomfort even to pagan thought.

By contrast, the Christian saw "life's dignity, nay, its blessedness, in its eternal perfectibility . . . proud in what through God he shall be."[4] Perfection turned into perfectibility, which fostered improvement. In that sense, process stems from incompleteness and thrives on imperfection, both of which make progress itself possible.

Since incompleteness and transformation are essential to it, process is not canonic. Instead, it weighs on a developmental worldview quite akin to Henri Bergson's concept of existence, which is not being, because "to exist is to change, to change is to mature, to mature is to go on creating oneself endlessly."[5] The way surpassed the end and spurred on a quest at the very heart of human life since the Middle Ages (Augustine: "Let us seek as we find, and let us find as we seek"; *De Trinitate* ix,1; also x,3). Beyond finite limitations, the new orators of infinity (with Bruno and More at the forefront) sought the inexhaustible Good along an endless path:

> Still falling short they never fail to seek
> (Henry More, *Psychatanasia*, III, iii, 13–14)[6]

III

Whether in the mind or on the roads of life, the "formative principle" was pervasive, and it affected the very archetype of human growth. The exclusive God-Man *We* ("*Faciamus*") of humanist panegyrics (Pico, Giannozzo Manetti) echoed the "flawless majesty" of the prelapsarian Adam, who "names" things because of a divine-like foreknowledge. In humanist images, the fallen couple about to start on its human journey (Masaccio, Michelangelo) is out to confront despair rather than experience.

Outside the garden of Eden, Pico let go of Adam the moment he fell. But Bruno was waiting for him: "Fate has not denied us the possibility of rising again. . . . Let us cleanse our interior affect, since after the formation of this internal world, it will not be difficult for us to make progress" (*Expulsion*, 114–16). After the fall, Adam's words are those of a human being. He discovered, as Elie Wiesel has recently written on the mystery of the Beginning, a purpose to his existence: to perfect the world which until then had been no more than created. To do that, God gave him the longest future in the history of mankind.[7]

While Bruno found that labor could spur progress beyond Edenic fictions, Milton presented Eden as a planted garden requiring work. The beginning implied a continuous growth that invalidated Adamic and post-Adamic distinctions.[8] It was the gift of the hand ("*Dono della mano*"; Bruno, *Opere*, 303) that set man apart as an active "maker" whose understanding of his own human condition would conquer fears and regrets alike. The mythic yielded to the chronotopic.

Intolerance of static models led Bruno to reject myths of perfection. The Golden Age became the realm of Leisure, where men were perhaps "more stupid than many of the beasts." As a matter of fact, "the gods had given intellect and hands to man" to let him operate not only according to his nature and what is usual but also "outside the laws of nature, in order that by forming or being able to form other natures, other paths, other categories, with his intelligence, by means of that liberty without which he would not have the above-mentioned similarity, he would succeed in preserving himself as god of the earth." Neither a matter of fate nor chronology, evolution thrives on "intelligence," "liberty," and "labor." In its progressive quest for fulfillment, the human spirit calls on Solicitude for "love of innovation" (*Expulsion*, 200, 205). Search had to find a home in infinite spaces beyond the range of ancient myths.

Having rid himself of lapsarian memories, Bruno set knowledge in the present: "The judgment of Eudoxus, who lived only shortly after the rebirth of astronomy, if indeed it was not reborn in him, could not be so mature as the judgment of Capillus living thirty years after the death of Alexander the Great, who adding years to years could add observations to observations." Later, Copernicus "saw ever more of those changes, being separated from Alexander's death by 1849 years." Great men spearhead history, while those who remain attached to the idea that "wisdom is with antiquity" actually live "as if dead through their own years" (*Ash*, 65–66). Likewise, it was noted that "true antiquity" is "the attribute of our own times, not of that earlier age of the world in which the ancients lived; and which, though in respect of us it was the older, yet in respect of the world it was the younger" (Bacon, *Novum Organum,* 1,84). The process of knowledge rested with explorations of tomorrow rather than any recovery of yesterdays.

Whereas Humanism dreamed of an antiquity without decadence and a modernity without future, the Baroque could accept the old only as a function of the new. History therefore became an open-ended process. Much as life consists of organic forms evolving in time, spirituality draws on activity rather than contemplation. For Bruno, the absolute was developmental, and Donne added that, "if there be any addition to knowledge, it is rather a new knowledge, then a greater knowledge; rather a singularity in a desire of proposing something that was not knowne at all before, then an emproving, an advancing, a multiplying of former inceptions; and by that meanes, no knowledge comes to be perfect" (*Sermons,* I, 260). Process therefore fostered possibility, and perfectibility measured hope (Bruno's capacity-to-be) rather than accomplishment (being-in-act).

At stake here is the struggle—metaphysical, physical, aesthetic—between permanence and fluency, Plato and Heraclitus. To the baroque mind, that conflict called for integration. At its best, art reconciled permanence with flux through forms that "presenced" epiphanic encounters between capacity-to-be and being-in-act. Whether it be acts of living (Vermeer, Velázquez) or of human reflection (Montaigne, Donne), baroque forms were more than snapshot views of transition. In fact, they captured what Alfred North Whitehead has called the perfect moment. In that fadeless lapse, time loses its "character of 'perpetual perishing'; it becomes the 'moving image of eternity.' "[9] As one representative image of the age, the outreaching gesture of Rembrandt's Aristotle caught a moment pregnant with the fullness of human experience.

IV

Martin Foss insists that the idea of perfectibility went hand in hand with that of infinity, which implies search without limits.

For the Greeks, infinity stood for chaos, and art enclosed the perfection of form under the heavenly dome of "here" and "now." Discussions on infinitist conceptions—from Epicurus to Lucretius—were peripheral to the mainstream of Greek thought and science, which were anchored to Aristotelian cosmology and Ptolemaic astronomy. The Supreme Being was a Divine Architect, that is to say, a spatial concept whose attributes were measure, limit, and harmony.

By contrast, Christianity opened the gate for "the way," and art chartered out temporal longings for transcendence. Before Copernicus and Bruno, however, a compromise was reached between the infinity of Christian quests and the finiteness of geocentric worldviews.[10] Even Augustine framed "seeking" within a heavenly harmony based on measure, number, and geometry (*De Ordine* II,xv,42; II,xi,34). However problematic, that alliance set a millennial standard.

The humanist culture of the earlier Renaissance was steeped in utopian intellectualism, which either presumed or postulated perfection. Treatises (Alberti), panegyrics (Leonardo Bruni), and artworks spelled forms of hypothetical maturity through the vocabulary of geometry (Piero della Francesca, Uccello), praise (triumphs, biographies, histories), and the epiphany of culture (in the pages of *The Courtier* and Raphael's frescoes in the Stanza della Segnatura, Vatican). In all of them, the style of the divine-like fixed the spatial stasis of perfection.[11]

Eventually, Copernicanism discredited the notion that our earth is unique and central to the whole. And the time had come to show that infinite space is not impossible but necessary. It is in the landscape of boundlessness that intellectual power "seeketh, yea, and achieveth the addition of space to space, mass to mass, unity to unity, number to number, by the science which dischargeth us from the fetters of a most narrow kingdom and promoteth us to the freedom of a truly august realm" (Bruno, *Infinite*, 377–78, 246). Amidst the forthcoming kingdom of an open universe, Francis Bacon spoke for a whole age:

> For twice a thousand years the sciences stood where they did and now remain almost in the same condition. . . . Whereas in the mechanical arts, which are founded on

> nature and the light of experience, we see the contrary happening, for these (as long as they are popular) are continually thriving and growing, as if the breath of life inspired them—at first rude, then convenient, afterwards adorned, but at all times advancing. (*Novum Organum* I,74)

Such an advancement shed new light on the dignity of "making." Paolo Rossi insists that "several typical categories of technical knowledge—collaboration, progressiveness, perfectibility, and invention—became categories to which Bacon attributed a universal value."[12]

Ancient doctrines on the perfectibility of art (Aristotle, Seneca, Averroes) did not spur progress in science beyond improvements over individual efforts, or developments from barbarism to culture (which would eventually decline in a mode akin to natural growth). By contrast, the Judeo-Christian tradition brought forth the idea of a salvation history pointed toward a transcendental future. Below heavenly promises, there was no link between temporal felicity and eternal destiny. Perfectibility, to rephrase Joseph Mazzeo, had to be glimpsed as a purely human potentiality and not as a divine gift miraculously bestowed.[13]

Bacon, instead, condemned cyclical notions of history and philosophical systems (either ancient or medieval), which he replaced with an unlimited faith in the growth of useful scientific knowledge. Science took on the temporal mode of the future, and technology translated its principles into practical achievements.

Actually, the modern concept of knowledge emerged through the systematic cooperation of scientists—Accademia del Cimento, 1657; Royal Society, 1662; *Académie des Sciences*, 1666—who shared research and inventions. Libraries crucial to the dissemination of scientific knowledge were founded in Milan (Ambrosiana Library) and Rome, where the Cesi and the Lyncean Academies sponsored the publication of Galileo's works, treasured theological as well as humanist texts, and gave equal attention to the book of the universe and to those of the ancients.

Since Leonardo da Vinci, modern knowledge has been

engaged in the study of new sciences (from botany to geology) whose texts had to be made available. Federico Cesi openly declared, as Pietro Redondi informs us, that his academy was devoted solely to the search for natural truths independent of theological and political controversy. In Rome, a "marvelous conjunction" of minds set to stir renewal in science (Galileo) and religion (Jesuits of the Collegio Romano). They all tested tradition either through expediency or deliberation. Mixtures of both often were necessary to keep at a distance from Cardinal Bellarmino and the Congregation of the Index at one extreme, and Galileo and the Academy of the Desirous Ones at the other.[14]

At the breaking point of a cultural heritage, not only "prodigious" minds (Galileo) but also more modest ones could take on authority. Earlier attacks against book learning (Montaigne) and obedience to rules (Bruno) were echoed in Giuliano Fabrici's frontal assault (which obviously was valuable for its timing rather than its novelty) on the Aristotelians more than on Aristotle himself:

> Philosophy should study the great text written by God, where the book is the world and experience the characters, and should not be subjected to the law of a litigious piece of writing which after two thousand years of interpretation is still not understood even by those philosophers who have sworn to believe what it dictates. And in sum, man should confine himself to pondering opinions with the weight of reason and not authority, while today he speculates stunned by the writings of one who taints him more now that he is dead than when he was alive.[15]

The Greeks had weakened the link between science and technology to the benefit of quasi-religious or philosophical systems divorced from the needs of men. The moderns, instead, moved in the opposite direction. And Bacon was not alone in shouldering the conviction that there was but a single tradition, wherein earlier theories and "isms" marked stages of a unified process that could tolerate neither limits nor rejections.

When measured against classical standards, infinity

spawned excess. For the Baroque, instead, it set the process of human experience in a natural environment where the new science, as Majorie Nicolson's inspired comments tell us, "released human imagination to a spaciousness of thought man had not known before. The Idea of Infinity had demolished the Circle of Perfection."[16] The *furor poeticus* found an apt counterpart in a new *furor astronomicus,* whose object was the boundlessness of divine creation. The "breaking of the circle" unraveled a cosmic process which could not be less than cornucopian. Whatever doubts the new coordinates of infinity and perfectibility may have caused, they had to yield to the very dynamics of evolution. Even denial became a way for adding strength to the broader experiences of the human condition.

V

It is perhaps a contradiction to close this study by quoting the philosopher of "duration." In a baroque vein, however, contradictions can be at once real and apparent. To find some sort of certainty, Henri Bergson writes that "he who installs himself in becoming sees in duration the very life of things, the fundamental reality. . . . Eternity no longer hovers over time, as an abstraction; it underlines time, as a reality."[17] The baroque mind did just that. To be true to its cornucopian outpouring, it had no choice but to capture the formative spirit of man's quest of perfectibility.

Notes

Introduction

1. Outstanding are Jean Rousset, *La littérature de l'âge baroque en France: Circe et le päon* (Paris, 1954); Frank Warnke, *Versions of Baroque* (New Haven, 1972); and Peter Skrine, *The Baroque: Literature and Culture in Seventeenth-Century Europe* (New York, 1978). For a treatment of the critical fortunes of the concept, see René Wellek, "The Concept of Baroque in Literary Scholarship," in *Concepts of Criticism* (New Haven, 1967), and Warnke, *Versions of Baroque*, 1–20.

2. This is Ulrich Weisstein's recommendation, *Comparative Literature and Literary Theory* (Bloomington, 1973), 76.

3. Luciano Anceschi, "Le poetiche del barocco letterario in Europa," in *Momenti e problemi di storia dell'estetica*, vol. 1 (Milan, 1959), 468–85.

4. *Spanish Baroque Art* (Cambridge, 1941), 2–3.

5. See Weisbach, *Spanish Baroque Art*, 3; Warnke, *Versions of Baroque*, 1, 40, dates baroque features of Montaigne's prose back to the early essays of 1575–80. In the 1920s, Morris Croll also illustrated baroque style through Montaigne's prose, in *Attic and Baroque Prose Style* (Princeton, 1969), 207. Jean Rousset, *La littérature de l'âge baroque en France*, 235, considers the literature produced between 1580 and 1625 as prebaroque.

6. Alexandre Koyré, *From Closed World to the Infinite Universe* (New York, 1966); Ernst Cassirer, *The Individual and the Cosmos in Renaissance Philosophy* (Philadelphia, 1972); Cassirer, *An Essay on Man* (New Haven, 1965); Hyram Haydn, *The Counter-Renaissance* (New York, 1950); Frances Yates, *Giordano Bruno and the Hermetic Tradition* (New York, 1964); John Nelson, *Renaissance Theory of Love* (New York, 1958); Marjorie Nicolson, *The Breaking of the Circle* (New York, 1960); Arthur Lovejoy, *The Great Chain of Being* (New York, 1960).

7. Giorgio Bárberi-Squarotti, "Per una descrizione e interpretazione della poetica di Giordano Bruno," *Biblioteca dell'Archivium Romanicum. Studi secenteschi* 1 (1961), 39–52; Carlo Calcaterra, *Il Parnaso in rivolta* (Bologna, 1961), 194–99; René Wellek, *Concepts of Criticism*, 91. Squarotti's analysis is literary, whereas Calcaterra leans toward the history of ideas and philosophy. Assuming that the Baroque is exemplified in the poetry of Marino, the latter states that "the new vision of the world, which is drawn in direct, clear

and straight lines represents the real anti-barocco" (187). With regard to the arts, see Paolo Portoghesi, *Roma barocca: Storia di una civiltà architettonica* (Rome, 1966); Eugenio Battisti, *Rinascimento e Barocco* (Turin, 1960); and Robert Klein, *Italian Art: Sources and Documents* (Englewood Cliffs, 1966). By contrast, Arnold Hauser associates Bruno with the philosophy of Mannerism, in his *Mannerism* (New York, 1965).

8. See my *Adam "New Born and Perfect": The Renaissance Promise of Eternity* (Bloomington, 1987).

9. On the subject, see my essay, "A Baroque Study of Montaigne: Italian Humanism and the Essay," *Comparative Literature Studies* 22 (1986), 413–43; H. Outram Evenett, *The Spirit of the Counter-Reformation* (Cambridge, 1968), 10–11, 16–18; Marcel Bataillon, "De Savonarole à Louis de Grenade," *Revue de littérature comparée* 16 (1936), 37–39.

10. See Warnke, *Versions of Baroque,* 9, and John Rupert Martin, *The Baroque* (New York, 1977), 12.

11. Luciano Anceschi, "Le poetiche del barocco letterario in Europa," 468; Harry Levin, "Leech-Gathering," in *The Critical Moment* (London, 1964), 69.

12. *Renaissance Perspectives in Literature and the Visual Arts* (Princeton, 1987), 6. I also find support to my cautious assessment of synchronic approaches at page 7: "Any theory arising from these inter-art comparisons must be empirically tested by a rigorous and detailed analysis both of art works and the literary text in place of the impressionistic responses and vague gesturing which have given synchronic enquiry its doubtful reputation."

13. *The Lion and the Honeycomb: Essays in Solicitude and Critique* (New York, 1955), 182–83.

14. *Essays in Aesthetics* (New York, 1957), 92.

15. See Gérard Genette, *Figures as Literary Discourse* (New York, 1982), 21. E. D. Hirsch also draws attention to the distinction-interaction between "the meaning of a text (which does not change) and the meaning of a text to us today (which changes)"; in *Validity in Interpretation* (New Haven, 1967), 255.

16. See André Malraux, *The Voices of Silence* (New York, 1954), 635.

17. George Steiner, "Human Literacy," in *The Critical Moment,* 29, writes that such luxuries "of detachment one should like to afford, but cannot." Harry Levin reiterates that "objectivity in matters involving human responses, may at best be an approximation"; in "Leech-Gathering," 68.

18. "La définition du terme 'baroque'," in *Proceedings of the III Congress of the International Comparative Literature Association* (The Hague, 1962), 174.

Chapter 1

1. *Studies in Iconology* (New York, 1972), 180. This view has friends (Charles De Tolnay) and foes (Frederick Hartt).

2. *Henry Moore on Sculpture,* ed. P. James (London, 1966), 185.

3. Charles de Tolnay, *Michelangelo,* vol. 4 (Princeton, 1960), 62, writes

that Michelangelo made of form "a vehicle for a major force going through it."

4.   Marsilio Ficino, *Marsilio Ficino: The Philebus Commentary*, trans. M. J. B. Allen (Berkeley, 1975), 298; *De raptu Pauli*, in *Prosatori latini del Quattrocento*, ed. Eugenio Garin (Milan, 1962), 950. Translation by author.

5.   See Jan Bialostocki, "Terribilità," in *Stil und Überlieferung in der Kunst des Abendlandes. International Congress on the History of Art* 21/2 (Berlin, 1967), 223–23; David Summers, *Michelangelo and the Language of Art* (Princeton, 1981), chapter 15; Pietro Aretino, *Lettere sull'arte di Pietro Aretino*, vol. 1 (Milan, 1957), 64–65. Translation by author.

6.   See Herbert Read on this point, in *Henry Moore* (New York, 1966), 257.

7.   Alberti, *On Painting*, trans. J. Spencer (New Haven, 1976), 97.

8.   Politian, *Oratio super Fabio Quintiliano et Statiis Sylvis*, in *Prosatori latini del Quattrocento*, 874–76.

9.   Frederick Hartt, *Michelangelo: La scultura* (Milan, 1972), 47.

10.   Adrian Stokes, *Michelangelo* (New York, 1956), 77, points out that "much of Michelangelo's sculpture seems to state that the outer stone is not to be considered as mere husk; it too has forms in embryo."

11.   In *Michelangelo: A Self-Portrait*, ed. R. Clements (New York, 1968), 12–13.

12.   Henri Focillon, *The Life of Forms in Art* (New Haven, 1942), 38.

13.   Charles de Tolnay, *Michelangelo*, vol. 4, 61; Giulio Carlo Argan, *Storia dell'arte italiana*, vol. 3 (Florence, 1972), 10–11. Bernard Berenson, *The Drawings of the Florentine Painters*, 2d ed. (Chicago, 1938), pointedly writes that Michelangelo strives "to pack into the least possible space the utmost possible action with the least possible change of place."

14.   *Studies in Iconology*, 177–78.

15.   Ficino, *De raptu Pauli*, in *Prosatori latini del Quattrocento*, 944.

16.   As translated by Creighton Gilbert, *Complete Poems and Selected Letters of Michelangelo* (New York, 1963). All subsequent quotations are from this edition. Enzo Noè Girardi has edited the critical edition of the *Rime* (Bari, 1960).

17.   Ficino, *Theologia platonica*, vol. 1, ed. Michele Schiavone (Bologna, 1965), 90. Translation by author.

18.   *Henry Moore on Sculpture*, 186.

19.   *Michelangelo*, vol. 2, 231.

20.   Adrian Stokes, *Michelangelo*, 78; Cesare Brandi, "Forma e compiutezza in Michelangelo," in *Stil und Überlieferung in der Kunst des Abendlandes*, 86; Henri Bergson, *Creative Evolution* (New York, 1944), 347.

21.   Charles de Tolnay, in "Michelangelo e il blocco," in *Momenti del marmo* (Rome, 1969), 100, writes on the sculptor's technique: "First of all, Michelangelo used to transform, by using the *cagnaccia*, the rigid and lucid planes of the block into a living substance. . . . he did not accept matter as inert stone; he immediately proceeded to inject life in it"; Focillon, *The Life of Forms in Art*, 44.

22.   *On Art and Artists*, trans. R. Fedden (New York, 1957), 209.

23.   *Poetry, Language, Thought* (New York, 1971), 36, 59.

24.   See Eugenio Montale, *Michelangelo poeta* (Bologna, 1976), 17.

25.   *The Diaries of Paul Klee, 1898–1918* (Berkeley, 1964), 112.

26.   See Johan Huizinga, *The Waning of the Middle Ages* (New York, 1954), the last chapter, "The Advent of the New Form," 323–35. also Ramón Menéndez Pidal, *La lengua de Cristobal Colón* (Madrid, 1942); Emilio Orozco Díaz, *Temas del Barroco* (Grenada, 1947), xvii. As Wilhelm Worringer writes, "the transcendental Gothic style, followed by the intermezzo of the Renaissance, is succeeded by another transcendental style, the Baroque," in *Form in Gothic* (London, 1957), 116; Maurizio Calvesi, *Treasures of the Vatican* (Geneva, 1962), 94, 124; Juan Luis Alborg, *Historia de la literatura española*, vol. 2 (Madrid, 1967), 720–22.

27.   *Marsilio Ficino: The Philebus Commentary*, 300.

28.   J. J. Winckelmann, *History of Ancient Art*, vol. 3 (New York, 1968), 264. Also, Mario Praz, *On Neoclassicism* (Evanston, 1969), 51–53; Charles Seymour, Jr., *Tradition and Experiment in Modern Sculpture* (Washington, D.C., 1949), 40; Albert Elsen, *Rodin* (New York, 1967), 174; Rainer Maria Rilke, *Rodin* (New York, 1945), 26, 29; Yourcenar, *Le Temps, ce grand sculpteur* (Paris, 1986), 61.

29.   *The Nude* (New York, 1956), 245, 257, 270, 277.

30.   *The Nude*, 197.

31.   Jean-Paul Sartre, *Essays in Aesthetics*, 86.

32.   *The Letters of Michelangelo*, vol. 1, trans. E. H. Ramsden (Stanford, 1963), 52–54. Letter dated June-October 1509; ibid., vol. 2, 16. Also, Kenneth Clark, *The Artist Grows Old* (Cambridge, 1972), 29.

33.   *Ideas para una filosofía de la historia de España* (Madrid, 1957), 292–93. The critic used the phrase in describing the Spanish ethos from St. John of the Cross to Don Quixote.

34.   See Charles Seymour, Jr., *Michelangelo's David: A Search for Identity* (Pittsburgh, 1967), 76; Glauco Cambon, *Michelangelo's Poetry: Fury of Form* (Princeton, 1985), 126.

35.   In Giuseppina Fumagalli, *Leonardo: Omo sanza lettere* (Florence, 1952), 158; *The Notebooks of Leonardo da Vinci*, vol. 2, ed. J. P. Richter (New York, 1970), 116.

36.   Ficino, *De raptu Pauli*, in *Prosatori latini del Quattrocento*, 948.

37.   See Etienne Souriau, "Time in the Plastic Arts," in Susanne Langer's *Reflections of Art* (Baltimore, 1960), 126.

38.   Michelangelo's late style, Gianfranco Contini writes, in fact reflects epistemological concerns, since *"una posizione stilistica . . . è una posizione gnoseologica"*; in *Esercizi di lettura* (Florence, 1947), 324.

39.   *La littérature de l'âge baroque en France*, 231.

40.   Preston Roberts, "A Christian Theory of Dramatic Tragedy," *The Journal of Religion* 31 (1951), 7, 12, 18.

41.   *The Beginning and the End* (London, 1952), 170.

Chapter 2

1.   See Croce's *Poeti e scrittori del pieno e del tardo Rinascimento*, vol. 2 (Bari, 1954), 89; *The Essence of Aesthetics*, trans. D. Ainsle (London, 1921), 44, which is a translation of *Nuovi saggi di estetica* (V. Bari, 1920). *Coleridge's*

Shakespearean Criticism, vol. 1, ed. T. Raysor (Cambridge, 1930), 223. On the relation between Bruno and Coleridge, see my "A Voice of Its Own Birth: Giordano Bruno and the Foundations of Coleridge's Poetics," *Comparative Literature Studies* 19 (1982), 296–318.

2. *De vinculis in genere* (1591–92), first published in Giordano Bruno, *Opera latine conscripta,* ed. Tocco III (Florence, 1890), as translated in Robert Klein's *Italian Art: Sources and Documents* (Englewood Cliffs, 1966), 187.

3. *De vinculis in genere,* 187.

4. *On the Boiler* (Dublin, 1946), 25–26.

5. In Filippo Baldinucci's biography, *The Life of Bernini* (London, 1966), 77.

6. *The Great Chain of Being* (New York, 1960), 293.

7. See Bruno Migliorini, "Etimologia e storia del termine 'barocco,' " in *Manierismo, Barocco, Rococo: Concetti e termini* (Rome, 1962), 39–49; Giovanni Getto, "La polemica sul Barocco," in *Letteratura italiana: Le correnti,* vol. 3. (Milan, 1956), 433; Georg Weise, "Considerazioni di storia dell'arte intorno al barocco," *Rivista di letterature moderne* 3 (1952), 7.

8. Marino, *Epistolario,* ed. A. Borzelli and F. Nicolini, vol. 2 (Bari, 1911), 55. Translation by author.

9. Eugenio Battisti, *Rinascimento e Barocco* (Turin, 1960), 265–67.

10. As a spokesman for Counter-Reformation precepts, Cardinal Paleotti wrote that, in the Greek sense, *verisimilitudine* in art is "apt to persuade others," much as discretion aims at "gaining praise"; in *Discorso intorno alle imagini sacre e profane,* in *Trattati d'arte del Cinquecento,* vol. 2, ed. Paola Barocchi (Bari, 1962), 370, translation by author. Also John Gordon Sweeney III, *Jonson and the Psychology of Public Theater* (Princeton, 1985), 5; G. L. Bernini: Fontana di Trevi, ed. Cesare D'Onofrio (Rome, 1963), 11; Vicencio Carducho, "Dialogues on Painting," in *A Documentary History of Art,* vol. 2, ed. E. Holt (New York, 1963), 210.

11. Cristoforo Landino, *Disputationes camaldulenses,* in *Prosatori latini del Quattrocento,* ed. E. Garin (Milan, 1952), 728.

12. See Harold Bloom, *The Anxiety of Influence* (New York, 1973), 7, 15.

13. *Problemi di estetica* (Bari, 1966), 136–37. See also G. N. G. Orsini, *Benedetto Croce: Philosopher of Art and Literary Critic* (Carbondale, 1961), 263–64.

14. *Letters from Petrarch,* trans. M. Bishop (Bloomington, 1966), 182–83.

15. On the subject, see Thomas Greene, *The Light in Troy: Imitation and Discovery in Renaissance Poetry* (New Haven, 1983), 263–64. See Jorge Luis Borges, *Other Inquisitions* (Austin, 1964), 11. As Wallace Stevens put it, "every poem is a poem within a poem: the poem of the idea of the poem of words": in *Opus Posthumous* (New York, 1977), 174. Having translated the Icarus sonnet (*The Heroic Frenzies*), John Addington Symonds confirmed that "whoever may have been its author, it expresses in noble and impassioned verse the exultation of those pioneers of modern thought, for whom philosophy was a voyage of discovery into untravelled regions." In *The Bibelot,* vol. 12 (New York, 1960), 316. Also Alastair Fowler, *Kinds of Literature: An Introduction to the Theory of Genres* (Cambridge, 1982), 267; Richard Waswo, *Language and Meaning in the Renaissance* (Princeton, 1987), 292.

16. *The Breaking of the Vessels* (Chicago, 1981), 13. Or, as Harry Levin put it, novelty rests with "the talented use of sources and conventions"; in

Contexts of Criticism (Cambridge, 1957), 63, in the essay "The Tradition of Tradition."

17. Giorgio Bárberi-Squarotti, "Bruno e Folengo," *Giornale storico della letteratura italiana* 138 (1958), 57, refers to Bruno's "plastic notion of language."

18. Emanuele Tesauro, in *Il cannocchiale aristotelico,* ed. August Buck (Berlin, 1968), 3, translation by author; Giorgio Bárberi-Squarotti, "Per una descrizione e interpretazione della poetica di Giordano Bruno," 42. It is interesting to notice that, while Francesco Patrizi attacked Aristotelianism before Bruno in *Della Poetica* (1555–86), Scaliger condemned Homer for lack of *decorum,* since he was too close to nature. On the subject, see Ettore Bonora, *Critica e letteratura nel Cinquecento* (Turin, 1964); Guido Morpurgo Tagliabue, "Aristotelismo e Barocco," in *Retorica e Barocco: Atti del III Congresso Internazionale di Studi Umanistici,* ed. Enrico Castelli (Rome, 1955), 119–96.

19. *The Complete Works of S. T. Coleridge,* vol. 2, ed. Shedd (New York, 1853), 111.

20. Mikhail Bakhtin, *Problems of Dostoevsky's Poetics* (Minneapolis, 1984), 110–11, 279. Walter J. Ong, *The Barbarian Within and Other Fugitive Essays and Studies* (New York, 1968), 71, writes: "Compared to the ancient world, the world of scholasticism is a visualist age. The ancient educational ideal of the orator here yields to a less auditory ideal as rhetoric is superseded by dialectic, and dialectic itself begins to lose the two-sided character of genuine dialogue and attenuate itself into a teacher's monologue."

21. Alexandre Lazarides, *Valéry: Pour une Poetique du Dialogue* (Montreal, 1978), 17.

22. Ficino, in *The Letters of Marsilio Ficino,* vol. 1, 46.

23. See Martin Kemp, "From 'Mimesis to Fantasia': The Quattrocento Vocabulary of Creation, Inspiration, and Genius in the Visual Arts," *Viator* 8 (1977), 385.

24. Cristoforo Landino, *Opere di Dante degli Alighieri . . . col Comento di Cristoforo Landini* (Vinegia, 1484), preface, fol. a, as translated in M. H. Abrams, *The Mirror and the Lamp* (New York, 1971), 273.

25. See E. N. Tigerstedt, "The Poet as Creator: Origins of a Metaphor," *Comparative Literature Studies* 5 (1968), 374. See also David Summers, *Michelangelo and the Language of Art,* 473 n. 38 and 495 n. 99.

26. *The Letters of Marsilio Ficino,* vol. 1, 190.

27. Willis Barnstone, *The Poetics of Ecstasy: From Sappho to Borges* (New York, 1983), 1–3: Giorgio Bárberi-Squarotti, "Per una descrizione della poetica di Giordano Bruno," 46, points out that the frenzies are "rationally conditioned by a precise goal that is mental"; John C. Nelson, *Renaissance Theory of Love,* 20.

28. Joseph Mazzeo, *Renaissance and Seventeenth-Century Studies* (New York, 1964), 39; Giulio Marzot, *L'ingegno e il genio nel Seicento* (Florence, 1944).

29. See Américo Castro, *The Structure of Spanish History* (Princeton, 1954), 660.

30. Jaroslav Pelikan, *Fools for Christ: Essays on the True, the Good, and the Beautiful* (Philadelphia, 1955), 128; Rudolph Otto, *The Idea of the Holy* (New York, 1968); Kenneth Burke, *A Rhetoric of Motives* (New York, 1950), 79.

31.   Stanley Fish, *Self-Consuming Artifacts: The Experience of Seventeenth-Century Literature* (Berkeley, 1974), 3.

32.   See Linda Ching Sledge, "Typology and the Ineffable: Henry Vaughan and the 'Word in Characters,' " in *Ineffability*, ed. P. S. Hawkins and A. H. Schotter (New York, 1984), 96–97; and Robert B. Shaw, "George Herbert: The Word of God and the Words of Man," in ibid., 86–87.

33.   E. McCurdy, *The Notebooks of Leonardo da Vinci*, vol. 1 (New York, 1968), 612.

34.   See Adelia Noferi, *Il gioco delle tracce* (Florence, 1979), 159–60; and Frances Yates, *Giordano Bruno and the Hermetic Tradition*, 324; Wallace Stevens, *Opus Posthumous*, 183–86. See also Stanley L. Jaki, *Science and Creation* (London, 1974), 262–63; José Ortega y Gasset, *Man and Crisis* (New York, 1962), 80.

35.   *Gli Asolani*, trans. R. Gottfried (Bloomington, 1954), 157, 154, 158. See Nesca Robb, *Neoplatonism of the Italian Renaissance* (London, 1935), 191.

36.   *Paradoxes and Problems*, ed. Helen Peters (Oxford, 1980), 55, 58.

37.   In *Paradoxes and Problems*, 19–20.

38.   See Arthur Lovejoy, *The Great Chain of Being*, 303.

39.   *Coleridge's Shakespearean Criticism*, vol. 2, 358.

40.   Marino, *Dicerie sacre: La strage de gl'innocenti* (Turin, 1960), 94. For a translation, see Linda Nemerow, "The Concept of Ut Pictura Poesis in Giambattista Marino's *Galeria* and the *Dicerie sacre*, with a translation of 'La Pittura' and 'La Musica,' " Ph.D. dissertation, Indiana University, 1980.

41.   Cesare Brandi describes the *lanterna* as a *"getto rotante che si avvita nel cielo,"* in *Struttura e architettura* (Turin, 1971), 59.

42.   On this point, Paolo Portoghesi has called attention to a very high seashell mounted on a pedestal in Borromini's house, *Borromini nella cultura europea* (Rome, 1964), illustration 52.

43.   Frances Yates, *Giordano Bruno and the Hermetic Tradition*, 278, provides a concise summary of the story: "The sun, the universal Apollo, the absolute light, is reflected in its shadow, its moon, its Diana which is the world of universal nature in which the enthusiast hunts for the vestiges of the divine, the reflections of the divine light in nature, and the hunter becomes converted into what he hunts after, that is to say, he becomes divine. Hence the wonderful image of Actaeon and his dogs, hunting after the 'vestiges,' which recurs again and again in the *Eroici furori*, until, by progressive insights, the dogs, thoughts of divine things, devour Actaeon and he becomes wild, like a stag dwelling in the woods, and obtains the power of contemplating the nude Diana, the beautiful disposition of the body of nature. He sees All as One."

44.   As translated by George Whalley, in *The Philosophical Lectures of S. T. Coleridge* (New York, 1949), 324.

45.   *Mountain Gloom and Mountain Glory: The Development of the Aesthetics of the Infinite* (Ithaca, 1959), 137, 140.

46.   Nicolson, *Mountain Gloom and Mountain Glory*, 315.

47.   *The Breaking of the Circle*, 201–2.

48.   Friedrich Schiller, *Naive and Sentimental Poetry: On the Sublime* (New York, 1966), 204.

49.   Karl Jaspers, *The Origin and Goal of History* (New Haven, 1965), 141.

50.   Peter Green, *Sir Thomas Browne* (London, 1959), 18.

51.   Since Bruno stated that poets are philosophers, one could comment on his poetics in light of Lovejoy's assessment of his philosophy, which gives the reader "an impression of immense originality, freshness and spontaneity; and nothing seems more alien to its temper than the spirit of asceticism, or other-worldliness, of contempt for the material, the natural , the human, which is commonly attributed to the Neo-Platonists and to medieval theology," in "The Dialectic of Bruno and Spinoza," *University of California Publications. Philosophy* 1 (1904), 160.

Chapter 3

1.   Ficino, *Marsilio Ficino: The Philebus Commentary*, 366. See discussion of the subject in chapter 1.

2.   Jean Rousset, *La littérature de l'âge baroque en France: Circe et le päon*, 231.

3.   *Aesthetics* (New York, 1964), 8.

4.   Karl F. Morrison, *The Mimetic Tradition of Reform in the West* (Princeton, 1982), 392.

5.   *Dicerie sacre: La strage de gl'innocenti*, 111.

6.   *Donne's Sermons*, ed. L. P. Smith (Oxford, 1920), 85. Also Kenneth Burke, *The Rhetoric of Religion* (New York, 1971); S. T. Coleridge, *Aids to Reflection*, in *The Complete Works of S. T. Coleridge*, vol. 1, 116.

7.   See Alfred North Whitehead, *Adventures of Ideas* (New York, 1933), 248; and Newton P. Stallknecht, *Studies in the Philosophy of Creation* (Princeton, 1934), x.

8.   Bruno's *minimo* also anticipated Coleridge's *prothesis* (a "co-inherence of action and being") and Valéry's *germe* (as the "highest and most universal degree of action and existence"); in *Aids to Reflection*, 218; *Oeuvres*, vol. 2 (Dijon, 1960), 658.

9.   *Aesthetics*, 14. See I. A. Richards, *Coleridge on Imagination* (Bloomington, 1960), 52; Giulio Carlo Argan, "Il realismo nella poetica del Caravaggio," in *Scritti di storia dell'arte in onore di Lionello Venturi*, vol. 2 (Rome, 1956), 36.

10.   See W. J. Bates's relevant statement in "Coleridge on Art," in *Perspectives of Criticism*, ed. H. Levin (New York, 1970), 132.

11.   *The Dialogic Imagination* (Austin, 1981), 84–85. Katerina Clark and Michael Holquist, *Mikhail Bakhtin* (Cambridge, 1984), 275, write that Bakhtin looked at genres "not just in their narrow literary context but as icons that fix the world view of the ages from which they spring." Also Tzvetan Todorov, *Mikhail Bakhtin: The Dialogic Principle* (Minneapolis, 1984), 83.

12.   Howard Hibbard, *Bernini* (Baltimore, 1974), 93.

13.   Helmut Hatzfeld, *Estudios sobre el barroco* (Madrid, 1973), 107, points out that even baroque transcendentalism did not break loose of time and space.

14.   Bakhtin, *The Dialogic Imagination*, 10–11. From a religious standpoint, one need only mention the progressive experience of spiritual exercises (Saint Ignatius) and the education to the devout life (St. Francis de Sales).

15. On the subject, see Francesco De Sanctis, *History of Italian Literature,* vol. 1 (New York, 1959), 304. Vittore Branca adds that, "after chivalric stories, survived in the world of memory and nostalgia, it is the world of our merchants to offer the most lively and aggressive champions in the struggle of those superhuman forces"; in *Boccaccio medievale* (Florence, 1956), 71–72. Also Manuel Duran, "Cervantes and Ariosto: Once More, with Feeling," in *Estudios literarios de hispanistas norteamericanos dedicados a Helmut Hatzfeld con motivo de su 80 aniversario,* ed. J. M. Sola-Sole, A. Grisafulli, and B. Damiani (Barcelona, 1974), 89.

16. See Salvatore Battaglia, *Mitografia del personaggio* (Milan, 1968), 247. E. C. Riley, *Cervantes's Theory of the Novel* (Oxford, 1964), 2–3, notes: "The main impetus came from Italy. It was an accident that the increase in critical consciousness among Spanish writers of the last two decades of the sixteenth century (a development apparent among English writers of the same period) coincided with the divulgation of Aristotelian poetic doctrines from Italy. . . . Theoretical considerations never exercised so tight a hold on Spanish writers as they did on the Italians, and in the 1590's Spain was a generation behind Italy in these matters, but their influence mounted steadily in the lifetime of Cervantes." Also Claudio Guillén, *Literature as System,* 77–78.

17. *Two Picaresque Novels,* trans. M. Alpert (Baltimore, 1969), 25. References are to this edition, with page number indicated in the text.

18. See A. C. Piper, "The 'Breadly Paradise' of Lazarillo de Tormes," *Hispania* 44 (1961), 270.

19. *Aspects of the Novel* (New York, 1954), 41.

20. Agnes Heller, *Renaissance Man* (London, 1978), 232; also François Jost, "La Tradition du Bildungsroman," *Comparative Literature* 21 (1969), 100.

21. Georg Lukács, *Soul and Form* (Cambridge, 1974), 18. For Hugo Friedrich, *Montaigne* (Paris, 1968), 343, Montaigne was determined to make visible "the perpetual movement of his spirit."

22. As Nietzsche put it, "there is no 'being' behind doing, acting, becoming. The 'doer' is merely a fictitious addition to the doing; the doing is all"; in *Nietzsche in Outline and Aphorism* (London, 1907), 28.

23. S. T. Coleridge, *The Philosophical Lectures,* ed. K. Coburn (New York, 1949), 344, wrote that Descartes cherished the "self-determined indetermination of voluntary doubt."

24. Guillén, *Literature as System,* 15; Warren, "The Styles of Sir Thomas Browne," *Kenyon Review* 13 (1951), 674.

25. See Joan Webber, *The Eloquent 'I:' Style and Self in Seventeenth-Century Prose* (Madison, 1968), 13. Also Morris Croll, *Style, Rhetoric, and Rhythm* (Princeton, 1966), 207–33.

26. *G. L. Bernini: Fontana di Trevi,* ed. Cesare D'Onofrio (Rome, 1963), 66–67. The play has been translated by Donald Beecher and Massimo Ciavolella with the title of *L'Impresario* (Ottawa, 1985).

27. "Gianlorenzo Bernini's *The Impresario:* The Artist as the Supreme Trickster," *University of Toronto Quarterly* 53 (1984), 239. In line with a modern approach, Jackson I. Cope describes antiform in Renaissance drama as "process-as-product," in *The Theater and the Dream: From Metaphor to Form in Renaissance Drama* (Baltimore, 1973), 3. Jean Rousset, *La littérature de l'âge baroque en France: Circe et le paon,* 232, writes that "la création est

encore visible dans l'achèvement, mais comme une phase intermédiaire au sein d'un développement."

28.   José Ortega y Gasset, *Velázquez, Goya and the Dehumanization of Art* (New York, 1972), 106.

29.   Américo Castro writes: "The Spaniard's finest creations have always been like this, works which combine in an integral relationship the agent, the action, and the thing done"; in *The Structure of Spanish History* (Princeton, 1954), 661.

30.   See Elias L. Rivers, *Quixotic Scriptures* (Bloomington, 1983), 109; Stephen Gilman, *Cervantes y Avellaneda: Estudio de una imitación* (Mexico City, 1951), 52; Carlos Fuentes, *Don Quixote, or the Critique of Reading* (Austin, 1976), 43–45.

31.   Martin Pops, *Vermeer: Consciousness and the Chamber of Being* (Ann Arbor, 1984), xv.

32.   See Christine Brooke-Rose, "The Readerhood of Man," in *The Reader in the Text,* ed. S. Suleiman and I. Crosman (Princeton, 1980), 142; Balachandra Rajan, "Andrew Marvell: The Aesthetics of Inconclusiveness," in *Approaches to Marvell,* ed. C. A. Patrides (London, 1978), 160; Rien T. Segers, "Some Implications of *Rezeptionsästhetik,*" in *Yearbook of Comparative and General Literature* 24 (1975), 20.

33.   Karl F. Morrison, *The Mimetic Tradition of Reform in the West,* 30.

34.   For Montaigne, as for Proust, readers were not "his" readers, "but readers of themselves," the book "serving as a sort of magnifying glass"; in *The Past Recaptured,* in *Remembrance of Things Past,* vol. 2, trans. F. A. Blossom (New York, 1934), 1113. Terence Cave, *The Cornucopian Text: Problems of Writing in the French Renaissance* (Oxford, 1979), 153, writes that such transfers made literary forms "doubly decodable"; the same text became "two different works" in which meaning depended on the reader's "classificatory choice."

35.   See Stanley Fish, *Self-Consuming Artifacts: The Experience of Seventeenth-Century Literature* (Berkeley, 1974), 101.

36.   See Roland Barthes, *New Critical Essays* (New York, 1980), 3; Valéry, *Leonardo. Poe. Mallarmé* (Princeton, 1972), 10.

37.   Giulio Carlo Argan, *The Europe of the Capitals,* 24.

38.   Christine Brooke-Rose, *A Grammar of Metaphor* (London, 1958), 132.

39.   Term coined by H. Weinrich, "Münze und Wort," in *Romanica. Festschrift für G. Rohlfs* (Halle, 1958), 508.

40.   Tesauro, *Il cannocchiale aristotelico,* in *Trattatisti e narratori del Seicento,* 21. Translation by author.

41.   *Metaphor and Reality* (Bloomington, 1973), 71–72.

42.   *Il cannocchiale aristotelico,* 82.

43.   *The Pentamerone of Giambattista Basile,* vol. 1, trans. N. M. Penzer (New York, 1932), 433–45.

44.   In the clash between then and now, Proust writes, "the latter has always been the victor but it was ever the vanquished" that stood out as the more beautiful; in *The Past Recaptured,* 997.

45.   For quixotic minds, the literal could be more problematic than the fantastic, especially if one were to agree with Roger Fry that "to be *innocente* is a fate too terrible to be accepted by a Spaniard"; in *A Sampler of Castile* (Richmond, 1923), vi.

46. See D. A. Miall, "Metaphor as a Thought-Process," *Journal of Aesthetics and Art Criticism* 38 (1979), 21; Terence Cave, *The Cornucopian Text,* 171.

47. See José Ortega y Gasset, *Obras Completas,* vol. 6 (Madrid, 1955), 259.

48. See Philip Wheelwright, *Metaphor and Reality,* 57.

49. Philip Wheelwright, *Heraclitus* (Princeton, 1959), 91–92, 95.

50. *Discorso sulle immagini sacre e profane,* 370. In this connection, Calderón's lines are revealing:

> Si será esto lo fingido
> Y lo otro lo verdadero?
>
> .   .   .   .
>
> Fingimos lo que no somos,
> seamos lo que fingimos
> (*En esta vida todo es verdad y todo es mentira*)

51. See Anthony Wilden, "*Par Divers Moyens on Arrive à Pareille Fin:* A Reading of Montaigne," *Modern Language Notes* 83 (1968), 596. Rosalie Colie, *Paradoxia Epidemica: The Renaissance Tradition of Paradox* (Princeton, 1965), 11.

52. Gérard Genette, "Narcissus baroque," *La nouvelle revue française* (September 1961), 55. Jorge Luis Borges, *Labyrinths* (New York, 1964), 196, writes on Hamlet that, if characters can be real and fictitious, we "readers or spectators" could be fictitious as well.

53. See Howard A. Slaatte, *The Pertinence of Paradox* (New York, 1968), 1, 94. See also Giulio Carlo Argan, "La retorica e l'età barocca," in *Retorica e Barocco: Atti del III Congresso Internazionale di Studi Umanistici* (Rome, 1955), 14; A. E. Molloch, "The Technique and Function of the Renaissance Paradox," *Studies in Philology* 53 (1956), 193.

54. The term "telescoping" was coined by T. S. Eliot, *Homage to Dryden,* 221. Quevedo illustrated literary telescoping in a sonnet against Góngora:

Microcósmote Dios de Inquiridiones

The immensity of God-like concepts dwindles down to a little world. The transformation of the noun into a verb generates a 'magnifying' action that makes meaning and size insignificantly small. Telescoping endorsed relativism of sight and knowledge, as Montaigne wrote: "The conception and semblance we form is not of the object, but only of the impression and effect made on the sense; which impression and the object are different things" (454). Bacon took an equally critical stand in more continental climates. However purified, "the human understanding is like a false mirror, which, receiving rays irregularly, distorts and discolours the nature of things by mingling its own nature with it. . . . the spirit of man is in fact a thing variable and full of perturbation."

(*Novum Organum* I, 41–42)

55. In Evelyn M. Simpson, *A Study of the Prose Works of John Donne* (Oxford, 1948), 316; *Paradoxes and Problems,* 20.

56. *In cannocchiale aristotelico*, 460, translation by author. See Barbara C. Bowen, *The Age of Bluff* (Urbana, 1972), 6; Terence Cave, *The Cornucopian Text*, 327–30.

57. For Paolo Portoghesi, "formation" substituted form; in *Roma barocca* (Bari, 1978), 68; also Carlo Ragghianti, *Arte, fare e vedere* (Florence, 1974), 130; Irving Lavin, *Bernini and the Unity of the Visual Arts*, vol. 1 (New York, 1980), 13; Austin Warren, *Richard Crashaw: A Study in Baroque Sensibility* (London, 1939), 206; Maurizio Calvesi, *Treasures of the Vatican*, 191–92.

58. Glenn O'Malley, "Literary Synesthesia," *The Journal of Aesthetics and Art Criticism* 15 (1957), 391–411.

59. See Jeremy Adler, "*Technopaigneia, carmina figurata* and *Bilder-Reime*: Seventeenth-Century Figured Poetry in Historical Perspective," *Comparative Criticism* 4 (1982), 107–47, especially 129–30. One of the most famous "and grandiose was the performance of an Italian opera, *Chi soffre speri*, by Rospigliosi (text) and Mazzocchi-Marazzuoli (music), given at the Barberini palace on 27 February 1639 before 3,500 spectators, including Cardinal Mazarin. Bernini provided the stage designs, which were so marvelous that his biographer thought their fame would endure forever. Between the acts, *The Fair of Farfa* was enacted by a great multitude of players, spilling over into the audience and garden. Every kind of scene from real life at a Roman carnival was made part of the gorgeous entertainment, while Cardinal Barberini entertained his guests. Among these was none other than John Milton"; Carl J. Friedrich, *The Age of the Baroque, 1600–1660* (New York, 1962), 86–87. See Peter Skrine, *The Baroque: Literature and Culture in Seventeenth-Century Europe*, 28; Roy Strong, *Festival Designs by Inigo Jones* (London, 1969), 1; Per Bjurstrom, "Baroque Theater and the Jesuits," in *Baroque Art: The Jesuit Contribution*, ed. R. Wittkower and B. Jaffe (New York, 1972), 100–101; Mark S. Weil, "The Devotion of the Forty Hours and Roman Baroque Illusions," *Journal of the Warburg and Courtauld Institutes* 37 (1974), 218–48; *Leo Spitzer: Representative Essays*, ed. A. Forcione, H. Lindenberger, and M. Sutherland (Stanford, 1988), 130–31.

60. See *Il Sacro Monte sopra Varallo* (Milan, 1981); Rudolph Wittkower, *Idea and Image: Studies in the Italian Renaissance* (London, 1978), 175–84; Pierluigi De Vecchi, "Annotazioni sul Calvario del Sacro Monte di Varallo," and Stefania Stefani Perrone, "Giovanni d'Enrico urbanista e architetto al Sacro Monte di Varallo in Valsesia," in *Fra Rinascimento, Manierismo e Realtà*, ed. Pietro C. Marani (Florence, 1984), 109–18, 129–42.

61. *The Diary of John Evelyn*, vol. 2 (Oxford, 1955), 261.

62. W. S. Heckscher, *Rembrandt's Anatomy of Dr. Nicolaas Tulp* (New York, 1958). For illustration and commentary on the 1656 anatomy lesson, see Kenneth Clark, *An Introduction to Rembrandt* (New York, 1978), 100, plate 109.

63. *On Painting* (New Haven, 1973), 43; Giuseppe Lipparini, *Le pagine della letteratura italiana*, vol. 9 (Milan, 1960), 86, translation by author; *Il cannocchiale aristotelico*, 19–21.

64. See Joseph Mazzeo, *Renaissance and Seventeenth-Century Studies*, 1–28. Even though she was yet to become the musicians' patroness at the time the sculpture was produced, Raphael's *S. Cecilia Altarpiece* (1513–14) already had established that kinship.

65. *The Spirit of Mediterranean Places* (Marlboro, 1986), 9.

66. *The Literature Machine: Essays* (London, 1982), 291–95.

67. *Dialogue Concerning the Two Chief World Systems,* trans. Stillman Drake (Berkeley, 1974), 105. I draw from Calvino's last critical text, *Six Memos for the Next Millennium* (Cambridge, 1988), 44–45.

68. As Luca Giordano wrote, Velázquez's canvas is "the theology of painting," and so are, to many, the *Captives* and the Cervantine novel with regard to sculpture and literature; in A. Palomino, *El museo pictórico y escuela óptica* (1724), ed. M. Aguilar (1947), 922. On Rembrandt, see Pascal Bonafoux's forceful comments, *Rembrandt: Self-Portrait* (New York, 1985), 8–9, 20.

69. *The Gods Made Flesh: Metamorphosis and the Pursuit of Paganism* (New Haven, 1986), 7.

70. *The Analysis of Beauty* (Oxford, 1955), 27–29.

71. Projecting Kantian influences toward twentieth-century art, Newton P. Stallknecht notes that free beauty identifies the artwork "as a realization in a chosen medium, of an idea that may be described as intransitive in that it does not point beyond itself"; in "Kant's concept of the *Esthetic Idea* and the Appreciation of Modern Art," in *Revue Internationale de Philosophie* 11–2 (1975), 185.

72. A. W. Schelling, in *Concerning the Relation of the Plastic Arts to Nature,* as translated by Michael Bullock in the Appendix to Herbert Read's *The True Voice of Feeling* (London, 1953), 333.

73. S. T. Coleridge, *Theory of Life,* in *The Complete Works of S. T. Coleridge,* vol. 1, 403; W. H. Auden, *The Enchafed Flood* (New York, 1950), 46.

74. *Aesthetics,* 47; *Leonardo. Poe. Mallarmé,* 16. In the more scientific language of the time, Henri Bergson updated that legacy: "Our personality shoots, grows and ripens without ceasing"; in *Creative Evolution,* 9–10.

75. Thomas McFarland, *Romanticism and the Forms of Ruin: Wordsworth, Coleridge, and Modalities of Fragmentation* (Princeton, 1981), 5. On the subject, see Jean Rousset, *La littérature de l'âge baroque en France: Circe et le päon,* 251–52.

76. Leo Spitzer, *Classical and Christian Ideas of World Harmony* (Baltimore, 1963), 23–24, 130.

77. For Gaston Bachelard, *The Poetics of Space* (New York, 1964), 113, "every form . . . retains life, and a fossil is not merely a being that once lived, but one that is still alive, asleep in its form."

78. Or, in Alfred North Whitehead's more recent statement, "existence is activity ever merging into the future," in *Modes of Thought* (New York, 1958), 232.

Chapter 4

1. Jean Rousset speaks of *"résultats obtenus,"* in *La littérature de l'âge baroque en France: Circe et le paon,* 232.

2. Carlos Fuentes, *Don Quixote or the Critique of Reading,* 12. As E. C. Riley puts it, "this very self-conscious author absorbs criticism in creation," in *Don Quixote* (London, 1986), 34.

3. *The Boundaries of Genre: Dostoevsky's Diary of a Writer and the Tradition of Literary Utopia* (Austin, 1981), 50, 121.

4. W. V. Quine, *The Ways of Paradox and Other Essays* (New York, 1966), 11; Thomas Docherty, *John Donne, Undone* (London, 1986), 18–21.

5. Morson, *The Boundaries of Genre*, 40.

6. Thomas Greene, *The Light in Troy: Imitation and Discovery in Renaissance Poetry*, 195.

7. As Baltasar Gracián put it, "there are mirrors for the face, but none for the mind; let discreet introspection be your mental looking glass"; *The Oracle: A Manual of the Art of Discretion* (New York, 1953), 117. And Thomas Browne had no doubts that his "substantial Man" (*Christian Morals* II,4) could give literary presence to the inner self.

8. See *The Devout Soul* (1643), in *The Works of Joseph Hall*, vol. 6, ed. P. Wynter (Oxford, 1863), 530–31. Also Louis Martz, *The Poetry of Meditation* (New Haven, 1969), 15.

9. *Self-Consuming Artifacts: The Experience of Seventeenth-Century Literature*, 3–4. Also Anne Drury Hall, "Epistle, Meditation, and Sir Thomas Browne's *Religio Medici*," *PMLA* 94 (1979), 236; Stanley Stewart, *The Expanded Voice: The Art of Thomas Traherne* (San Marino, 1970), 76; Louis Martz, *The Poetry of Meditation*, 16; John L. Lievsay, *The Seventeenth-Century Resolve: A Historical Anthology of Literary Form* (Lexington, 1980); Helen C. White, *English Devotional Literature: Prose, 1600–1640* (Madison, 1951), 237; H. Outram Evennett, *The Spirit of the Counter-Reformation*,45.

10. Northrop Frye, *The Anatomy of Criticism* (New York, 1955), 53, 326; also Laurence Stapleton, *The Elected Circle: Studies in the Art of Prose* (Princeton, 1973), 16.

11. James Sutherland, *On English Prose* (Toronto, 1957), 28.

12. Terence Cave, *The Cornucopian Text: Problems of Writing in the French Renaissance*, 332.

13. Bakhtin, *The Dialogic Imagination*, 411.

14. See Marthe Robert, *Origin of the Novel* (Bloomington, 1980), 4–5.

15. Renato Poggioli, *The Spirit of the Letter* (Cambridge, 1965), 345, refers to unwritten poetics in his discussion of the modern novel. Focusing on the Renaissance, Rosalie Colie adds that "from 'real' literature as opposed to criticism and theory, of course, we recover what is far more important, the *unwritten* poetics by which writers worked and which they themselves created"; in *The Resources of Kind* (Berkeley, 1973), 4, 29–30. Recently E. C. Riley, *Don Quixote*, 5–6, has focused on the "marginality" of Cervantes, who wavered "between a frankly stated pride in his literary achievements and a sense of poetic insufficiency."

16. See Juan Bautista Avalle-Arce, *Don Quijote como forma de vida* (Madrid, 1976), 34; Miguel de Unamuno, "*Qué es verdad*" (1906), in *Ensayos*, vol. 1 (Madrid, 1970), 801, writes: "For a Spaniard, the reality that is believed in is worth more than the reality which is not belived in."

17. Michael Seidel, *Satiric Inheritance: Rabelais to Sterne* (Princeton, 1979), 62.

18. Jonathan Brown, *Images and Ideas in Seventeenth-Century Spanish Painting* (Princeton, 1978), 88, writes: "The present title was not given to the picture until 1843, when the elevation of servants above their masters may have followed in the wake of republican sentiments that swept nineteenth-century Europe." That being the case, we would have a sort of boundary title established by popular acclaim. For Karl Just, *Diego Velázquez and His Times*

(London, 1889), 414, the title of *Las Meninas* derives from the fact that "the noble damsels were for the Spaniards the most attractive of all the figures," since "they were the dark-eyed daughters of their race, lovely young blossoms of the old Castilian stock."

19. See Madlyn M. Kahr, *Velázquez: The Art of Painting* (New York, 1976), 106; Michael Levey, *Painting at Court* (New York, 1971), 148; J. H. Elliott, *Imperial Spain, 1469–1716* (London, 1963), 294.

20. See Raymond S. Willis, "Sancho Panza: Prototype for the Modern Novel," *Hispanic Review* 37 (1969), 210.

21. Américo Castro, *The Structure of Spanish History*, 59.

22. As Quevedo wrote, "the desire to be different ruined Caesar's Rome, just as the desire to be different from themselves ruined men"; in *Marco Bruto*, in *Obras Completas*, vol. 1, ed. F. Buenda (Madrid, 1966), 827. Translation by author.

23. On the subject, see Leo Spitzer's polemical footnote, *Linguistics and Literary History*, 84, directed against Américo Castro's essay "Cervantes and Pirandello" in *An Idea of History: Selected Essays of Américo Castro* (Columbus, 1977), 15–22.

24. Stephen Gilman, "An Introduction to the Ideology of the Baroque in Spain," *Symposium* 1 (1946), 103.

25. See José Ortega y Gasset, *Meditations on Don Quixote* (New York, 1961), 154; Raymond S. Willis, "Sancho Panza: Prototype for the Modern Novel," 227.

26. Ruth El-Saffar, *Novel to Romance* (Baltimore, 1974), 164, writes that Cervantes "took a peek into the future, into the chaotic uncertainties of individual perception unguided by authority and without the reassurances that rational thought or empirical data could offer, and shut the door again." As Michael Seidel comments on the subject of satire, "change is a complex notion, and its sometimes hidden processes seem to release a conserving instinct in a culture or a literature. Therefore one of the more convincing measures of change is the extent to which some will go to resist it"; in *Satiric Inheritance: Rabelais to Sterne*, 81.

27. See Arnold Hauser, *The Social History of Art*, vol. 2 (New York, 1951), 207–25. Also Barry Wind, *Velázquez' Bodegones: A Study in Seventeenth-Century Spanish Genre Painting* (Fairfax, 1987), 13–14.

28. Hugo Friedrich, *Montaigne* 156.

29. W. H. Auden, "The Hironic Hero: Some Reflections on Don Quixote," in *Cervantes: A Collection of Critical Essays* (Englewood Cliffs, 1969), 81.

30. See Svetlana Alpers, "Interpretation without Representation, or the Viewing of *Las Meninas*," *Representations* 1 (1983), 40.

31. Alastair Fowler, *Kinds of Literature: An Introduction to the Theory of Genres and Modes*, 92, notes that, "in prose fiction, the pretense of factuality at first dominated titles." Also Edward W. Said, *Beginnings* (New York, 1975), 3; John G. Weiger, *The Substance of Cervantes* (Cambridge, 1985), 41. E. C. Riley tells us that "there was no accepted word in Spanish for long prose-fiction works. *Libro* or *historia* usually had to do." Cervantes "could not have written *Don Quixote* at all without a keen sense of the difference, and the relationship, between what we now think of as 'romance' and 'novel,' although he did not know any such terms"; in *Don Quixote*, 11.

32. See Madlyn Millner Kahr, *Velázquez: The Art of Painting*, 137–38;

and Jonathan Brown, *Velázquez: Painter and Courtier* (New Haven, 1986), 261–62.

33. *Essays and Soliloquies* (New York, 1925), 101.

34. Unamuno, *Our Lord Don Quixote* (Princeton, 1976), 439.

35. *The Tragedy of a Character*, in *Short Stories*, trans. F. May (New York, 1965), 94–97.

36. "L'ironia comica nella poesia cavalleresca," in *Saggi, poesie, scritti varii* (Verona, 1960), 101.

37. See Thomas Mann, "Voyage with Don Quixote," in *Cervantes: A Collection of Critical Essays*, 53. As Jean Starobinski has recently noted on Montaigne, "writing transforms the initial reader's experience into an author's experience. Simultaneously, it turns the original obedient reading into a critical reading"; in *Montaigne in Motion* (Chicago, 1985), 27. John G. Weiger, *The Substance of Cervantes*, 3, has written that "the praise of poetry concerns itself with the nature of art; the praise of *Don Quixote* limits itself to the reception given the work by the public, irrespective of its essence and intent."

38. See S. J. Freedberg, *Circa 1600: A Revolution of Style in Italian Painting* (Cambridge, 1983), 8; Jonathan Brown, *Velázquez: Painter and Courtier*, 17.

39. "Boundaries of Narrative," *New Literary History* 8 (1976), 5. See also Svetlana Alpers, *The Art of Describing: Dutch Art in the Seventeenth Century* (Chicago, 1983).

40. As translated in E. L. Eisenstein, *The Printing Press as an Agent of Change*, vol. 2 (London, 1979), 479.

41. See Lionello Venturi, *Four Stages toward Modern Art* (New York, 1964), 28.

42. *Velázquez' Bodegones: A Study in Seventeenth-Century Spanish Genre Painting*, 70. For the symbolism of genre painting, see his chapter "Naturalism and Metaphor," 81–114.

43. Cardinal Paleotti, *Discorso intorno alle immagini sacre e profane*, in *Trattati d'arte del Cinquecento*, vol. 2, 354.

44. Giuliano Briganti, Ludovica Trezzani, and Laura Laureati, *The Bamboccianti: The Painters of Everyday Life in Seventeenth-Century Rome* (Rome, 1983), 2.

45. André Malraux, *The Voices of Silence*, 470; John Rupert Martin, *Baroque*, 53; Giuliano Briganti, *Pietro da Cortona* (Florence, 1962), 32; Gérard Genette, "Boundaries of Narrative," 5–7; Georg Lukács, in *Writer and Critic and Other Essays* (New York, 1971), 127, writes that "description merely levels reality." On the subject of children in art, see Mary Frances Durantini, *The Child in Seventeenth-Century Dutch Painting* (Ann Arbor, 1983), especially 280–83. On Naples, see Romeo De Maio, "The Counter-Reformation and Painting in Naples," in *Painting in Naples 1606–1705 from Caravaggio to Giordano*, ed. C. Whitfield and J. Martineau (London, 1982), 35.

46. Helmut Hatzfeld's definition, in *Estudios sobre el Barroco*, 541; Benedetto Croce, *Saggi sulla letteratura italiana del Seicento* (Bari, 1962), 191; see also his *La Spagna nella vita italiana durante la Rinascenza* (Bari, 1962) and *Nuovi saggi sulla letteratura italiana del Seicento* (Bari, 1931); Giuseppe Galasso, "Society in Naples in the Seicento," in *Painting in Naples 1606–1705 from Caravaggio to Giordano*, 27.

47. *Metatheater: A New View of Dramatic Form* (New York, 1963), 72.

48. *Panopticon romano* (Milan, 1967), 187.

49. See José Antonio Maravall, *Teatro y Literatura en la Sociedad Barroca* (Madrid, 1972), 97–103; Américo Castro's *The Spaniards* (Berkeley, 1971), 110–11. In the Venetian *laguna*, Fulgenzio Micanzio echoed: "Everybody wears innumerable masks, which are changed according to circumstance"; in *Annotazioni e pensieri*, in *Storici e politici veneti del Cinquencento e del Seicento*, ed. Gino Benzoni and Tiziano Zanato (Milan, 1982), 844. Translation by author.

50. *Dramas, Fields, and Metaphors: Symbolic Action in Human Society* (Ithaca, 1974). On more strictly literary grounds, see Gustavo Pérez Firmat, *Literature and Liminality: Festive Readings in the Hispanic Tradition* (Durham, 1986).

51. See Maurizio and Marcello Fagiolo dell'Arco, *Bernini: Una Introduzione al Gran Teatro del Mondo* (Rome, 1967), 181; Donald Beecher, "Gianlorenzo Bernini's *The Impresario*: The Artist as the Supreme Trickster," 238; and his introduction to *The Impresario*, 16.

52. See Linda A. Stone-Ferrier, *Images of Textiles: The Weave of Seventeenth-Century Dutch Art and Society* (Ann Arbor, 1985), xvi–xvii, 229–30.

53. See Jonathan Brown, *Velázquez: Painter and Courtier*, 2–3; E. Haverkamp-Begemann, "Introduction," *Rembrandt after Three Hundred Years: An Exhibition of Rembrandt and His Followers* (Chicago, 1969), 23–26.

54. Famous are the *presepi* in the Museo San Martino, Naples; Museo Nazionale di Palazzo Bellomo, Siracusa; and the private collection of Giuseppe Alvigini, Biella. On the subject, see F. Mancini, *Il presepe napoletano* in the series *Forma e colore*, n. 47 (Florence, Sansoni); Angelo Stefanucci, *Il presepe nel Sud: La stella di Betlemme* (Milan, 1975); M. Mariani, C. Faldi, and C. Strinati, *La cattedrale di Matera nel Medioevo e nel Rinascimento* (Milan, 1978), 63–68; Mario Praz, in *Il giardino dei sensi: Studi sul Manierismo e il Barocco* (Vicenza, 1975), 214–16. As Harry Levin would say, "such is the folklore of civilization: neither the biography of writers nor the pseudo-biography of their characters, but the stuff of collective experience as it has been sensitively registered and compactly preserved"; in his discussion of realism and reality, *The Gates of Horn* (New York, 1963), 469. On Pulcinella, see Goethe's *Italian Journey* (New York, 1962), 205; Croce, *Saggi sulla letteratura italiana del Seicento*, 241–43; Anton Giulio Bragaglia, *Pulcinella* (Rome, 1953), 63; Giuseppe Galasso, "Society in Naples in the Seicento," 27. Mikhail Bakhtin, *The Dialogic Imagination*, 57; the critic insists that "the parodic-travestying literature of Southern Italy was especially rich and varied. Comic-parodic plays and riddles flourished there." On recent comments on the Neapolitan ethos, see Domenico Rea, *Fate bene alle anime del Purgatorio: Illuminazioni napoletane* (Milan, 1977), 82–83.

55. In 1607, Thomas Tomkins published an allegorical play about language (*Lingua*), which enacts the tongue's disastrous struggle to become a kind of autonomous sixth sense. The lesson is that speech should not be isolated from reason and experience.

56. Thomas Docherty, *John Donne, Undone*, 202, writes: "When George

More had Donne imprisoned and held his own daughter until April 1602, there was an attempt being made to 'undo' the name of Donne and to challenge its power to appropriate Ann More."

57.   Richard Waswo, *Language and Meaning in the Renaissance*, 140–56; Geoffrey Hartman, *Saving the Text* (Baltimore, 1981), 133. Also Bakhtin, *The Dialogic Imagination*, 61; Ramon Saldivar, *Figural Language in the Novel: The Flowers of Speech from Cervantes to Joyce* (Princeton, 1984), 50–51. In *Linguistics and Literary History*, 52, Leo Spitzer adds: "Words are no longer, as they had been in the Middle Ages, depositories of truths nor, as they had been in the Renaissance, an expansion of life: they are, like the books in which they are contained, sources of hesitation, error, deception—'dreams' "; in his essay "Linguistic Perspectivism in the 'Don Quijote.' " Spitzer adds that the baroque artist "says something with full consciousness that one cannot actually say it. He knows all the difficulty of translation fron intention to expression, the whole insufficiency of linguistic expression"; in *Die Literarisierung des Lebens in Lopes Dorotea* (Bonn, 1932), 11–12.

58.   Secondo Lancellotti, *L'oggidì overo gl'ingegni non inferiori a passati*, in *Trattatisti e narratori del Seicento*, 295. Translation by author.

59.   *On Humor*, trans. A. Illiano and D. P. Testa (Chapel Hill, 1960), 142.

60.   In *Trattatisti e narratori del Seicento*, 20.

61.   Marjorie Nicolson, *Science and Imagination*, 2.

62.   *On Humor*, 145.

63.   Jean Rousset, *La littérature de l'âge baroque en France: Circe et le päon*, 253.

Chapter 5

1.   Katerina Clark and Michael Holquist, *Mikhail Bakhtin*, 347.

2.   See my *Adam "New Born and Perfect": The Renaissance Promise of Eternity*, chapter 3.

3.   *De remediis utriusque fortune*, in *Four Dialogues for Scholars*, trans. Rawski (Cleveland, 1972), 31.

4.   *Letters from Petrarch*, 302.

5.   *The Letters of Machiavelli*, trans. A. Gilbert (New York, 1961), 142. On the *studiolo* theme, see André Chastel, *The Myth of the Renaissance* (Geneva, 1969), 167–69.

6.   Michel Foucault, *The Order of Things* (New York, 1970), 42. Hugh Kenner, *Paradox in Chesterton* (New York, 1947), 26–27, states: "The tendency toward these errors may be discerned in a simple example. Man is said to be good. It is plainly folly, however, to say that man is therefore as good as God. . . . Analogy explains, paradox describes."

7.   See Ramon Saldivar, "Don Quixote's Metaphor and the Grammar of Proper Language," *Modern Language Notes* 95 (1980), 260. Long after Petrarch, Tesauro reiterated that "madness is nothing else than a metaphor, which replaces one thing with another. It therefore happens that madmen are usually endowed with excellent minds, and the most subtle minds, like poets and mathematicians, are particularly prone to become mad. . . . a mental

image too highly assimilated and felt, often turns into a fantastic construction, which, through aging, becomes madness"; in *Il Giudicio*, in *Trattatisti e narratori del Seicento*, 17. Translation by the author.

8. Jean Starobinski, *Montaigne in Motion*, 27.

9. Julius S. Held, *Rembrandt's Aristotle and Other Studies* (Princeton, 1969), 22–23, 32.

10. The Book of the Courtier, trans. C. Singleton (New York, 1959), 121–22.

11. His whole collection was catalogued for sale in 1656. See Kenneth Clark, *An Introduction to Rembrandt*, 18–19, 69–70.

12. See Anne Hollander, *Seeing through Clothes* (New York, 1978), 372.

13. See E. Haverkamp-Begemann, "Introduction," *Rembrandt after Three Hundred Years*, 21.

14. Svetlana Alpers, *Rembrandt's Enterprise: The Studio and the Market* (Chicago, 1988), 26.

15. *Rembrandt's Aristotle and Other Studies*, 40.

16. Madlyn Millner Kahr, *Dutch Painting in the Seventeenth Century* (New York, 1982), 131.

17. Richard McKeon, "Plato and Aristotle as Historians: A Study of Method in the History of Ideas," *Ethics: An International Journal of Social, Political, and Legal Philosophy* 51 (1940–41), 70.

18. Julia Kristeva, *Semeiotike* (Paris, 1969), 144.

19. See W. R. Valentiner, *Rembrandt and Spinoza* (London, 1957), 68.

20. In a commentary on Cicero, as translated in Arthur Lovejoy's *The Great Chain of Being*, 63. Also Ludwig Edelstein, "The Golden Chain of Homer," in *Studies in Intellectual History* (Baltimore, 1953), 64.

21. Nikolaus Pevsner, *Studies in Art, Architecture and Design*, vol. 1 (London, 1968), 42.

22. *The Knowledge of Man: A Philosophy of the Interhuman* (New York, 1965), 60.

23. *Obras Completas*, vol. 7 (Madrid, 1964), 152.

24. See Kenneth Burke, *The Rhetoric of Religion* (Boston, 1961), 12.

25. Tesauro, *Il cannocchiale aristotelico*, 85.

26. Martin Buber, *Between Man and Man* (London, 1947), 203; in *I and Thou* (New York, 1958), 11, Buber writes that "all real living is meeting." In Bakhtinian terms, dialogism "insists that we are all necessarily involved in the making of meaning"; Clark and Holquist, *Mikhail Bakhtin*, 348.

Chapter 6

1. Martin Foss, *The Idea of Perfection* (Princeton, 1946), 8. I draw substantially from this study.

2. Alfred North Whitehead uses the phrase "God in the image of a personification of moral energy"; in *Process and Reality: An Essay in Cosmology* (New York, 1960), 520.

3. *Christianity and Classical Culture: A Study of Thought and Action from Augustus to Augustine* (New York, 1944), 482.

4. In his monumental study of late antiquity and early Christianity, *Ancient Ideals,* vol. 2 (London, 1900), 405; also his *The Classical Heritage of the Middle Ages* (New York, 1957), chapter 2, "The Passing of the Antique Man," 18–32.

5. *Creative Evolution,* 10.

6. I draw from Marjorie Nicolson's *Mountain Gloom and Mountain Glory: The Development of the Aesthetics of the Infinity,* especially the chapter "New Philosophy," 113–43.

7. *Messengers of God: Biblical Portraits and Legends* (New York, 1976), 28, 6.

8. On the topos of the "test," see Harold Fisch, *A Remembered Future* (Bloomington, 1984), 4. For Louis Martz, "Adamic perfection depends upon the power of choice, which inevitably includes the right to err as well as the right to make amends for error. To Milton man's perfection lies in man's ability to grow, however painfully, in wisdom and understanding"; in *Poet of Exile: A Study of Milton's Poetry* (New Haven, 1980), 141. As Peter Lindebaum notes, "the whole emphasis on a difficult Eden and the insistence on the importance of prelapsarian sexual love" also suggests that "Eden is not qualitatively different from our postlapsarian existence"; in "Lovemaking in Milton's Paradise," *Milton Studies* 6 (1975), 300. Balachandra Rajan, *The Lofty Rhyme* (London, 1976), 74, writes that action is "the price that has to be paid not for perfection, but for human perfection." Barbara Lewalski, "Innocence and Experience in Milton's Eden," in T. Kranidas, *New Essays on Paradise Lost* (Berkeley, 1969), 116–17, adds that the "life of innocence" became an exaltation of "humanism, maturity, civilization in happiest conjunction with vitality, change, growth." The archetypal test "does not reflect the cycle of the seasons so much as the special conditions of human existence, the time of human life."

9. *Process and Reality: An Essay in Cosmology,* 514, 526.

10. See Nicolas Berdyaev, *The Beginning and the End,* 197–98.

11. On the subject, see my *Adam "New Born and Perfect": The Renaissance Promise of Eternity.*

12. My brief outline relies on the critic's outstanding short book, *Philosophy, Technology, and the Arts in the Early Modern Era* (New York, 1970), especially the chapter "The Idea of Scientific Progress," which contains detailed bibliographical footnotes on the subject. Also, the fundamental essays in P. Wiener and A. Noland, *Roots of Scientific Thought* (New York, 1957).

13. *Renaissance and Revolution: The Remaking of European Thought* (New York, 1965), 277.

14. *Galileo Heretic* (Princeton, 1987), 80–83, 324–25.

15. "Dell'ambizione del letterato," in A. Mascardi, *Saggi accademici dati in Roma nell'Accademia del Serenissimo Principe cardinale di Savoia* (Venice, 1630), 77; as translated in Pietro Redondi, *Galileo Heretic,* 75.

16. *The Breaking of the Circle,* 165.

17. *Creative Evolution,* 344–45.

Index